ISLAM AND SOCIAL WORK

Debating values, transforming practice

Sara Ashencaen Crabtree, Fatima Husain and
Basia Spalek

BAKER COLLEGE OF
CLINTON TWP. LIBRARY

BASW
BRITISH ASSOCIATION
OF SOCIAL WORKERS

This edition published in Great Britain in 2008 by

The Policy Press
University of Bristol
Fourth Floor
Beacon House
Queen's Road
Bristol BS8 1QU
UK

Tel +44 (0)117 331 4054
Fax +44 (0)117 331 4093
e-mail tpp-info@bristol.ac.uk
www.policypress.org.uk

© The Policy Press 2008

British Library Cataloguing in Publication Data
A catalogue record for this book is available from the British Library.

Library of Congress Cataloging-in-Publication Data
A catalog record for this book has been requested.

ISBN 978 1 86134 947 7 paperback
ISBN 978 1 86134 948 4 hardcover

The right of Sara Ashencaen Crabtree, Fatima Husain and Basia Spalek to be
identified as authors of this work has been asserted by them in accordance with
the 1988 Copyright, Designs and Patents Act.

All rights reserved: no part of this publication may be reproduced, stored in
a retrieval system, or transmitted in any form or by any means, electronic,
mechanical, photocopying, recording, or otherwise without the prior
permission of The Policy Press.

The statements and opinions contained within this publication are solely those
of the authors and not of the University of Bristol, The Policy Press or the
British Association of Social Workers (BASW). The University of Bristol, The
Policy Press and BASW disclaim responsibility for any injury to persons or
property resulting from any material published in this publication.

The Policy Press works to counter discrimination on grounds of gender, race,
disability, age and sexuality.

Cover design by Qube Design Associates, Bristol
Front cover: image kindly supplied by www.istockphoto.com
Printed and bound in Great Britain by Hobbs the Printers, Southampton

Dedicated to my children. Also, to the loving memory of Jack Crabtree, companion, comrade and mentor; and finally my regal mother,
Elvira Ranz y Diez de Artázcoz. **SAC**

To Sakina and Zakary – precious souls who bless my life and help me look to the future; and to Abba and Ammi, with immense gratitude, for their open-mindedness, patience and prayers. **FH**

Dedicated to the memory of Jo Campling. **BS**

Contents

List of case studies, figures and tables

Case studies

Figure

Tables

Acknowledgements

A number of people assisted in the development of this book, many of whom cannot be named for confidentiality reasons. Nonetheless I would like to thank all the anonymous individuals in the UK, the Far East and the Middle East who contributed their stories, some of which provided the bases of the case studies included. In this vein I would also like to thank one particularly intrepid, albeit unnamed, Arab social worker in the United Arab Emirates, whose passion for the protection of local children was evident in our interviews and the generous sharing of two harrowing cases, one of which is reproduced in this book as a case study.

I am also indebted to those Muslim academics who have helped me to develop my understanding of Islam in the context of social welfare. Dr Ismail Baba, Dr Belkeis Altareb and Dr Abdullahi Barise are three names that immediately come to mind in this respect. Furthermore, this book would certainly have been greatly impoverished, and almost certainly impossible to complete, without the invaluable help of my two colleagues, Dr Fatima Husain and Dr Basia Spalek. I would also like to thank Professor Jonathan Parker at Bournemouth University who has bestowed help and enthusiasm unstintingly whenever it was needed. In addition, I would like to acknowledge with gratitude the generous research support allocated to me over the years from the Universiti Malaysia Sarawak, Zayed University and The Chinese University of Hong Kong, which provided me with the funds and space to be able to explore my growing interest in the synergy between social work and faith.

Finally, I would like to wholeheartedly commemorate two remarkable people without whom this book would certainly never have been written. First, I would like to mention Jo Campling, whose level-headed advice and commitment to the project helped to bring this book to fruition. Second, I remain grateful, as ever, for the critical observations, the accomplished editing assistance and continuous encouragement given to me by my late husband Professor Jack Crabtree. Both Jo and Jack went beyond the call of duty to continue work on this book up to the final days of their lives, both of which were lost through untimely illness. Last but not least I would like to thank the editorial staff at The Policy Press for offering such an efficient but friendly service that always felt totally person-centred.

Sara Ashencaen Crabtree

ONE

Introduction

Aims and scope

On the book shelves of those with a genuine interest in social work, the chances are that there will be at least one well-thumbed text on the issue of 'race' and ethnicity and how this relates to, and the impact it has on, social work practice. So complex is this area that it continues to provide a rich source of academic inquiry, resulting in impassioned debate. The best known of these polemics rightly continue to feature on every social work student's reading list, and therefore we shall not spend too much time in revision here.

Under these circumstances, it may seem rather unlikely therefore that there can be anything new to add to this topic; especially where social work could well be viewed by other professions as being extremely well supported by the volume of information available on the market. However, at the same time, never before in living memory has there been so much focus devoted to a proliferation of articulated concerns from the media, politicians and the general public regarding the question of the social integration of Muslim minority ethnic groups in the West (Solomos, 2003).

This is normally framed in relation to the perceived irreconcilable conflict between the cultural values and practices of European nations and those of migrants from other cultures. The tension generated in civil society by this kind of rhetoric was demonstrated in the notorious case of the late Dutch politician Pim Fortuyn. His xenophobic and Islamophobic stance reverberated in Dutch society, this being rooted in the argument of the erosion of national values by an influx of intolerant Muslim migrants (Marranci, 2004).

Another more recent example, also from the Netherlands, was the murder of Theo Van Gogh, a controversial film director, by an individual who had embraced extremist interpretations of Islam some time after being trained as a social worker; a rich irony that will not be lost on readers (Ahmed, 2005).

In the UK the problem of the 'immigrant other' is being played out at many levels, including immigration itself, detention, security, the variables of socioeconomic status and those structural barriers restricting access to often inadequate public services. With regard to the UK's Muslim communities, recent debates have centred on issues of security following the terrorist attacks in New York and London. Consequently analysts, policy makers and politicians have begun to question the UK's multicultural model that according to some has resulted in segregated communities with little or no interaction across communities and ethnicities. Pervasive general suspicion, heightened by media headlines and an increase in Islamophobic attacks, has been supplemented by the questioning of some Muslim women wearing the *niqab* and of the lack of access for women to some mosques, a topic that we discuss in further detail in Chapter Two.

The UK government's continuing policy emphasis on family and parenting, together with the recent focus on the 'problem' of young people, has put all families under the spotlight. However, with young Muslim men being scrutinised for their allegiances, and the perceived inappropriateness of some young Muslim women's personal choices, the sphere of 'Muslim' family life, relationships and transmission of values is being additionally questioned. Although South Asian families have been characterised as having a collective ethos and strong intergenerational and familial bonds, for South Asian Muslim families this stereotype is changing. And since it has been suggested that parents need to keep a closer eye on their sons, the family is becoming in some respects the first level of a security buffer.

According to Poynting and Mason (2006), in considering legislation evoked by the European nations in response to the terror attacks of 11 September 2001 (9/11), it was the UK that reacted in the most extreme way, as for example through the invoking of a state of emergency in order to pass the 2001 Anti-Terrorism, Crime and Security Act.

Furthermore, following the 7 July bombings in London in 2005, there has been considerable discussion within the media and political arenas about the extent to which second- or third-generation Muslim men, particularly South Asian men, have been assimilated into British culture. For instance *The Times* featured an article where the reporter stated the following, 'Now moving towards its third generation since the initial Bengali immigration, this community remains, as far as I can see, unassimilated' (Crampton, 2005). Elsewhere, a reporter in *The Sunday Times* claimed that the young men who are the genus most susceptible to Islamic extremism in this country are second-generation British Pakistanis, due to the lack of a sense of identity (Taseer, 2005).

However, debates around assimilation appear to miss out key issues that arise when considering British Muslim identities and male

Muslim youth subcultures. Muslims constitute the most socially and economically deprived faith group in the UK. Statistics show that Muslims are the most likely faith group to experience poor housing conditions, and that 42% of Muslim children live in overcrowded accommodation, compared with an overall figure of 12% for the general population. Commensurately, a further 12% live in households with no central heating, compared with 6% for all dependent children, and that 35% are growing up in households where there are no adults in employment, compared with 17% for all dependent children (Choudhury, 2005, p 14). Furthermore, almost one third of Muslims of working age have no qualifications, the highest proportion for any faith group, and 17.5% of young people between the ages of 16 and 24 are unemployed compared with 7.9% of Christians and 7.4% of Hindus (Choudhury, 2005, p 16).

The economic and social deprivation experienced by a significant number of young Muslim men means that they, like other socially and economically deprived male youth, are likely to form subcultures, which are also likely to have strong masculinist ideals underpinning them (Young, 1999). Indeed, Archer (2003) argues that young Asian men may construct a 'strong' Islamic identity for themselves as a way of resisting the 'weakness' that they perceived to be associated with the category 'Asian'. Similarly, Saeed et al (1999) argue that the concept of *ummah* (the universal community of the Faithful) means that a global Islamic community supersedes national or ethnic identities. Young people may be claiming an Islamic identity for themselves, because this places them within a global community, thereby reducing their sense of marginalisation.

Islamist extremists who are intent on recruiting young British Muslim men combine masculine imagery with religion in order to try to connect with potential recruits. For example, Mohammed Siddique Khan, the eldest London bomber, recorded a video message to explain his reasons for the attack, and within this message it is clear that he was 'doing masculinity' saying:

> Jihad is an obligation on every single one of us, men and women; (whereas) our so-called scholars of today are content with their Toyotas and semi-detached houses … they are useless. *They should stay at home and leave the job to real men – the true inheritors of the* Prophet. (BBC News, 2005; Spalek, 2007, p 204; emphasis added)

The general background of underprivilege suggests that multiple strands of oppression bearing down on the lives of Muslim individuals and families give rise to a formulation of resistance among sectors of society, which in turn are regarded as an increasing threat to social stability. If social work is to work effectively with the communities they serve, the complex and interwoven factors of 'race' and ethnicity, identity, class and gender need to be more fully disentangled, analysed and addressed within the profession.

It has often been pointed out that Islam is the fastest growing religion in the West (Barise, 2005; Hodge, 2005). At the same time there is a serious dearth of social work texts dedicated to illuminating the needs of Muslim families in social work intervention. Judging from the social work literature available, there is little that is specific to Muslim individuals and families. Accessible information that does pertain to Islamic world views is often of a highly generalised nature, and therefore presents problems in terms of practical application.

The premise of our book, therefore, is based on the belief that many social work practitioners lack the basic background knowledge they need to be able to work more confidently with Muslim communities. Our aim here is to offer readers a clearer understanding of Islamic principles and practice, which continue to influence and underpin the lives of Muslim individuals and families. However, these in themselves do not help social workers to find strategies towards developing culturally sensitive ways of working with Muslims. Consequently, we also attempt to provide some useful suggestions to social work practitioners working with clients who identify themselves as Muslims. Accordingly, short case studies are included that serve to highlight relevant issues and principles; many of these have been taken from our own practice. In addition, a key point throughout has been to draw a clear distinction between Islamic principles and practices, and those that are specifically grounded in culture. Regardless of the commonality of the Muslim identity such differences vary across ethnic groups, which may hold widely differing customs and general outlooks on life.

Furthermore, in writing this book we have consciously tried to avoid subsuming the lives, experiences and perspectives of Muslims under the broader umbrella category of black perspectives (Ahmad, 1990). Since significant segments of the British black and minority ethnic population identify themselves as Muslim in the 2001 Census (ONS, 2002), these multiple standpoints may well overlap. However, we feel that it would be a mistake to fail to identify what is specific to Islam and to Muslim families, as this would only serve to prevent social workers from being able to identify the particular issues that are relevant to Muslims alone.

Here, therefore, we overtly focus only on the needs of Muslim clients who may come from a wide variety of socioeconomic, cultural, national and regional backgrounds. For many, the fundamental tenets of Islam serve as a unifying force, regardless of 'race', ethnicity and localised or cultural differences, although these of course are in turn highly influential.

Definition of terms

In this introductory chapter we attempt first to define the terms we commonly employ throughout the text, as well as to establish the parameters of the book and how we intend to address emerging topics in relation to social work with Muslim clients.

Just as there is no such thing as value-free research, or indeed politically unmediated social work practice, so too are the terms that authors adopt subject to politically loaded meanings, all of which represent potentially hazardous, contentious areas for further debate. Although we have consciously not fenced the text in with a barrage of terminology to perplex readers, nonetheless we have been at some pains to find nomenclature that is both accurate and non–oppressive, and which we attempt to use consistently throughout the text.

Accordingly, in discussing the divide between certain racial and ethnic groups primarily in the UK, we have preferred to adopt the term 'minority ethnic'. In addition to this, the simple and factual term 'Muslims' seems to be preferable to the long-winded term 'Muslim families and individuals', in general, except where families are specifically referred to. Such terms are not necessarily politically loaded; however, this is not necessarily the case in relation to some terms, such as 'orthodox', which implies a universal norm. For this reason we prefer to substitute for this the more neutral but descriptive term 'conservative'. Equally, we feel that the term 'Muslim extremism' is also one loaded with emotive and stereotypical images, and have duly refrained from using this in favour of 'extreme interpretations of Islamic principles' or 'concepts', as the case may be.

Organisation of the book

Moving away from the brief topic of definitions, in this section readers are guided across the subsequent chapters by a short description of the content. Accordingly, Chapter Two takes a broad perspective in order to discuss the diversity of the Muslim *ummah*. In so doing, we have borrowed lenses from the sociological and anthropological disciplines through which to view the current position of migrant and settled minority ethnic communities in Western Europe, and more particularly in the UK. Moreover, we also consider issues of relevance that are emerging from Muslim communities in the wider international area. These all serve to contextualise some of the more crucial contemporary debates revolving around multiculturalism and social inclusion, as well as that of nationalism and conservative interpretations of Islam.

Education is the topic of Chapter Three, particularly in relation to the training needs of social workers in the UK, and what can be done to enhance educational effectiveness in this area. Social work values and practice are considered in relation to Islamic principles and epistemology. Once again, concepts and cases are drawn from the international Muslim community, as well as closer to home.

Chapter Four focuses on the centrality of the family in Islam, as the main unit of socialisation of individuals in the Islamic world view. The wide-ranging morphology of Muslim families is considered. So too are gender norms, especially in terms of child-rearing, and the demarcation of the roles between the sexes. The prevailing stereotypes in the West of Muslim women and men are also discussed in relation to perceived dilemmas for social workers in relation to the professional value-base.

Having set the general scene, subsequent chapters are devoted to specific practice issues. Chapter Five therefore, considers social work with children and families, in terms of domestic violence and child abuse, as well as related concerns surrounding protection and welfare.

Chapter Six considers health issues in the Muslim family, which are likely to involve social work intervention at some point. Controversial practices such as female genital mutilation are reviewed according to different cultural interpretations. More conventionally, needs associated with disability and care-giving are considered in addition to those concerning mental illness, and, finally, the issues of death and dying are discussed.

The penultimate chapter considers a competing area of social need that affects the well-being of Muslims in the UK, that of crime and Islamophobia. This is of especial relevance following the aftermath of terror attacks in the UK, US, Spain and Bali. This chapter also explores the issue of crime in the Muslim community from various perspectives, in addition to the phenomenon of religious conversion among prisoners within the penal system including interpretations of *shari'a* law and secular laws in Muslim societies.

The final chapter draws together the separate strands of debate summarising how social work values may be transformed into culturally sensitive, professional practice.

Addressing 'race' and ethnicity in social work

In identifying how we treat the issue of 'race', ethnic and faith identity it becomes necessary to briefly revisit how this general topic has been treated in social work literature to date. This has commonly focused on the concepts of 'race' and culture with the aim of enlightening white practitioners to the cultural practices and lifestyles of clients from black and minority ethnic groups. Robin Sakina Mama (2001) identifies two main approaches used in the attempt to disseminate knowledge about other cultures. The 'emic' approach, for example, delivers specific knowledge of a particular culture, in addition to offering a set of strategies and guidelines for practitioners (Mama, 2001, p 376).

This method, however, has led to the critique that in so doing clichéd stereotypes of cultures are thereby perpetuated through the essentialising of individuals down to a set of properties regarded as typical of that culture (Mama, 2001). This is only a short step away from pathologising such clients in terms of perceived 'cultural deficits' (Ely and Denney, 1987, p 70). Clients who do not come from a dominant cultural or ethnic group are often then viewed as coming from a context that is problematic in terms of family functioning, general lifestyles and cultural values. These real or assumed differences are then regarded as liable to make social work intervention more likely (Ahmad, 1990; Ely and Denney, 1987).

This serves to underline why social work literature has also frequently highlighted racist overtones in social work practice, such as in relation to the patronising, colour-blind attitudes that overlook institutional and structural inequalities that have an impact on the lives of black and minority ethnic individuals in the West (Dominelli, 1994, p 36).

The 'etic' approach by contrast adopts a more universal perspective in attempting to develop broad concepts that are regarded as germane to the particular culture under study. However, this too is problematic in failing to address the issue of diversity within the cultural context, as is the case of Muslim communities, where homogeneity is assumed (Ahmed, 1994; Mama, 2001).

Tsang (2001) in turn argues that the 'cultural literacy model', as embodied in anti-discriminatory practice, and which, to an extent, straddles both the emic and etic points of view, has become the dominant approach in cross-cultural social work education. Unfortunately here, once more, the general features and properties are assumed to belong to all individuals of that particular culture in question.

Apart from the fallacies of overgeneralisation, such an approach also fails to take into account the ethnicity, socioeconomic background, ethical and value perspectives of white authors and practitioners through an ethnocentric perspective that assumes 'that ethnicity belongs only to the client' (Tsang, 2001, p 234).

However, the notion of culturally competent social work, as developed in the US, is gaining recognition in the UK as a viable framework that is easily transferable into effective practice (Becher and Husain, 2003).

In this book we have considered both the emic and etic approaches, and have attempted to draw out the most useful aspects of each, while trying to avoid the pitfalls. Following Tsang's point, we take into account our own cultural heritage as highly influential in informing our perspectives and our analyses, as will be explained further.

This, therefore, has led to an approach that is consciously wide in scope, international in perspective and yet deliberately targeted towards meeting the needs of primarily those British social work students and practitioners who wish to enhance their knowledge and stimulate their critical understanding in a reflective exercise while hopefully sharpening their practice skills.

Social work, ethnocentrism and the influence of postmodernism

Social work developed from the roots of social reform in the 19th century, which in turn was led by a small but energetic number of philanthropic enterprises, such as those connected with the Quakers and the Fabians (Payne, 2005). The appetite for massive industrialisation and the profit motive was belatedly being reflected in some quarters of society by a concern for a more humanitarian regard for the children, women and men who made the manufacturing might of Britain possible. The modernist assumption of universal social progress would be an idea that postmodernism would later take issue with, where a proliferation of critiques would emerge from the humanities, the social sciences and, later, popular culture against modernist and ethnocentric perspectives. Later in the 20th century the dominant, white, masculine and single-voiced viewpoint and authority of modernity would be challenged and fractured. This fragmentation enables multiple experiences from the margins of 'race', gender, culture and now faith, to be heard. This multiplicity stands effectively as the hallmark of postmodernist trends.

In this guise postmodernism, in relation to the celebration of diversity, appears as a benevolent and empowering force. Indeed, one to be openly embraced by the social work profession as being more egalitarian and therefore more in keeping with social work values of equality and advocacy.

Yet postmodernism has taught us that such apparent bedrocks of certainty offer an unreliable foundation to build on. Writing of the apparent crisis in social work in the US, David Stoesz has accused the profession of failing to keep faith with its social contract to tackle mainstream social problems, such as poverty, child welfare and disability. This failure, he argues, is rooted in a pseudo-academic haze of 'postmodernist relativism' (Stoesz, 2002, p 22).

In short, his argument is that social work has flirted too closely with postmodernism and has therefore abandoned the profession to strategic irrelevance in meeting the needs of individuals, families and communities.

The language of market-driven productivity that Stoesz speaks of, is taken up by Lena Dominelli who identifies social work as a victim of an increasingly globalised capitalism, in which social bonds and collective groups are fragmented by a postmodernist market economy (Dominelli, 1996, p 154). Here anti-racist social work, feminist social work and consumer perspectives stand in radical opposition to social work characterised by bureaucracy, managerialism and the 'fragmented service provision' in the postmodernist era (Dominelli, 1996, p 157). In a similar vein, Michael Preston-Shoot has described a grim scenario where the social work role in the postmodernist climate has become 'chaotic, fragmented and alienated and alienating' (Preston-Shoot, 2000, p 88). In such a climate, social workers are tied to the purchase of care packages rather than building core therapeutic relationships with clients. This move the author describes as being the 'dehumanisation of individuals', both clients and social workers (2000, p 90).

Separate from the issue of postmodernism however, but nonetheless commensurate with the criticisms of social work, has been the critique of how the criminal justice system is changing its focus. The rise of the 'actuarial regime' in criminal justice refers to the governance of populations through statistical analyses of risk (Simon, 1988; Ewald 1991; O'Malley, 1992). The fragmentation of human identity, which forms a primary example of depersonalisation, is manifestly evident in the actuarial approach. This takes place by viewing people according to statistical risk-based distributions rather than in terms of their personal properties, such as 'race' and ethnicity, class and sex. In social work terms, such emphases are a pronounced departure from understanding the individual in an ecosystems orientation, which seeks to identify actors and the variables of situations within the context of their environment (DuBois and Miley, 2005).

However, to return to postmodernism the critiques levied emphasise the essential inability of the postmodernist trend to enable clients and social workers to form effective coalitions that can challenge existing hierarchies of power in order to create social change. In the rejection of generalisations and the politics of solidarity this trend has confronted the aims of collectivisation in that it regards political power as dispersed rather than having a central locus. In such a diffused and ambiguous atmosphere, all are implicated in power plays, both those who are apparently disempowered, as well as those who attempt to unmask power differentials (Hartsock, 1990). Racism and other forms of discrimination cease to become potent and structural forces in people's lives, but instead collapse into being seen as merely competing discourses and perceptions.

However, postmodern perspectives that focus on the fluidity and diversity of identities can lose sight of those discriminatory norms that help to produce and perpetuate oppression. By stressing the locally produced and contingent nature of any knowledge claims, regimes of power in relation to whiteness, patriarchy, heterosexism, secularism, disablism and ageism remain unchallenged and therefore largely intact. The postmodern focus on the localised and transitory nature of any social norm suggests that such an approach cannot sufficiently challenge those wider norms that perpetuate inequalities (Fricker, 2000). As McClaurin (2001) argues, there is a materiality to identity that should be acknowledged, stemming from broader relations of power.

If, however, postmodernism is unable to provide impetus towards action that overtly alters the relations of power in client–worker interactions, such as can be found in terms of racism, it can instead create space in which the processes of social work are analysed, and this may lead to change.

Fook suggests that a 'critical' reflective approach is essential for *praxis* in enabling practitioners and educators to explore the extent to which theory fits with action (Fook, 1996, p 4; Preston-Shoot, 2000, p 89). Thompson concurs, saying that reflectivity steers a prudent middle path between the rejection of theory, and a rigid over-reliance on theory (Thompson, 2005, p 147).

Reflectivity in social work

The relativistic nature of postmodernism via reflectivity permits social workers to consider how a 'reality' is perceived through the perspective of another, and thus can be taken into account when planning an intervention. In other words, if the need to 'put oneself in other people's shoes' is an essential attribute of any practitioner, this is because it is the core value of empathy (Preston-Shoot, 2000, p 94). Of utmost importance even for those working in ethnically and culturally homogeneous societies, it is even more vital when working in heterogeneous or unfamiliar cultural terrain, as social work practice with clients from Muslim minority groups might be viewed.

Reflectivity in this book has guided us as authors, enabling an exploration of social work practice (including at times our own) in the context of Islam, through analysing our own personal and professional points of view

In addition to critical reflectivity, we have found the postmodernist strategy of reflexivity to be a useful device (Alcott, 1991; Lyons, 1999). Reflexivity means the identification of speaker location and is used to good effect in ethnographic work, typical of anthropology, in determining how the author's perspective influences the research process and outcome. In this text we have additionally adopted reflexivity, bringing in the interplay of our authorial voices, in which individual perspectives and personal histories have added to our critical analyses.

To clarify our intentions, we are not attempting to reach a uniform consensus with each other at all costs in this book. The topics discussed are too complex and multilayered for that to be easily achieved. In addition, our own particular backgrounds are sufficiently diverse to make such an endeavour an impractical one, even if consensus were considered to be the ultimately desirable outcome.

Having embarked on our own continuous learning curve, we believe that our approach offers a more multifaceted way of looking at and approaching social work practice with Muslims. In keeping with our dialogic aims therefore, readers are encouraged to think critically through the issues raised for themselves, and in relation to formulating their own professional responses. Consequently we do not offer a 'cook-book' set of instructions to be unthinkingly adopted by readers. We argue, we advise, we suggest, but we do not rigidly prescribe.

Thus by identifying our speaker locations through reflexivity, our experiences and assumptions are made more explicit to the reader in understanding how these may have coloured our perspectives on issues.

The purpose of such an exercise should not be, as Patai states, merely 'rhetorical manoeuvres' on our part, but instead the link between the personal properties and location of a researcher and their analysis should be sufficiently explained (Patai, 1991, p 149; Hirsch and Olson, 1995, p 19).

To this end, we would like to clarify our own speaker locations and to explain how these have informed our views of social work and social welfare with Muslims.

Sara's story

I am British by birth and female, born to a white, professional, mixed European family living in London. My first stirrings of interest in Islamic traditions are owed to my aristocratic Spanish mother, who throughout my childhood enjoyed recounting stories of the glories of the Moorish civilisation (and their encounters with the Catholic sovereigns) in historic Andalucía. As a child there hung a beautiful poster of the Alhambra on my bedroom wall, whose purpose was to portray the quintessential magnificence of Iberian architecture. In reality, the Alhambra is of course the most famous of antique Moorish palaces, in which superb abstract decoration, in keeping with Islamic principles, is taken to its artistic zenith.

Years later I was intrigued to find that in the Arabian Gulf this historical period continued to be immortalised in the name 'Al Andalus'. Nowadays this title is liberally bestowed on primarily educational establishments seeking to bask in the ideal of an elite borrowed from a lost and noble culture – one, furthermore, that had been shaped by the harmonious contribution of Muslims, Christians and Jews living for centuries under a particularly enlightened Islamic governance.

Returning however to the far less romantic and much more prosaic, my professional interest in the topic of this book has developed from two main, but complementary, areas emerging from practice and academia, respectively.

Thus prior to and after qualifying as a professional social worker in the early 1990s, I was employed in a range of social work settings in both London and nearby Hertfordshire. During this time I worked with a wide range of clients, including Muslims. I found that with the latter I was often hampered in not having the basic cultural knowledge I needed to work with them effectively. This was primarily because detailed and targeted information was rarely available on the needs of this group in the social work curricula.

Consequently, I regret that social gaffes probably took place while I was trying to develop appropriate intervention with courteous Muslim families, whose confidence in non-Muslim social workers may have been somewhat shaken by my well-meaning ignorance. Several years later, in between academic posts and the writing of my doctoral thesis, a relocation to the Luton area as a temporary locum social worker brought me into close contact with Muslim clients, who now formed the bulk of my caseload.

Due to my previous experiences my Asian team manager regarded me, maybe somewhat unwisely, as something of a minor expert on social work with Muslim minority groups. And since, in the opinion of the management, there was no other person better qualified in the immediate vicinity, most cases involving Muslim clients ended up on my desk.

In fairness, however, I found that most Muslim families in Luton were deeply relieved to have someone to work with, who at least had a basic familiarity with their customs and points of view, and almost invariably I was warmly welcomed once these informal credentials were accepted.

My academic experiences, on the other hand, were instrumental in exposing me to some of the rich diversity that exists in the Islamic world. For over a decade from 1995 I took up lectureships in local universities in Malaysia and the United Arab Emirates, both of which are predominantly Muslim nations, albeit that Malaysia boasts a thriving multicultural, multi-faith population as well.

Both nations provided a distinctive lesson in terms of personal and professional adaptation to two very different Muslim societies. Each had a distinctive social context and different population needs, together with dissimilar social welfare services, informed by alternative underlying assumptions of service provision. Equally, education for potential social care workers was distinctive in offering contrasting educational environments, curricula and general educational targets.

What I learned primarily from these experiences was a due appreciation of indigenous social work based on differing client beliefs and needs. Moreover, I discovered that there is a distinct gap between Islamic principles, as found primarily in the Holy Qur'an, and those beliefs and customs that were not basically Islamic, but instead were embedded in localised, traditional responses. In some cases the latter pre-dated Islam or ran parallel with it, an area that is considered in more detail in this book.

I also began to realise, with some concern, that although many of the issues I covered in classroom situations seemed relevant according to an international social work curriculum, there was sometimes a cultural dissonance between theory and my Muslim students' perceptions and perspectives. This provided me with some serious food for thought and in due course generated further research (Ashencaen Crabtree, 1999, 2008 [forthcoming]; Ashencaen Crabtree and Baba, 2001).

Another career relocation took place, this time to the rigorous, academic hothouse of Hong Kong, where my research agenda focused on minority ethnic groups. Once more I gravitated towards work with Muslims, specifically families, who live a fairly invisible existence within this ethnically homogenised and very competitive society. Preliminary findings from my research in Hong Kong indicated that although some families had gained a firm foothold in Hong Kong, many others led highly marginalised lives. Muslim families in Hong Kong are variously hampered by poor educational opportunities, unemployment problems, poverty and language barriers. These findings therefore appeared to hold some interesting points of resonance with the situation in the UK. And thus this prompted another move: back to the UK to take up new academic challenges and which has finally brought me full circle.

Thus while my professional and personal journey from the West to the East and back again has been a fascinating one, it has not always been an easy road to travel. Sometimes I have felt that bridging cultural divides has been a very difficult and occasionally perilous journey, which has at times proved a bruising experience on both sides of the client–practitioner, student–teacher divides.

However, fundamentally it has also represented a dialogue and one that is essential to engage with, *if* the dichotomies and dilemmas of differing and diffused national, cultural and religious identities are to be addressed successfully within an accountable and contemporary social work discipline.

Fatima's story

I was born in Karachi, Pakistan, into a practising and rather devout Dawoodi Bohra Muslim family. Both my parents were born under the British Raj in what is now India and were from the privileged educated minority with a tradition of producing lawyers.

My mother and her family fled India soon after partition, as did my father, and arrived in Pakistan as 'Muhajir' or refugees. I left Pakistan at the age of six and from then until my final arrival in Britain in 1997 my life has been marked by dislocation and external identifiers such as 'foreigner', immigrant, woman of colour and so forth in a number of countries on three different continents. Even today, questions about belonging, about citizenship and which box on ethnic monitoring forms best defines me are ever present. And in Pakistan, my country of birth, my ethnic label is still that of 'Muhajir'. Further complexity in my subjective position is added by my identity as a Muslim. I am a member of a minority denomination (the Bohras) within another minority (Shi'as) within a larger Muslim minority that, currently, is often and consistently vilified in the West.

With family members residing in Bangladesh, India, Pakistan, Scotland, New York, Texas and Canada, and expressing different levels of allegiance to being Bohra, mainstream Shi'a and orthodox Sunni, as well as agnostic and atheist, family gatherings have often been characterised by heated discussions about nationalism, the politics of belonging, faith allegiances and the importance of belief in one God. At the same time, acknowledging and appreciating – as well as confronting – my family background of privilege in a society ridden by class divisions, poverty and illiteracy has been a constant challenge.

Living in Western countries, I have had to respond from a very early age to questions such as 'Do you have trees in Pakistan?', 'Why does Islam treat women so badly?', 'Why is polygamy allowed?' and 'Why is it that it's always the children of "foreigners" who have problems?'. And have suffered comments such as 'You aren't really like them, you don't smell', 'Paki go home' and 'You know what we do with people like that' – this a response by a US immigration officer to my family name, Husain, after the first Gulf war. Not to mention the raised eyebrows, stares and questions from fellow Muslims (male and female) and devout family members who sometimes struggle to comprehend my positioning as a Muslim. It is precisely my position as a Muslim woman in the West that led me to study gender and Islam for my PhD, having been inspired by North African fiction, as well as thinkers and writers such as Fatima Mernissi and Mohammed Arkoun. I have also been deeply influenced by post-colonial and feminist theoretical perspectives, in particular Albert Memmi, Franz Fanon and Trinh T. Minh-ha.

Today I am a researcher working principally on issues related to the lived experiences of minority ethnic families and communities in the UK and Europe. I am also a single mother bringing up two mixed-race and inter-faith children in a society that is increasingly becoming fractured along class, 'race' and community divides.

Reflexivity is a guiding principle through which I approach research and communicate with people. Critical to my understanding of the communities I research is an understanding of self and my own subjective position in society, as well as an awareness of how others might perceive me, both as a researcher and a person.

Each and every position I take or identifier I use is subjective, situational and fluid, and each is significant to who I am and what I do. However, the dichotomous position that has been consistent in my life, both professionally and personally, is that of outsider/insider, a positioning that has served me well in researching communities, families, children, women, young people and men who are marginalised and disadvantaged.

Basia's story

I am a British-born, white female whose parents are Second World War refugees, who as children were forced to flee Poland when the Soviet army invaded eastern Poland. As a child I attended Polish school every Saturday, where I learned to read and write in Polish, where I learned about Polish history and culture, and where I sang the Polish national anthem.

I am a criminologist based at Birmingham University, England, and my research interests include Muslim communities in relation to criminal justice issues. Birmingham is a multi-ethnic, multicultural city, and having a significant number of Muslim students on the criminology courses that I ran, made me think about the extent to which criminology as a subject discipline reflects Muslim identities. It has been claimed that criminology 'was born with the death of God' (Morrison, 1995, p 5), and so part of my research has involved a focus on faith communities and criminological knowledge production.

Reflexivity is a key part of my approach to research, drawing very much on feminist research principles, whereby the values and characteristics of the researcher are made visible. Reflexivity is viewed as being a key way of ensuring rigorousness and reliability when carrying out research, as it might be argued that the beliefs and behaviours of social scientists influence the perception and documentation of social experience.

My subject positions are multitudinous, including my being white, a woman and a Western researcher, as well as a wife, friend, daughter and sister. All of these positions are significant, as these constitute the sites at which the social world is experienced and acted on, and so will have an impact in different ways on the research process. Moreover, while some aspects of my subjectivity might be linked to marginalised, outsider positions, which help to produce oppositional knowledge, other aspects of my self-identity might serve to maintain and reproduce dominant racial and cultural discourses and power relations. As a result, I am very keen to reflect on the multiple dimensions to my self and to explore the ways in which these can interact with the research process. Reflection for me is part of a personal ethics particularly as in the present political climate we are asking Muslim communities to reflect on their faith and citizenship and yet it seems this reflection is largely lacking on the part of Western governments, public officials and extensive parts of the media.

TWO

The Muslim *ummah*: context and concepts

Introduction

In providing an overview of Islam and diversity within Islam, this chapter acts as a basic introduction to a highly complex subject area that has been extensively discussed. The contextual nature of Islam is emphasised and particular references are made to the historical migration and settlement of Muslim communities in Europe and the UK. The authors are aware that any discussion of Islam and Muslims can be contentious and loaded, and therefore we attempt to open a window to the complexity of discussions referring to what it means to be 'Muslim'. We thereby seek to provide a reflective position for social workers and other social welfare professionals in their work with Muslim colleagues and service users.

First published in 1997, Huntington's description of the clash of civilisations might today be perceived as a prediction come true, with global power struggles increasingly defined by homogeneous categories of 'us' versus 'the other'. In this sense 'us' constitutes the 'civilised West', while the other may be perceived as an 'orthodox, hate-filled Islamic' mass. Dichotomised discourses such as Huntington's have been reinforced by both radical Muslims, such as Abu Izzadeen, who challenged British MP John Reid (Johnston, 2006), and those who have rejected Islam. One such case is of Ayan Hirsi Ali, the current favourite of the neo-conservative world based at the conservative think tank the American Enterprise Institute in Washington DC. Her rejection of her upbringing is not couched in terms of growing up in Somalia within a specific social and political context, but of Islam as an evil ideology that threatens the preferred ideal of Western democracy.

This perceived clash of civilisations forms the background of global conflict, political expediencies and 'Islamic' terrorism as it is played out in the 24/7 media in seeking an edge in readership and viewers, leading by way of sensational headlines and sound bites. It is this context that plays consistently in the background as people (Muslims and non-Muslims alike) try to live their daily lives in contemporary multicultural British society.

The establishment of an Islamic community

Islam, the third of the monotheistic religions, followed closely in the ideological steps of Judaism and Christianity with Abraham as the grand patriarch. Mohammed (570-632 BCE), the Prophet of Islam, brought to the Arabian peninsula a new social order that had its base in the revealed divine word. In defying the social order of the time, and the polytheistic Hijazi society, Mohammed (pbuh) created a new community of believers: the *ummah*. If the divine revelation could be considered a strategic intervention (Arkoun, 1994), then it can be stated that Mohammed through the symbolism of Islam created a social and political framework that challenged the order and power of the day, moving away from tribal allegiances towards allegiance to a divine entity: God or Allah. Mohammed's articulation of the divine word was fundamental in establishing a society distinct from, yet embedded in, existing cultural traditions (for example by incorporating a pagan ritual, the *Hajj*, into the new Islamic symbolism).

While the Islamic calendar may divide historical time into 'before' and 'after', Islam as a religion has roots that lie deep in a monotheistic past; however, the historical framework is rooted in localised cultural and political factors (Arkoun, 1994). It is often the conflation of the two that leads to references to a monolithic Islam, and this conflation, sometimes difficult to separate, is increasingly used in current political discourses and policy formulations.

The Qur'an, the *hadith* and the *shari'a*

The Muslim *ummah* was formed based on the divine discourse as revealed to Mohammed. These revelations were recounted by Mohammed to his followers and disciples who later wrote them down, creating the written text of the Qur'an: the *al kitab*. The sacred word of the Qur'an is the foundation of Islam and is considered by the majority of Muslims to be the word of Allah, the divine word par excellence (Shimmel, 1992).

During the life of Mohammed, the *ummah* directly addressed him with questions, problems and issues to be clarified. However, when revelation stopped with the death of Mohammed, the community strove to fill this gap by remembering and writing down the Prophet's own words and actions. These texts form the *sunna* or the prophetic tradition. The *sunna* comprises *hadith*, or sayings of the Prophet, and authenticated *hadith* are considered infallible examples of how believers should conduct themselves. The *hadith* therefore are read by Muslims in close connection with the Qur'an.

Similarly, in a desire to establish and implement a way of life guided by the Divine, the *shari'a* was written as a Muslim law guide. The *shari'a* or 'the Way' is not the word of God but is a divinely inspired guide that extends and elaborates on the teachings of the Qur'an and *hadith*. The *shari'a* was formulated in the seventh century, seeking to inspire legal practice with Islamic principles, and is also referred to as 'Islamic family law'. The *shari'a* has been incorporated to some extent in most Muslim societies or nations. Although, as discussed further in Chapter Four, women's groups in some countries are campaigning against versions of the *shari'a* that are part of national legislation but which are considered to undermine women's quest for justice and equality (Mehdi, 1997; Anwar, 2005). Conservative fringe groups in the UK have also called unsuccessfully for the establishment of *shari'a* law. Additionally in 2005, the premier of the province of Ontario, Canada, rejected a call for the establishment of Islamic tribunals to arbitrate in civil and marriage disputes after successful lobbying by Muslim women's groups. More recently Dr Rowan Williams, the Archbishop of Canterbury, has also raised the idea of adopting aspects of *shari'a* law in the UK, causing a storm of controversy in the media (BBC, 2008).

The Qur'an, the *hadith* and the *shari'a* form the foundation of 'Islamic' thought and practice. The Qur'an is considered the divine text and thus closed and unchangeable, but the *shari'a* has been open to interpretation and elaboration, leading to some level of transformation within specific socio-cultural contexts. While some have argued that the Qur'an should be viewed as a strategic intervention within a particular historic context, it, the *hadith*, *shari'a* and Mohammed, as a true follower of Islam, are held in high reverential regard by most Muslims. This veneration is understood with great difficulty by many non-Muslims in the Western world and has led to mischievous provocation, such as the Danish cartoon affair, or the DKNY jeans with Qur'anic verses on the back pocket, Nike shoes with a symbol resembling Allah in Arabic, together with the designer dress produced in 1994 with embroidered Qur'anic verses on it.

Islam and Muslims

The word 'islam', as derived from the Arabic root 'SLM', is defined as 'submission, resignation to the will of God', whereas the verbal forms of 'SLM' mean 'to submit, surrender, resign', as well as 'to be secure' and 'to be protected from harm'. Additionally the word for peace, 'salam', is derived from the same root.

In the context of the religion, *islam* can be defined as 'giving one's whole self over to God', and other connotations associated with the word include transcendence: a move towards God and to a higher level of existence. A derivative of SLM, 'muslim' is defined as someone who submits to the will of God, or acts in loving obedience to God, and not necessarily a follower of Islam. This distinction is explained in some detail by Arkoun (1994) with respect to Qur'anic references to Abraham as not Jewish or Christian but as a 'muslim'. In the Qur'anic context then, *muslim* indicates an 'ideal religious attitude' towards God, a complete obedience exemplified by Abraham's willingness to sacrifice his son. Therefore, it is possible to talk about *islam* and *muslims* at two different levels. The first is the *Abrahamic islam*: a religious experience, a purity of communication with God that pre-dates rituals and legislation, and that is reaffirmed in the experiences of Mohammed. The second are the notions of *Islam* and *Muslim* as defined and written within the historical, social and political framework of the revelation. Again we find these words, which are steeped in significance and connotation, existing at two different levels that are often intertwined as meanings become conflated and the *din* and *dunya* (sacred and profane) are woven together.

These definitions are relevant in contemporary discourses as these words are used freely to define social, political and national movements, and often synonymously. What is an Islamic Republic, for example as in the Islamic Republic of Pakistan? What shades of meaning are there when one refers to 'Muslim communities' as opposed to 'Islamic communities'? 'Islamic terrorists' or 'Muslim terrorists'?

These terminologies are constantly being debated, and although these discussions might not appear to be directly relevant in the context of a social work intervention, it is worth noting that how we identify and refer to others, and how others self-identify, is constantly shifting and changing. Ethnic monitoring in the UK has been transformed with the faith question, with many Muslims preferring to self-identify as 'Muslim' rather than use an ethnic identifier (for example, British Muslim versus Asian of Pakistani origin). Additionally, at the margins there are voices questioning the notion of a Muslim identity that is British – a challenging topic that we shall consider later in the chapter. Consequently a discussion of identifiers and their significance is critical in developing an understanding of the complex nature of what is happening in contemporary society, both nationally and globally, as our consciousness continues to be pervaded by references to 'Islam' and 'Muslims'.

Fundamental principles of the *ummah*

The debate about the historical context versus the unchanging divine word forms another backdrop in understanding the complexity of what it means to be Muslim. Grasping the basic nuances underpinning these issues will hopefully assist the reader in considering the multiplicity of factors that interact in creating a Muslim consciousness. Although there are many competing voices attempting to articulate the meaning of being Muslim, it is still legitimate to attempt to extract factors that contribute to the creation of a unifying *ummah* and a common Islamic discourse. At its most simple, this leads to a consideration of the five fundamental duties, the so-called 'pillars of Islam' that are obligatory for all believers.

The first principle is of the *shahadah* or bearing witness to the monotheistic nature of Islam and the prophecy of Mohammed. The *shahadah* sums up the central points of Islam, that there is only one God and that Mohammed is His prophet. The recitation of the *shahadah* is usually considered sufficient to confirm conversion to Islam.

The second fundamental duty is that of prayer or *salat*. This is the most important duty and structures daily life for Muslims. While the Qur'an does not mention the number of daily prayers that should be undertaken, so far as is known the ritual prayer was practised five times a day by the Prophet Mohammed. The times of these prayers are fixed according to the daily movement of the sun, whereby Muslims are required to stop whatever activity they are engaged in and pray at the designated times: before sunrise, midday, late afternoon, at sunset and after nightfall. The ritual prayers are performed facing the holy site in Mecca and while all denominations of Islam accept the five daily prayers, some have reduced the five ritual prayers to three designated time slots (before sunrise, midday and after sunset).

The third principle is that of *zakat*, an alms tax aimed at benefiting the poor and needy in society, which is discussed in greater detail in Chapter Three. This obligation is clearly delineated in the Qur'an, which indicates the amount payable together with how the collected money should be disbursed.

The fourth pillar, which seems to be increasingly observed with greater strictness, is that of fasting or *saum*. Ramadan, the ninth month in the Muslim lunar calendar, is the month of fasting when practising Muslims refrain from eating, drinking and smoking from sunrise to sunset. It is quite common that Muslims who might not follow any other rituals during the year will fast for the entire month. While the basic premise of fasting is consistent across all Muslim communities, there are some who interpret the fast with exacting rigour. It is therefore important to develop an understanding and awareness of the basic principles (see Case study 1), and have access to a source of knowledge to follow up on issues that may consequently be raised.

Case study 1: The importance of contextual knowledge

In a recent consultation with British secondary school teachers about their teaching experiences, one teacher mentioned how some of her Muslim pupils wanted to constantly spit in class during Ramadan, stating that while fasting they were not permitted to swallow their own saliva (Husain, 2007). When the teacher contested their actions, these pupils from the British Somali community became aggressive and accused the teacher of 'dissing' their religion. At first the teacher tried to explain that spitting was not allowed in the classroom irrespective of who was doing it.

Unsure of how to adequately resolve the situation and understanding that additional information was needed, the teacher discussed the situation with her colleagues. A Muslim colleague of South Asian origin then explained some of the different interpretations and practices that take place during Ramadan. In the presence of the Muslim colleague the teacher then spoke to the pupils who were involved and explained that swallowing saliva did not invalidate the fast. The understanding reached was that in the classroom there were rules that all pupils had to abide by and that while she respected the pupils' fasting practices, she knew that this particular practice varied across communities and cultures. Because of this variability in practice, they agreed that spitting would be suspended during class. The presence of or knowledge that can be gleaned from a 'cultural expert' is often useful for professionals who may be unfamiliar with the details of cultural and religious practices within families and communities, even if only to highlight differences in practices.

Another example emerges from a national Arab university where the first author taught. A white American convert to Islam took up cudgels with the predominantly foreign-run faculties for continuing classes during Ramadan, instead of suspending them during the Holy month. She was duly informed by an Arab student that her interpretation was wrong and that abstention from normal daytime activities, despite the extra fatigue, was not religiously condoned as a condition to fasting. Unfortunately, however, matters can deteriorate quickly where misunderstandings and miscommunications abound in relation to issues of rigid interpretations of faith (Case study 2).

Case study 2: The 'anti-Islamic' academic

A non-Muslim social work academic visited a Muslim student on placement for a routine supervisory session. During this visit the academic enthusiastically commented on population demographics, moving on to expand on the topic of increasing longevity in most developed countries. The student retorted that according to her understanding of the Qur'an the lifespan of individuals could not exceed a certain age (70 years old). Perplexed by this anachronistic point of view, the academic pointed out that the demographics of their particular society showed that this was far from the case, but on the contrary proved a generally accepted point. She went on to offer the explanation that of course when the Qur'an was written 70 years would probably have seemed the maximum age any human could reach. The Bible held the same opinion, but clearly this was no longer true for people living in the modern age.

The student angrily retorted that the Qur'an was written 'for all time' and its words were not just relevant to one historical period. The academic, realising she had inadvertently put a foot wrong, apologised for any offence caused but suggested that perhaps the student would care to check the demographic figures for herself.

Assuming that all was now peacefully resolved, the academic was later very bewildered to discover that the student had decided to publicly denounce her to numerous other Muslim students as 'anti-Islamic'. This allegation served to escalate classroom tensions to the point of achieving severe disruption for the rest of the semester, to the detriment of the students and the academic alike.

Returning from our case study digressions into belief and practice, we consider the last pillar of Islam, which is the pilgrimage to the *Ka'aba* in Mecca, Saudi Arabia. Taking place at a particular time of the year, millions of Muslims will travel, at least once in their lifetime, to perform the rituals of the *hajj*. Ancient Arab rites have thus been transformed and sacralised into the ultimate spiritual experience for Muslims. The *hajj* is not only a purification ritual but also unifying ritual: a coming together of Muslims from all over the world and thus affirming the existence of the *ummah*. Such unity, for instance, profoundly affected the black activist Malcolm X on his pilgrimage in 1964, where he experienced 'the equality of all believers regardless of race, tribe, or nation' (Esposito, 2002, p 54).

While the *hajj* remains the ultimate pilgrimage for all Muslims, there are other pilgrimages that are of relevance to different denominations. Certain local and cultural variants of Islam incorporate visits to the shrines of saints, and in particular the visitation of the holy sites in Iraq is strongly associated with Shi'a Muslims. Such differences are not generally known about beyond the Muslim world; yet the invasion of Iraq by Western coalition forces, and the increase in sectarian violence in Iraq, has highlighted the diversity and tensions that exists between denominations within the monolithic concept of Islam.

Although differences in the practice of fundamental duties do exist, the five pillars of Islam, *shahadah, salat, zakat, saum* and *hajj* are the unifying threads that bind the *ummah* together. In so doing they provide a set of core rituals and practices that enable consistency and continuity to exist on both spiritual and historical levels.

Sacred spaces

In every social grouping there is a specific ideology or frame of reference that is used to form and structure society and to establish the boundaries of that social structure. This is also true for the groupings of Muslim societies within the overarching notion of the *ummah*, where to 'be' and 'live' as a Muslim entails defining clear boundaries governing social activities. One basic division, not unique to Muslim societies, is that of 'public and private space'. The public space is male dominated, and the private space, being dominated by family life, is comprised in general of the 'world of women' (Mernissi, 1983); this is a topic we revisit in more detail in Chapters Four and Five in drawing out the implications for women and children.

Furthermore, public spaces within Muslim communities can be further divided into two distinct spaces: the socioeconomic and the socio-sacral. The latter space within Muslim communities is the mosque, which serves not only as a religious space for performing the rituals of prayers but is also a social space. As a religious space, the mosque facilitates and strengthens the spiritual bond between an individual and the divine entity. As a social space the mosque provides a space where people can gather to discuss religious, social and political issues. As discussed in Chapter Three, this is the supreme space of social reconciliation where believers seek empowerment and reconciliation as a collective.

Mosque attendance is largely a male activity, although most purpose-built mosques have a separate section for women. This is a possible consequence of the ideological division of public and private spaces into male and female domains. In some countries, such as Senegal, women are forbidden entry into mosques altogether. Certainly, some mosques will not allow women into the male sections of mosques even outside of prayer times. Culturally accepted by some, this division remains a contentious issue with Muslim women's groups, who argue against this practice by using the example of the *Ka'aba* in Mecca, where men and women pray side by side as equals before Allah.

In the contemporary era with purpose-built mosques in every major British city, the nature and function of the mosque has not changed but instead has been expanded, with some mosques providing a range of social support as well as religious education for children. As elsewhere mosque attendance remains largely a male activity with some mosques in Britain not providing any space for women to worship. This issue was sensationally highlighted in the media recently when a women's group vocally campaigned to be permitted into such mosques and was followed avidly by camera crews. Predictably it was also raised in a speech on multiculturalism by Prime Minister Tony Blair in relation to British values (Blair, 2006).

However, it should also be noted that the wider development of mosques on the British landscape has altered over time. The first real mosques pre-dated the initial wave of Muslim migrants in the 20th century. Proper mosques, however, had already been established in the cosmopolitan cities of London and Liverpool in the late 19th century under the energetic patronage of a Dr Leitner, a Hungarian academic and Orientalist, and 'Shaykh Abdulla' Quilliam, an English convert to Islam, appointed by the Shah of Persia as his consul for Liverpool (Nielsen, 1999, p 4). Nonetheless, in general mosques evolved in Britain from the more common arrangement of creating a place of worship in houses, following the need for a sacred space by male migrant workers from Muslim countries (Peach, 2006).

Sex segregation nevertheless carries further ramifications in relation to worship and gender differentials. Muslims are required to pray at the designated time, wherever they are. To enable this, the mosque's sacred space is easily transferred to the prayer rug which functions as a transportable sacred space permitting believers to recreate the link with the divine anywhere. For women who do not go or are not allowed into mosques, the prayer rug is their only way to create the sacred space needed to perform the prayer ritual. However, as Nielsen notes, given this gender segregation it has not been uncommon for the content of prayers to be quite different between men and women, in which those of women are considered far less authentic and more superstitiously grounded than the more profound piety of men (Nielsen, 1999, p 23). Thus we can see that equal entry to mosques by females along with males carries implications in terms of physical access and access to sacred content, which accordingly affects the status of pious Muslim women in relation to the dominant male elite in the *ummah*.

Gender and Islam

The discussions and debates about the status of women in Muslim societies can be endless and all consuming. It is also very easy to utter banalities about this issue but an underlying fact is that the Qur'anic revelations did not modify the prevailing social conditions governing elementary kinship structures, the control of sexuality and the distribution of wealth and power in a society (Levi-Strauss, 1967). This is certainly not unique to Muslim societies and Lerner states that patriarchy, or the gendered distribution of power in societies, is a historical phenomenon that 'arose out of a biological determined given and became a culturally created and enforced structure over time' (Lerner, 1986, p 42).

Within the Muslim world polemics on this issue range widely. These extend from the conservative discourses, such as that of Maududi, from South Asia, who declared that a woman's 'natural' place was in the home as mother and nurturer, to feminist discourses that challenge this orthodoxy, as well as Western feminist discourses of female oppression (Mernissi, 1983; Ait Sabbah, 1986; Maududi, 1986). Many of these issues are further developed for readers in Chapter Four. However, in the brief discussion permitted here, it is argued that the situation of 'women in Islam' should be examined in the context of each society and every ethnocultural group. In the battle for female emancipation, whether in the 'West' or in 'Islam', the biological, anthropological, historical and socio-cultural condition of women has yet to be completely mastered (Arkoun, 1994).

The debate on the status of Muslim women in Western societies has for the moment become focused on women's clothing, in particular the veiling of Muslim women. Some Muslim feminists have analysed the concept of veiling in great detail, noting nuance and how the intersection of class, status and denominational affiliation play significant roles. Indeed, it should also be noted that the politicisation and 'Arabisation' of Muslim communities in the West have also had an impact on women's clothing. Suffice to say, at this point that the appropriation of women and, in particular, their bodies as symbolic spaces to be elevated, abased or to be fought over is not a uniquely Muslim concept but one that is as old as patriarchy itself (Lerner, 1986; Minh-ha, 1989; Jeffery, 1998).

Culture, faith and tradition

The different levels and layers of history, ethnicity, culture, tradition, ideology and denomination all contribute to creating what can be viewed as an unvarying, unified Islam and *ummah*. However, as one slowly peels away the onion-skin layers, it becomes apparent that, although marginal voices call for some kind of return to a pure Islam and *ummah* that existed during the time of the Prophet, the original framework was strictly coloured by the local context that existed at the time the revelations were received by Mohammed. Therefore, in discussing Islam or Muslims it is imperative to establish the precise contextual references. In the Muslim world, the notion of a monolithic Islam, devoid of cultural nuance and traditional texture, conflates diversity; as does the stereotype of a single essentialising characteristic defining the so-called 'West'. Consequently, it would be obvious to most that when speaking of the notorious cartoons of Mohammed, it is nonsensical to refer to them as 'the European cartoon affair' when it initially involved the Danish media.

Moreover, the dichotomy inherent in the idea of 'us' versus 'them', or 'the West' versus 'Islam', is one that is exploited by extreme voices on both sides of the divide. Consequently for 'Islamic' extremists and conservative clerics, as well as the political neo-conservatives and extreme nationalist movements (such as the British National Party in the UK), the notion of static and closed social communities is used as a convenient untruth that serves both sides equally well in promoting self-serving agendas.

Denominational diversity

Denominationally, Islam is as rich and diverse as the variety of branches of Christianity. The first split in the *ummah* took place soon after the death of the Prophet. The conservative branch of Sunni Islam accepted the leadership of the three orthodox Caliphs, while the Shi'a rejected the Caliphs and recognised the Prophet's son-in-law, Ali, as the first *Imam* and the legitimate spiritual heir to Mohammed. This divide is significant and resonates deeply within the global *ummah* with some Sunni sects claiming that Shi'a are 'non-Muslims'. Certain Muslim countries have been marked by sectarian Sunni–Shi'a violence, with the majority Shi'a countries being Iran, Iraq and Yemen. In recent times these sectarian differences have been played out on the global stage in Iraq; in Pakistan armed groups on both sides have been involved in Sunni–Shi'a violence for decades.

Within the Sunni tradition there are four main schools of thought and jurisprudence; however, the differences between these groups are minor. The majority of Muslims in Britain are Sunni, and it is worth noting that Sunni and Shi'a mosques are distinct, with worshippers frequenting their denominational mosques, similar to the ways that Catholics and Anglicans frequent their own churches. The Shi'a tradition comprises the majority Twelve Imam Shi'as and the Ismailis. There are further distinct groups of Ismailis. Apart from these main Shi'a groups there are other smaller, related sects that are localised minorities within larger Muslim societies.

Away from the dogmatic definitions and the conservative ritualisation of religious practice arose another current in Islam, that of ascetic mysticism known as Sufism, which today continues to attract many converts in the West (Esposito, 2002). Marked by a pure devotion to God and love for humanity, Sufism is practised by both sexes and is characterised by the influence of poetry and devotional music. David Waines (2003) sets out the often tortuous but profoundly spiritual 'inner' path of Sufism by drawing on the legendary tale of Hayy b. Yazqan, an allegory written by the multi-talented Abu Bakh Ibn Tufayl, a philosopher, teacher and physician born near Granada, al-Andalus, in the year 581 BCE. In the story, the hero Yazqan starts life as a feral child reared by a doe, yet through innate human ingenuity, aided by sense data, finally attains a state of enlightened and ecstatic metaphysical wisdom (Waines, 2003, pp 133-4).

Sufi sects exist in most Muslim countries and in some instances their influence permeates into localised socio-cultural practices. Equally however, Sufism is open to adopting new, local practices, and consequently has been criticised for this and for their devotional focus that considers emphases on 'laws, rules, duties, and rights to be spiritually lacking' (Esposito, 2002, p 57).

One contrasting denomination that has become highly influential in recent decades is Wahabism, the majority Sunni sect in Saudi Arabia. It is characterised by orthodox purity and, in the view of many, conspicuously tribal traditions regarding gender rights. Nonetheless, its message is increasingly promoted through the building of mosques and the regard the *ummah* has for Saudi Arabia as the guardian of the holiest shrines (the *Ka'aba* in Mecca and the Prophet's mosque in Medina) in Islam. It has, however, also achieved some notoriety in relation to the association with Osama bin Laden (Esposito, 2002). Historically the iconoclastic Wahabism has known a bloody past in its puritanical quest for purity, waging war on Muslim dissenters and unforgettably destroying many sacred Islamic sites, including 'the sacred tombs of Muhammad and his Companions in Mecca and Medina' (Esposito, 2002, pp 51-2). John Esposito goes on to add that this legacy inspired the Taliban's deplorable, philistine destruction of the superb, ancient Buddhist sites that Afghanistan once boasted of, and which was duly condemned by Muslim leaders worldwide.

Nationalism and fundamentalism

Radical Islamic movements are a recent development in the history of Islam, which can be traced back to the colonial era in the creation of nations with majority Muslim societies and the secularisation of political discourses. The notion of Islamic 'fundamentalism' includes many groups, which combine religious revivalism with political ideology together with social welfare, offering an alternative to secularised ideologies.

Up until the 1970s these revivalist movements were localised and existed within the context of nation states where groups, such as the Muslim Brotherhood in Egypt, filled a vacuum created by secular regimes that had failed to provide a sense of identity or educational and social welfare structures that would benefit the poor and needy. Therefore, underlying the creation of these movements was a class struggle and a sense of social justice that sought to follow Islamic principles to improve the social condition of the impoverished and illiterate majorities. Certainly, these movements also viewed historical developments as part of a greater cosmic struggle between good and evil, between the righteous who followed Islam 'properly' and those who corrupted or rejected it.

Three major factors have contributed to the expansion of these movements from contextualised local politico-religious movements to international players with an increasingly strong grip on the consciousness of a global *ummah*. The first factor was increasing levels of repression in their home nations, which led many leaders into exile and settlement in Western European countries or North America where they were able to express their ideologies with more freedom. The second factor was the broader struggle between Western democracy and communism. This led to the funding and creation of the *Mujhadeen* (Holy Warriors) in the 1970s, whose role was to fight the Soviet Union whose forces had invaded Afghanistan in support of the repressive but capsizing Afghan government. The third and final factor was the post-colonial migration of large segments of the *ummah* to Western European countries where the consequences of migration, settlement and minority status have strengthened the voice for a unified global *ummah*.

The extraordinarily misconceived and tragic recent history of Afghanistan is one worth reviewing in relation to its complexity and the later ramifications that continue to throw a malignant pall over world events today. From 1979 to 1989 the Soviet occupiers of Afghanistan, being both communist and atheist, were strongly opposed by Afghan resistance leaders preaching *jihad* (the meaning of which indicates the struggle to follow a virtuous, moral life and one free from injustice and oppression, which may or may not include armed opposition) (Esposito, 2002, p 117). Their followers, the *Mujhadeen* were trained, armed and funded through Western assistance, channelled via Pakistan's military intelligence agency, specifically under the direction of the US President, Ronald Reagan, and aided by the more modest assistance from British Prime Minister, Margaret Thatcher – both viewed as 'enthusiastic' supporters of the Afghan *jihad* (Waines, 2003, p 270).

Thus was created the most unholy alliance of competing and lethal intervention from the Soviet and opposing Western alliance, synergised with Muslim zeal, in the form of a rising, international cadre of Muslim resistance fighters ready to sacrifice their lives in the *jihad* and to free part of their *ummah* from oppression and occupation. Elements of the *Mujhadeen* would eventually mutate into the infamous Taliban, but in the meantime the fallout in terms of the death toll and social upheaval of the Afghan conflict would be enormous.

> In the crudest terms, the ten-year *jihad* against the Soviets and the subsequent decade of inter-Afghan conflict cost more than a million lives, one and a half million wounded or maimed and some seven million refugees ... Afghanistan was cruelly blessed with more personal weapons of all types ... than similar inventories of both Pakistan and India combined. (Waines, 2003, p 273)

Migration and Muslim communities in Europe

The migration of Muslims to continental European countries has followed a similar pattern in which, according to Nielsen (1999), four main waves of migration have occurred. The first was that which would found historical Andalucía under the Moors. The second was that of the Mongol armies, which overran much of the Balkan states in the 13th century and whose permanent residents in the former USSR (Union of Soviet Socialist Republics) would be known as the Tatars. The great Ottoman Empire was the next in line and would leave a residual Turkish population, mostly around Eastern Europe and Greece. Modern Europe is now experiencing the fourth and latest wave, and in this section we will primarily concentrate on the post-colonial migration to the UK, before a brief review of the situation in Continental Europe.

The majority of Muslims in the UK are of South Asian origin and arrived in the UK to fill acute labour shortages in British industry, particularly in the textile towns in the North of England. Another surge of migration took place in the 1970s when East African Asians arrived in the UK after expulsion from Uganda under the dictatorship of Idi Amin, as well as from other countries such as Kenya, Tanzania, Zimbabwe and Malawi. The last major migration of Muslims occurred in the 1980s and was from particular areas of Bangladesh. Most of the early migrants from South Asia were young men and family reunification took place at a later date. Nielsen notes that a study of the Pakistani community in Oxford showed that the women were keen to join their menfolk to '"save" them from moral corruption', some of whom were establishing relations with local Englishwomen and on occasion contracting marriage as well (Nielsen, 1999, p 27).

Muslims of South Asian origin are mostly Sunni Muslims from Pakistan. The large Bangladeshi community is primarily from the Syleth region and have settled mostly in the East End of London. This has long been a traditional settlement area for migrants, such as the 17th century Huguenot refugees, as well as Jewish migrants, and now Bangladeshis followed by Somalis.

Other Muslim groups have arrived from multiple locations, such as the Turkish, Kurdish, Iranian, Iraqi and Moroccan communities, as well as those from different African countries including Somalia, Sudan and Nigeria. Not forgetting the former Balkan states: Bosnians and Albanians, in addition to white Anglo-Saxon converts to Islam.

Thus, when social work professionals work with Muslim individuals and families they should consider the different countries of origin, and the cultural-specific as well as regional-specific factors that have an impact in different ways on the way faith is manifested. Even within the same groups, such as Muslims of Pakistani origin, linguistic and denominational differences as well as levels of education have a significant influence on how Islam is promoted and practised.

BAKER COLLEGE OF
CLINTON TWP. LIBRARY

To reiterate, the majority of the Muslim population of the UK is concentrated in large urban areas, although until the last census in 2001, there were only estimates given of the overall number of Muslims in the general population. For the first time the 2001 Census included a question on religion, reflecting the importance of religion and a faith identity for many minority ethnic communities (Modood et al, 1997). According to the 2001 Census, the Muslim population of the UK was 1.6 million, or 2.7% of the population (Peach, 2006). Of this at least 68% of the Muslim population is of South Asian origin (Indian, Pakistani and Bangladeshi); however, it is clear that there are great ethnic, national and linguistic differences in the South Asian Muslim populations, as well as across the Muslim *ummah* as a whole.

The majority of the Muslim population in the UK is Sunni; however, there are no clear estimates to the numbers of different denominations. According to Peach (2006), based on the vernacular languages used in mosques, the majority are defined not just by denomination but by the use of a South Asian language or dialect. Peach concludes that the characteristics of the Muslim population reflect the ethnic majority, namely Britain's South Asian populations. The UK has more precise statistics on ethnicity and faith than those European countries which do not promote ethnic monitoring and record keeping. In fact some countries, such as France, consider it to be divisive to the promotion of a national French identity.

The diversity of Muslim communities in the UK is reflected in the range of practices and the development of mosques, where there are a wide range of Sunni mosques that are affiliated with different denominations. Recently, plans to build a mosque by the Tabligh-i-Jamaat in the East End of London were rejected, as the local Bangladeshi Muslim population, along with other local communities, felt that it was a radical movement. Mosques in Britain have been divided by linguistic and regional differences, for example sermons in mosques in the East End of London might be delivered in Bengali or Sylethi (a regional dialect) as the majority of the congregation is of Bangladeshi origin.

Within the Shi'a community, which traditionally establish *Imambargahs*, a place of worship but also where the martyrdom of Imam Husain[1] is commemorated, the language in which sermons are delivered will depend on the linguistic background of the congregation. Certainly Sunni and Shi'a will, if the option is available, worship in their own religious spaces, much as the Anglicans, Roman Catholics and Baptists, for example, tend to do.

For Shi'a Muslims there is always the fear of marginalisation and reprisal, based on historic events together with current perceptions of the faith. Those who listen regularly to the news will have heard of the Shi'a–Sunni conflicts in Iraq as well as Pakistan, but there is also a tendency for these tensions to be played out within the wider Muslim community. While these differences are often hidden and sometimes marginal, contextualising the wide range of Muslim communities as a monolithic whole may lead to great insensitivities, not only for social care practice but in the overall understanding of how Islam is interpreted and practised by different groups.

When they came to power in 1997 the Labour government attempted to create a unified voice for all Muslims in the UK, assisting in the establishment of the Muslim Council of Britain. For the government this eased their ability to communicate with 'the Muslim community', but many Muslims, and in particular those from minority denominations, feel that they cannot identify with such an organisation and regard its establishment as a matter of political expediency rather than as a sincere effort to engage in genuine dialogue.

The Muslim population in Britain suffers from significant socioeconomic and educational disadvantages. In particular, the asylum seeker and refugee communities, such as the Somali community, remain the most vulnerable in society. Characterised by strong family formation, high rates of marriage and a larger household, the Muslim population has the youngest age structure, with around 33% of the population under the age of 16 and as high as 38% for Bangladeshi Muslims (TUC, 2005).

The Muslim population in general is regarded as poorly qualified, as well as hampered by high rates of unemployment and economic inactivity. Muslim women are generally absent from the workforce and the rates of female economic inactivity do not take into account 'homeworking' (Modood et al, 1997). Recent data suggest that as many as one in three Muslim children may live in workless households (0-19 Update, 2003). A recent study shows that minority ethnic communities are marked by poverty with 73% of children of Pakistani and Bangladeshi origin living in poverty (Platt, 2002). Of the minority ethnic populations in the UK (distinct from refugee and asylum seeker communities), the Bangladeshi community is the most disadvantaged in terms of housing, education and income.

Other parts of Europe show some similarities with this depressing picture, as well as some significant differences. The Muslim population in France reflects its colonial past (as is true of Britain), in that the majority of Muslim migrants settling in France came originally from existing and former areas of influence in North-West Africa, particularly Morocco, Algeria and Tunisia. Apart from these Maghreb Muslims, other Muslims would follow in the 1970s, such as Turks and black African Muslims from Mali, Mauritania and Senegal (Wihtol de Wenden, 1996, p 53).

The challenge for the *ummah* in France has related to the underprivileged position of French Muslims in general, where education levels have been low and unemployment figures high. However, the secular values underpinning the Republic are an additional ideological obstacle to negotiate in presenting a prima facie and irrefutable cultural difference. In this vein, it is interesting to see that a recent poll conducted in the US reveals that American Muslims appear to be more assimilated into society than those in Britain and Europe (McAskill, 2007). This is partially attributed to the better living standards experienced by the *ummah* in the US, in addition to the higher levels of religion in American society, which is regarded as more compatible with Muslim belief systems than North European secularism.

On the issue of national allegiance, the invasion of Kuwait in 1990 by Saddam Hussein provided an interesting litmus test for Franco-Maghrebians (Wihtol de Wenden, 1996). Their vote in a French poll on the topic indicated a strong disapproval of American military intervention, yet they also thoroughly disliked Saddam Hussein's missile attack on Israel. Furthermore they showed a particular concern towards maintaining a viable future for themselves in France (Wihtol de Wenden, 1996). The French perspective towards its Muslim population has since altered. This has moved from regarding such minorities as suffering from adaptation problems to French society, towards a greater concern towards the issue of Muslim youth exclusion (Wihtol de Wenden, 1996).

Spain continues to have a poignant passion for its Islamic past, which it is argued is one that is both idealised and ahistorical in the minds of most people of Spanish descent, who are proud to claim their stake in such a romantic, ethnically diverse and richly cultured past (Abumalham, 1996). Yet, sadly, Abumalham goes on to argue that this is sharply delineated by a very different and pervasive attitude towards deprived Muslim minority groups in contemporary Spain. Unlike the educated, discreet and assimilated Muslim professionals in Spanish society, labouring Muslim Maghrebian migrants, mostly single males, are in danger of being seen as an underclass of social undesirables, living in shanty towns, 'ignorant of the Spanish language and social norms', who due to 'labour marginalization' problems tend towards criminal activities in relation to smuggling and drug trafficking (Abumalham, 1996, p 29).

In a great and tragic irony, the multicultural, intellectual harmony that existed in Sarajevo, Bosnia, has been compared to that of the glories of medieval, Islamic Spain prior to the ferocious, ethnic-cleansing Serbian attacks stridently encouraged by the nationalist Serbian President, Slobodan Milošević, on their Muslim neighbours:

> Our hauntingly beautiful, beloved Bosnia became a symbol
> of intractable ethnic hatred and hyper-intolerance, of all that
> is worst in the human community. (Shenk, 2006, p 8)

As David Waines recalls, barbarity and cruelty laid to waste this peaceful and productive society culminating in the worst massacre since World War Two when 7,000 Muslim men and boys were slaughtered in Sreberenica (2003, p 207).

Germany hosts the second largest number of Muslims in Europe, although unlike France and Britain this is not owed to its former imperialist influences, but rather to the modern labour market. In the 1960s Muslim immigrants, mostly from Turkey, came in droves in the capacity of cheap *Gastarbeiter* (guest-workers) (Waines, 2003, p 258). Although the assumption of many migrants was that they would eventually return to their homeland, the second generation who were born in Germany are now taking up German citizenship and establishing themselves in society more firmly than their parents did. One irony for Turkish migrants specifically, is that they may feel more able to practise their religion freely than they are able to do in Turkey, which remains influenced by the sweeping secular reforms of Kemal Ataturk in the early 20th century (Henkel, 2004). Viewed ambivalently by many Muslims globally, Ataturk established the modern Turkish state, abolished the spiritual leadership of Sunni Muslims (the Caliphate), and replaced *shari'a* with European laws (Fuller and Lesser, 1995, p 39; Waines, 2003, p 221).

The case of the Netherlands provides an interesting counterpoint to the rather bleak picture of Muslim ghettoisation in Europe, in that, although rife with integration and assimilation problems today, at first the picture for Muslim migrants in the Netherlands appeared rosy, or at least in the eyes of the indigenous population. Initially the Dutch assumed that past strategies of maintaining a policy of *equal but different*, in which specific social, political, religious and cultural groups lived and worked in separate 'social compartments', would also work in the case of Muslim migrants (Gowricharn and Mungra, 1996, p 116). This tactic employed the historical concept of 'pillarisation', in which minority groups could achieve an upwardly mobile, vertical thrust through the influence and help of peers further up the hierarchy. Assimilation into wider society was believed to occur at the top levels of the pillar, and through strong leadership and self-organisation of the group this served to draw individuals and families further up the chain of integration in turn (Gowricharn and Mungra, 1996; Spruyt, 2007).

Such a strategy worked for other religious groups like the Catholics in Dutch society, and it was thereby assumed that the way forward was for Muslims to create their own pillar. However, pillarisation failed in the case of Muslim migrants for various reasons, including the fact that such migrants were far less internally homogenised than the Dutch Catholics, as well as not having a sufficient vertical infrastructure to create an effective pillar in the first place due to ongoing educational and economic problems (Gowricharn and Mungra, 1996; Spruyt, 2007). The generous welfare system in the Netherlands that supported many Muslim migrant families could not ameliorate the yawning divisions between their condition and perspectives of life compared with those of indigenised Dutch citizens, on whose consciousness was being imposed the deeply unpleasant idea that 'second- and third-generation Muslims were less integrated than the first generation' (Spruyt, 2007, p 320). Furthermore, this generation seemed overtly hostile to Dutch society and values, which would eventually result in open conflict and erupting violence.

Politicisation and the quest for identity

In the UK, the Salman Rushdie affair marked a turning point in the politicisation of Britain's Muslim communities. As Waines comments, 'It has been observed that had Salman Rushdie's *The Satanic Verses* been written, say, by a Moroccan Muslim and published in France, there would have been no controversy' (Waines, 2003, p 259). However, apparently the fact that Sir Salman Rushdie was born in India was an intense aggravation and an offence to British Muslims, given that over half the British Muslim population originates from the Indian subcontinent.

In addition to the Rushdie episode, socioeconomic disadvantage, structural racism and the quest for a unifying empowering identity have in turn exposed a gaping hole in Britain's multicultural model. This gap in recent years has been quickly filled by marginal and extreme voices that promise strength in a collective voice that is pure and distinct from a local context, in which many Muslims, particularly the young, feel increasingly marginalised. A case in point relates to the alienated response of the Pakistani community in Manchester towards the first Gulf conflict, when Saddam Hussein was elevated in their view to an iconic Muslim hero battling in a righteous *jihad* against the Manichean and crusader force of George Bush and his British allies (Werbner, 1994). The plight of the invaded Kuwaitis was accordingly completely eclipsed as being merely part of the greater *ummah*, since it was argued by these proponents, 'They are Muslims. What difference does it make who their ruler is?' (Werbner, 1994, p 216).

The image of Saddam Hussein taking on the might of the West was apparently an appealing one for much of the Muslim diaspora, however corrupt, brutal and flawed his regime evidently was. This serves to illustrate just how alluring the promise of a *just* society based on Islamic principles is, in being cleansed of 'localised contamination' from a majority non-Muslim social and political structure. Harking back to a 'golden age' of Islam is compelling for those seeking to understand their marginalisation and socioeconomic oppression. This powerful image resonates intensely for Muslim populations, who are painfully conscious that hundreds of years of cultural, intellectual and military superiority in preserving and adding to the knowledge of the ancient civilisations came to an end during the period of the Renaissance (Fuller and Lesser, 1995). Europe, having absorbed and been nurtured by these extraordinary examples, was coming of age and would no longer look back for inspiration to the foster parent of eclectic Islamic culture.

Today in Britain, politico-religious, ideological movements have grounded themselves in the localised experiences of Muslim communities and seek the creation of a collective through the individual compliance to rituals and practices. Where secular models have failed these movements have become the voice of political and social change, and to some extent have succeeded in providing a sense of identity, belonging and continuity, as well as an agenda for radical change (Esposito, 2002).

It is argued that these radical movements are in a symbiotic relationship with Western nations where a Eurocentric interpretation of Islamic history and of Muslim–Christian history prevails. This history, characterised by fear and disdain, is still present in the consciousness of European Christian nations and is expressed socially and culturally at many levels (Hourani, 1991). Indeed, it is the combination of this fear and the loudness of extreme, opposing voices that provides the headlines for the media in speaking to millions, thereby providing a space where marginal voices become normative but where the majority of 'average' voices are silenced.

However, it is also asserted that the loss of its historical supremacy has left behind a sense of profound loss and trauma in the Muslim collective consciousness (Fuller and Lesser, 1995). The stunning past success in the spread of Islam, which travelled so far from its original birthplace, was regarded by Muslims as an incontrovertible sign of God's favour. Although much of the evangelical rewards were retained, in that so many of the world's population are practising Muslims, Islam's place as a dominant global power decayed as did over time its great seats of learning through the forces of modernisation, as well as through the impact of colonialism.

Muslim migrants living in the contemporary West are faced with both the general problems of all immigrants in finding their niche in a new society where they may be discriminated against, but additionally have a unique set of obstacles to overcome as well, argues Jørgen Nielsen (1999). First, *shari'a* was never originally visualised as applying to minority Muslim groups living in non-Muslim societies, and to attempt this is clearly problematic (Nielsen, 1999; Waines, 2003). Additionally, the *ummah*, in comprising a wide diversity of people from Asia (including the Middle East), Africa and Europe, inherently creates uncertainties when unravelling which practices are pivotal to Islam, and therefore to be retained and strengthened, over which are traditional, localised customs that may or may not be incompatible with the competing rights and needs of others in a multicultural society (Nielsen, 1999).

Human dignity and *insan al-kamil*

In this comparatively short discussion about Islam, it is apparent that 'Islam' and 'Muslim' are not static, ahistorical notions fixed in time and space, but are dynamic and in a continuous state of flux. History, nationality, locality and language all colour individual lives and create a rich tapestry of the *ummah*. Although areas of ambiguity, paradox and contradiction do exist, the tapestry would have little meaning if separated into its component threads.

This dynamic vision of Muslims and Islam is underpinned by unifying characteristics and values, which act as guiding principles in leading an Islamic way of life. Accordingly, although so far we have reviewed many problems and conflicts, as well as historical legacy and Islamic precepts, the diverse and the unified aspects of Islam remain key elements in comprehending Islamic perspectives. Consequently, apart from the fundamental five pillars there are other important concepts to consider, such as that of *ashan*, mutual care and respect, an idea that is clearly compatible with social work values. In addition there is also *izzat*, meaning respect or honour, an idea that resonates strongly among most Muslims, and although open to adverse interpretations is of value in understanding Muslim attitudes and consciousness.

Above all, at an individual level, Islam in its purest form seeks, like social work, to promote human dignity, with the additional mandate of raising consciousness to a higher spiritual level. Despite contention and localised variations of custom, the accepted principles and rituals act as a guide for individuals to follow the 'straight' path. This is one that promotes the aspiration of the ideal and complete human, *insan al-kamil*, and in conformity with the other monotheistic religions aspires to lead believers to eternal life.

Note

[1] Husain was the grandson of the Prophet Mohammed. He is considered to be the third 'Imam' by Shi'ite Muslims. Imam Husain, his immediate family and a small group of followers were killed by the Ummayid Caliph, Yazid, in what is now Karbala, Iraq.

Social work education and Islam

Addressing discrimination in social work education

Social work training in the UK is undergoing many transitions that will bring it into closer alignment with social work education taking place internationally. The three-year degree programme is one such development and will serve to move the vocation more firmly into the professional arena. In addition to this, the move to register social workers as practitioners, a common procedure in many English-speaking countries, is yet another step towards increased accountability. Each in turn will more clearly define the professional identity of social work and its orbit of influence and responsibility, although at the same time this will probably result in tighter control over the social work remit in the UK. In this event, the unfortunate repercussions are likely to be outside of mainstream social work areas, militating against progressive initiatives at community and grass-roots levels.

Social work education will also be under pressure to maintain a commitment to improving programmes to address the increasingly complex needs of a multicultural and multi-faith society. It remains to be seen how the institutes of higher education in Britain will meet the challenges of providing appropriate education for social work trainees.

A commitment to understanding and addressing cultural diversity has held a strong profile in social work curricula for some time. It is also one strongly promoted by the International Federation of Social Workers (IFSW) in relation to the Global Qualifying Standards for Social Work Education and Training, as outlined on their web pages (www.ifsw.org/en/p38000255.html). How this enterprise should best be managed, however, remains open to debate and experimentation, and has been subject to various strategies in the discipline both nationally and internationally over the years.

Accordingly, Frank Keating (2000) sets out to chart the development of anti-racist perspectives in their various evolutions, as they have been introduced into social work education in Britain. In doing so he argues that this momentum has paved the way for a more far-reaching examination of other forms of discrimination and oppression (Keating, 2000). He furthermore argues that anti-oppressive training, a further development, now requires a broader framework and one that takes into account multiple forms of oppression and their repercussions on individuals, families and communities (Keating, 2000).

The anti-discriminatory approach has been strongly fostered in social work training, and followed in the wake of anti-racism that was in turn an attitude of raised consciousness that tied in with new legislation such as the 1976 Race Relations Act. Both approaches sought to utilise alternative ways to a common end seemingly by addressing discrimination towards clients within service provision (Thompson, 1993). A further offshoot of both anti-discriminatory and anti-oppressive strategies involves the commitment towards closer understanding of minority cultures, this being endorsed as the 'sensitive' way forward (Payne, 2006). However others are critical of such approaches, arguing that they may produce social work 'technicians' capable of responding to multicultural client groups within the status quo of existing state-run bureaucracies, but who operate in a politically and morally neutral vacuum (Williams, 1998, p 220).

This vacuum of cultural competency, being devoid of the personal, is a problem compounded for non-white social work professionals, who can find themselves in jeopardy in the quest to 'be authentic as a practitioner', as Narda Razack (2001, p 220) writing from the context of the US argues. This may occur where there is a personal need by such professionals to address oppressive experiences within the bureaucratic confines of predominantly 'white, middle-class, psychoanalytic' agencies (Razack, 2001, p 220).

Employing a 'token' social worker of colour in an otherwise all-white professional agency can be read as offering a message of token interest in clients from minority ethnic groups, rather than offering a commitment to addressing the needs of such clients, including their insidious experiences of institutional and personal racism (Razack, 2001, p 224).

Tokenism results in personal and professional isolation. Individuals from particular backgrounds, in which the parameters and nuances of religion or culture are not easily comprehended, may be at greater risk of isolation. This could represent a particular concern for Muslim practitioners, whose world view and social orientation may differ markedly from those of non-Muslim fellow students and colleagues. Under these circumstances, such practitioners will find themselves pressed to advocate both on their own behalf as well as their clients'. The latter may in turn be lumped indiscriminately with other client groups, who share apparent similarities (ethnicity, for example) but whose actual backgrounds are for the most part dissimilar. An alternative but equally likely scenario is one where the religious identities and cultural backgrounds of individuals are viewed as being so alien that the basic commonalities of human development, personal need and circumstances are overlooked.

Globalisation and social work

In relation to ethnic diversity, a further point for social work education will increasingly lie in the obligation to adequately address the issue of globalisation. This will become a matter of increasing importance if the profession is to be sufficiently poised to take advantage of the opportunities created by this phenomenon.

In discussing globalisation in the classroom setting, issues of 'difference and complexity' will need to be sufficiently addressed (Suárez-Orozco, 2005). This, however, should not prove to be very difficult in that social work purports to take these points into strong consideration as a matter of course. For globalisation incorporates not merely the ebb and flow of economies across international borders, but that of human migration as well (Lyons et al, 2006). In addition to this, globalisation indicates how cultural transformations develop, as manifested, for example, through the reforging of separatist ethnic identities, such as can be seen in Spain, Britain and the former Soviet Union.

A further effect is seen in the metamorphoses of cultural identities. Some countries may have partially assimilated values and practices from dominant nations along the axes of world power. In so doing, this is likely to generate some reconfigurations of traditional perspectives into the incorporation of new cultural identities and social interpretations. Where such transitions are taking place the effects are also often felt in relation to social welfare, and thus give rise to new forms of social work practice, which meld established ideas with the new. These evolving responses in welfare provision thereby become examples of the processes of professional indigenisation.

In opposition to these paradigms are some ethnic and cultural groups that defiantly reject the encroachment of dominant cultural forms, as can be seen occurring in the Middle East towards principles, practices and policies deemed Western or, specifically, American. These too have their ramifications for social work, in which the linkages between social work values and traditional or cultural values may be regarded as, at best, tenuous. A further example of this incongruent fit between values may be found in relation to certain societies where a proportion of individuals are deemed of less value and of lower status than others.

Globalisation in the West seems for many a double-edged sword. In Britain the processes of globalisation raise fears over the perceived threat of immigration. It is often assumed in the media that there is a rising flood of asylum seekers who threaten to swamp the welfare services of the country of settlement. Yet it is equally thanks to globalisation that the diminishing ranks of personnel available to run essential parts of the British health and social care sectors are swelled by trained doctors, nurses and social workers from overseas. In the case of medical staff, there are concerns that they are often poached from developing nations whose resources are further drained.

With these large-scale events as a continuous backdrop it is all the stranger, therefore, that social work educational resources in Britain have concentrated so much on the local, at the expense of a more international perspective. Charlotte Williams, for instance, critiques social work education in Europe as 'fundamentally ethnocentric', this despite the overt needs of multicultural populations (Williams, 1998, p 211).

In addition, Lyons et al (2006, p 197) comment that in both the US and Britain the international content in the social work curricula has been treated with mostly a qualified measure of tolerance, leaning towards 'occasional responsiveness'.

This equates with our view: that too often in Britain international professional experience is not sufficiently regarded as valuable within social work. Although student placements may be arranged in overseas settings on occasion, these are usually seen as an esoteric undertaking, of uncertain future application, in comparison with more conventional, neighbourhood placements. In the meantime, those with international experience are often regarded as ill-equipped to teach social work in Britain, on the grounds of being insufficiently familiar with the local context. This, arguably, is quite a loss to the body of expertise that could otherwise be gained.

What is not sufficiently recognised is that social work in Britain is not particularly more complex or diverse than the social work practices and policies that are taking place in many other nations; it is parochialism at its worst and ethnocentric arrogance to assume so. To reiterate, the psychosocial needs of clients are not so markedly dissimilar across nations at a fundamental level, as Maslow's hierarchy of needs would indicate. In this vein, Brij Mohan, following Leroy Pelton, argues that commonalities need to be identified among individuals that stand over and above the regrettable splintering of collective interests along the lines of 'race' and gender, into 'differential power equations and interest groups' (Mohan, 2002, p 6).

Furthermore, in reference to a more global perspective in the profession, ideally social work values and practitioner skills are adaptable and transferable across boundaries, including international ones, enhancing rather than diminishing knowledge and skills. Last, but not least, there may be much to learn, and even benefit from, in knowing more about the morphology of indigenous social work as practised beyond our specific native land, such as *gotong royong* (forms of grass-roots community building) in Malaysia (Ashencaen Crabtree, 1999) or use of traditionally *wasta* mediation in conflict resolution, such as can be found across the Arab nations (Al-Krenawi and Graham, 2001).

Consequently, to paraphrase Tsang once again, if we are determined to keep our parochial blinkers firmly in place, ethnicity and cultural location will always be seen as belonging to the 'other', and never to ourselves (Tsang, 2001).

Teaching cultural diversity

A basic contradiction occurs where, despite a certain disinterest in international social work, great strides have been made to tackle racism within the British social work curriculum. It is debatable how far this anomaly has had an impact on the ability of social work students to fully embrace cultural diversity and commensurately to tackle racism within societies in global transition, particularly as it has been argued that Islamophobia, as a pertinent example, is in fact a particularly powerful manifestation of a phobic reaction to multiculturalism per se (Marranci, 2004).

Following a well-recognised line of reasoning, Johnson and Yanca (2004) argue that appreciation of the culture of clients is best reached through a fuller recognition and analysis of our own in a reflective process. Theirs is not a solitary voice on this matter but a point of view that is echoed by other writers arguing from within the discipline of social work and beyond. Virginia Lea (2004), for example, considers the value of helping trainee teachers to identify their own personal 'cultural scripts' influencing their cultural assumptions and professional conduct. Reflection enables them to duly recognise and facilitate processes of revision as they occur through experiential learning in encounters with cultural diversity (Lea, 2004).

Within social work itself, the use of an ethnographic approach towards the understanding of the 'texture of the client's life' can be used to draw out the client's personal experiences, and the meaning that they attach to them (Thornton and Garrett, 1995, p 68). Ethnography is not confined to the personal only, but can in turn be linked to structural oppression, such as racism, sexism, ageism and classism across multiple and intermeshing levels of influence.

The 'critical incident technique', as undertaken in the Australian context and elsewhere, may also be adopted in considering 'race' and ethnicity. This in turn is reminiscent of the cultural script portfolio, but is far more rigorous in terms of analysis. In this formal exercise an event in social work practice that has resulted in a shift of practitioner consciousness is identified and discussed in depth. Through these means the premises, transformation and outcome are made explicit in the process of analysis and self-discovery (Fook, 1996).

Finally, Robin Sakina Mama (2001) expounds on a pedagogic strategy taking place in the US, whereby social work students are introduced to cultural diversity first through increased self-awareness and second by introducing students to appropriate readings and a variety of the cultural practices, belief systems and customs of specific minority ethnic groups. The session is led by a weekly guest speaker representative of, and authoritative about, the particular ethnic group and associated issues pertaining to them.

Dominant pedagogies

Despite this wide range of learning strategies, it is nevertheless close to a truism to say that in the classroom setting dominant groups tend to impose dominant values (Taylor, 1997). In the West, for instance, epistemological concerns pertaining to the acquisition and generation of knowledge have favoured mechanistic (and, some would argue, masculinist) approaches (Bowers and Flinders, 1990).

Social work has traditionally tended to take a more open view of what may constitute knowledge. This has tended to emphasise the experiential aspect from both the client's and the practitioner's points of view in order to identify good practice. However, this too has been under much criticism as being unscientific and of spurious value in terms of accountability towards the client and the public purse. Instead, a much more quantifiable and positivistic approach has been demanded by some, in which evidence-based practice has been regarded as providing a much-needed correction to an assumed lack of rigour in the discipline. Many schools of social work, particularly in the US, are now committing themselves to teaching intervention techniques predominantly based on evidence-based practice, as being congruent with a recognised and dominant form of validity as used in the 'elite' physical sciences.

Nevertheless, this move has equally been subject to some powerful critiques, in which even for its proponents there are obvious difficulties to negotiate. There is the problem of the dichotomy between an objective and quantifiable method of empirical data collection versus the subjective-interpretative experience that has traditionally underpinned person-centred social work (McNeill, 2006). Large-scale empirical data tell the practitioner nothing of individual differences; and intervention that is not tailored to specific requirements *and* the personal and cultural values of clients, is liable to prove alienating and ineffective (Humphries, 2003).

Beth Humphries (2003) goes on to pose two important questions that encapsulate concerns for social work undertaken within broad multicultural parameters. The first question is: who can be 'a knower' of social work knowledge? Are there other ways of acquiring knowledge about client groups that work towards the goal of creating effective services that truly take into account both commonality of need and actual difference? The second question follows on: if we assume that we know what works in the West, in relation to the rest of the world 'what else *works* [and] to what end?' (Humphries, 2003, p 85).

Social workers internationally offer us examples of alternative practice with clients from specific backgrounds, such as Muslims. Many of these practices offer a challenge to accepted social work ideas and values. In this book we attempt to address these questions, as posed by Humphries, through the critical engagement of social work values with practice issues, with the additional aim of attempting to achieve a fuller understanding of the belief systems and the wisdom of Islam to the further enrichment of the diversity that is social work.

Social work values

Social work is arguably more ethics-based and directly concerned with values than any other profession, including medicine and law (Reamer, 1995). Professional ethics, however, have a tendency to become enshrined into static lists of operational directives and prescriptions. They do not in themselves form a substitute for values, which are instead ideals made dynamic through application and analysis in an exercise of praxis (Hugman, 2005).

Professional values, in the main, are expected to become internalised in practitioners, and thus may come to be regarded by the owner as merely common-sense concepts operating towards good practice. Few practitioners are consciously aware all the time of how values inform their decisions and shape their intervention. Yet, clearly they do, and in so doing are subjected to amendment, reinforcement and deepening subtlety and complexity – in a process that continues throughout the personal and career development of individuals.

In social work, practitioners regularly encounter situations that challenge held values; this is often the case with regard to conflict at multiple levels of engagement, often in relation to professional values, agency codes of conduct and personal values. Equally, in social work, most practitioners will have had experience of encountering paradoxical situations, where one value countermands the other, leading to an uncertainty about how to proceed. Under these circumstances most social workers will opt for a teleological utilitarian approach to the problem, in which the likely consequences of actions are assessed and balanced in the selection of the best possible outcome for involved parties.

Values and ethics change over time according to the social and political climate. Sarah Banks (2006) demonstrates this succinctly through a comparative examination of values, as laid out by the Central Council for Education and Training in Social Work (CCETSW) in 1989, in relation to a final updated version by the General Social Care Council in 2002. In the 1989 version the emphasis was on anti-racism and other forms of oppression. By 2002 the emphasis had shifted towards the protection of clients and their rights, together with professional accountability (Banks, 2006). The latter, and more encompassing, remit is currently congruent with the majority of identified values in the profession internationally. Moreover, Banks, in a comparative exercise of social work literature, goes on to identify three particular domains of professional values and ethics as outlined in Table 1.

Increasingly, two main issues are becoming more prominent in relation to social work values and ethics. The first lies in the awareness of cultural diversity within society, irrespective of concerns regarding

Table 1: Professional and ethical domains
1. *Respect for dignity and worth of all human beings*: includes promoting the rights of individuals and groups towards self-determination
2. *Promotion of welfare or well-being* of service users and society
3. *Promotion of social justice*: including addressing inequalities and the fair distribution of goods and services towards individuals and groups

Source: Banks (2006, pp 47-8)

racist discrimination. It inevitably means that at least some of the values held within one dominant group will not necessarily be shared by other groups. This has ramifications for social workers in working with groups who hold alternative values and belief systems, as well as for those wishing to practise social work, but without necessarily accepting all the values held by the profession or agency they are employed by.

The second emerging issue is the increased awareness of the spiritual needs of clients (and indeed practitioners as well, in many cases), and how these should be addressed in training and service delivery. This is a topic that we shall return to later in the chapter.

Internationally, we can find examples of social work driven by values that are not prominent within a Western context. Al-Krenawi and Graham (2001), for example, discuss the use of an informal 'cultural mediator' to intervene in the growing discord between a social worker and his Bedouin Arab clients in Israel. The problem revolves around four families, all of whom are closely related. Due to a quarrel one husband banishes his wife from the family home, retaining custody of the children under traditional prerogatives. This gives rise to offence in the second family and retaliation in which the second wife is ejected; and the exact same response is enacted in the third and fourth families respectively. The social worker, himself an Arab, intervenes, demanding the immediate return of the children to their mothers under Israeli law. This threat escalates tensions still further and it now becomes a tribal dispute, until, that is, the mediator is brought in to work with the families and the social worker, where order is restored.

The choice of the mediator in this social context stands in keeping with cultural notions, being a highly respected senior, inevitably male person of recognised community standing and pious outlook. He is therefore equipped to address traditional cultural issues pertaining to family honour and male prerogative, while juxtaposing these powerfully with Islamic principles. These fortunately are congruent with Israeli law in believing that young children under these circumstances are in need of the care of their mother.

However, apart from being an instructive anecdote, the main point in using this example is to demonstrate how the values evidenced by the client groups and cultural mediator, in this particular case study, offer an alternative set of priorities, from which the reader may gather that it is not the welfare of the children that is of paramount consideration here, nor the equal rights of access to children by both parents. Instead, what is considered of more importance within this cultural context is the balance and harmony of the immediate community. Thus relations of power between the families, according to status and position, should be symmetrical for equilibrium, as Al-Krenawi and Graham (2003) point out in a later paper on this topic. The initial quarrel creates an imbalance that triggers off a chain reaction of equivalence, which is at first negative, but then finally works towards an outcome of positive restoration and united families.

Despite being of Arab heritage, the social worker in this case study has been trained in models that are not indigenous, the results of which are clearly shown to be a disastrous mismatch of values, and indeed communication styles, between himself and his clients, which serves to inflame rather than alleviate the situation. The authors, not surprisingly, draw from research literature to contend 'that Israeli social work education "does not orient students towards reducing prejudice or enhancing their cultural sensitivity"' (Al-Krenawi and Graham, 2001, p 670).

A further example that is pertinent to social work is taken from the same region, and involves the education of Arab children in Israel. This serves to highlight some of the incongruence in values based in a traditional culture versus those of the majority Israeli culture. Mariam Dwairy (2004) argues that the prevailing self-orientated, individualistic ethos in services, in which young people are encouraged to be assertive, is directly in conflict with collective values prevalent in Arab communities, where 'assertiveness is frowned upon as a rude, selfish or even aggressive behavior', being one that is liable to expose perpetrators to family rejection and punishment (Dwairy, 2004, p 428).

A level of assertiveness, however, is required in the interests of pursuing autonomy and self-determination, both of which are highly prominent values in social work. Consequently, these are promoted by Western-trained social workers in work with clients. However, apparently some thorny paths must be negotiated first if Israeli social workers are to work successfully with Arab clients who may be unfamiliar with professional frames of reference that are normally Western-orientated and individualistic, as is the case in the Israeli context. Such considerations are not likely to be confined to Arab client groups alone, obviously, but instead hold wide-reaching implications for minority groups living within cultures with alternative and dominant discourses.

Islamic values

The issue of cultural diversity apart, the principles governing Islam itself are often regarded as being essentially compatible with social work values. This presents a viable challenge to some of the very negative

Islamophobic notions that abound, as David Hodge (2005) points out in reference to the 'denigrating images connoting ignorance, oppression, fanaticism and violence' (Hodge, 2005, p 7).

A further challenge to Islamophobia, which is often noted as a xenophobic fear of the Muslim 'other', is further offered by Naina Patel et al (1998) in the clarification of some of the beliefs that underpin Islam. These are viewed as overlapping the professional value-base of social work, and are paraphrased in Table 2.

Table 2: Islamic values
1. Emphasises the well-being and welfare of the community
2. All people (men and women) are regarded as equal
3. There is a relationship between individual freedom and the community's obligations to the individual
4. Conscience and conformity dictate the individual's sense of responsibility and obligation
5. Consultation between people is important in relationship building

Source: Patel et al (1998, p 199)

Patel et al's observations (1998) are next aligned with a slightly truncated version of the principles of Islam and daily practices in Table 3.

This is complemented by the daily and universal ritual practices of Muslim devotees, as defined in Table 4.

Table 3: The six pillars of faith
1. in Belief God (Arabic name, Allah) being the One Creator and Sustainer of all beings
2. Belief in and reverence of the angels who never disobey God, unlike humans
3. Belief in all of the revealed scriptures of God (including the original books revealed to the Prophet Moses and the Prophet Jesus)
4. Belief in and reverence of all prophets of God from Adam to Mohammed (peace be upon them) without discriminating among them
5. Belief in the hereafter
6. Belief in human free will, as well as the fact that nothing can happen without God's permission

Source: Adapted from Barise (2005, p 4)

Table 4: Five pillars of ritual practice
1. Declaration of faith (*shahadah*): there is no god but Allah and Mohammed (peace be upon him) is the Prophet of Allah
2. Prayers (*salat*): to be performed five times a day facing the holy *Ka'aba* (the first mosque built on earth) in Mecca
3. *Zakat* (self and property purification): to pay a proportion of goods for the welfare of the community
4. Fasting (*saum*) during the month of Ramadan: abstaining from all food and drink from dusk to promote religious consciousness, and allied virtues of restraint and compassion
5. Pilgrimage to Mecca (*hajj*): at least once in the life of all able-bodied adults

Source: Barise (2005)

In the following sections we discuss the values, outlined by Patel et al (1998) in relation to the principles of Islam and described by Barise (2004), with a further analysis of the suggested congruence between these two discrete canons. An exception is made with regards to a discussion of equality between the sexes. This being a large and complex area, it is the topic of Chapter Four, where it is unpacked in more detail.

The welfare of the community

In relation to the topic of well-being and welfare, Banks, in addition to other writers, is concerned not only with the empowerment of the individual, but the demand for social justice towards the community in the shape of social welfare (Banks, 2006).

In Islam there is an equal concern to balance these two claims in which an individual should strive for perfection through selflessness, altruism and giving happiness to others as a pious Muslim (Al-Krenawi and Graham, 2000). Nowhere are these ideals shown in collective action more succinctly than in the Islamic conception of welfare.

Zakat forms one of the five pillars of faith in Islam. This requires that Muslims pay a proportion of their wealth to the community for the purposes of providing public assistance to the needy (Barise, 2005). This moral imperative is of course not solely confined to Islam; much the same can be found in Christianity and Judaism for example. However, in the Christian context, the parting of goods is a private and pious, but essentially charitable, act. Hartley Dean and Zafar Khan (1997) argue that, by contrast, atonement is not the purpose of *zakat* in Islam. This has a more altruistic purpose altogether, for it is social justice itself that is served by a redistribution of wealth among the *ummah*. The very word *zakat* indicates its rationale in meaning both growth and purity.

The hoarding of wealth is believed to lead to economic malaise. *Zakat* purifies the wealth of the individual, but it also keeps the social, economic and political body or structure of the *ummah* from deterioration. To employ a metaphor that is often used for the purpose, *zakat* taps the parts of the body where the blood is congested and transfers it to those parts which are weak or anaemic (Dean and Khan, 1997, pp 197–8).

In the Christian tradition, the beneficiaries of charitable donation have no specific rights to assistance; however in the Islamic world this is not the case at all, and the needy, as equally worthy in their own right, have every right to claim from wealthier sections of society.

This has implications for citizenship issues, specifically in terms of the rights of the individual and the community's obligations towards them, a further point mentioned by Patel et al (1998). In terms of welfare assistance, it may also explain the generous welfare provision extended to citizens in the affluent society of the United Arab Emirates, for instance. There an affluent Muslim state can offer easily accessed welfare provision towards its underprivileged citizens, such as Emirati widows and divorced women, as well as other designated individuals; public assistance usually exceeds any comparable state welfare that can be found in the West. However, it is fair to note that such public assistance is the right of Emirati citizens solely and is not normally extended beyond those parameters.

Individual freedom and social conformity

Islam, as the Judaeo-Christian tradition, emphasises the interplay of the conscious mind in relation to the governing of conscience and the awakening of insight. These forces are instrumental in enabling individuals to exercise their choices as moral agents in society.

Equally, the monotheistic triumvirate of Islam, Judaism and Christianity all emphasise the importance of social concern and commitment by the individual that in turn leads to social conformity and justice (Burr, 2005).

With reference to Muslims in particular, to go against the overarching principles of society and religion, is in effect to behave as a bad Muslim: a most serious indictment. Thus for Muslims, while hypocrisy may exist naturally, there should, however, be no psychological or ontological gap for tensions to exist between social accountability and the individual inclination, as Dean and Khan so eloquently put it:

> It [Islam] eschews the dualism of the Western Enlightenment and thereby the inherently ambiguous distinctions between body and soul; between the secular and the religious; between state and church; between politics and morality; between public obligation and private belief. Islam is at one and the same time a religion and an ideology. (Dean and Khan, 1997, p 194)

Others would argue against this definition of singularity, in wishing to add that Islam does distinguish between body and soul or spirit (as in, *ruh*: 'prayer is food for the soul'). For fasting in Ramadan is a way to distance oneself from the physical body and to concentrate on prayer and spiritual nourishment through the strengthening of one's relationship with Allah. Finally there also exists a distinction between sacred time, which is eternal, and profane time, which is temporal and earthly.

Furthermore, for Muslims conflict is open to resolution ideally through informal as well as strategic consultation. To aid these processes, the social networks in the *ummah* are reinforced through the processes of spiritual connection and socialisation.

An excellent example is the in-mosque greetings of peace during major feast celebrations. Even enemies are compelled to be cordial. The feast seasons themselves often provide the context for settling instances of marital or family discord, very often with the assistance of concerned family members, neighbours or friends (Al-Krenawi and Graham, 2003, p 296).

A final conclusion is that to be a Muslim, one must act as one; and this of necessity means adhering in full and proper measure to all the expectations and prescriptions that are attached to the state, which include a declaration of faith (*shahadah*), as the first of the Five Pillars (Barise, 2005).

Conflict in values

What has been argued so far is that outwardly it would seem that the principles of Islam fit well with the three value domains of social work, as outlined by Banks (2006). However, there are some significant points where there is a departure, and one of the more prominent may lie in relation to the social work values of respect for individuals and the ethos behind anti-discriminatory stances. This becomes particularly prominent in relation to clients whose personal lives or orientation may be unacceptable to some practitioners adhering to particular religious points of view.

Islam, for instance, is not tolerant of homosexual orientations in principle, although obviously as a personal issue it may be practised in private. This, however, most clearly does represent a problem area for social work, as prejudice in this area stands in obvious violation of non-oppressive practice. So how does one square the circle on this issue?

Indeed, there are many issues that may be offensive to Muslims, as well as others, such as abortion, some forms of single parenthood, premarital sex, some types of adoption and euthanasia, to name but a few contentious areas. Social workers, however, are expected to work with most, if not all, of these aspects without discrimination. To attempt to force the issue, as an individual, that certain problems or client groups are not acceptable within one's own personal brief, is to attempt to redefine the basic core values of the profession as it is manifested within particular national boundaries.

Where there is a yawning gap between the practitioner's principles and the professional ethos, many would argue that it seriously militates against achieving effective work with clients. Unsurprisingly some in the profession may feel that under these circumstances the onus would be on the objecting practitioner to find an alternative outlet where they could practise within their own personal boundaries, such as in certain community initiatives and pastoral care.

Others might suggest that such practitioners should be reserved for work within mainstream social work with client groups who share their belief systems. However this tends to happily assume that faith clients who lead lifestyles unacceptable to devout Muslim practitioners will not be encountered. Michael Merry points out the fallacy in such thinking in discussing a similar issue for educators in the US (Merry, 2005).

Similarly, if we assume that religious customs and beliefs are altogether innocuous and seek merely to promote the good of the community its beliefs express, we unavoidably participate in the oppression of gay and lesbian Muslims (Merry, 2005, p 29).

Merry's observation is a crucial one, for many Muslims would argue whether a gay or lesbian can at the same time be a Muslim. This is an issue we return to later in Chapter Five . Yet Merry does raise an important point: moving faith practitioners out of mainstream social work practice and education, unless they can commit themselves completely to a non-oppressive professional ethos to all clients without distinction, diverts a difficult problem into a socio-religious, cultural cul-de-sac but does little to resolve matters satisfactorily.

Conflict between religion and social work is not confined to any one specific faith group. In discussing a new social work programme offered to ultra-orthodox Jewish women in Israel, Garr and Marans (2001) cite the reaction of one student towards the issue of a client's unwanted pregnancy, which was to immediately wish to discuss the matter with the student's own rabbi. The authors reflect on this reaction in the following way:

> The student focused on her own religious value system. As social work educators, the authors focused on identifying the client's needs. Dilemmas such as this emphasized the need for an effective method to teach that the best interests of the client must determine the treatment plan. With this student population we found a greater resistance than usual in changing the focus from themselves to the client, their needs and value system. Our presumption is that this resistance was reinforced by the centrality of religion in their lives. (Garr and Marans, 2001, p 463)

Putting client needs first is another essential social work value that fundamentally underpins good practice; however, as the Israeli authors point out, this can be problematic, and is a point that is thoughtfully considered by Malaysian Muslim psychiatrist Ramli Hassan (1993). Here he summarises a paradox: that of the professional ethos of unconditional acceptance of the client in the counselling situation, in relation to his moral obligations as a Muslim working with Muslim clients. This, he believes, should be to shepherd them back onto the correct path according to the dictates of religion:

> In such a relationship, the Muslim psychiatrist is first and foremost a Muslim and a psychiatrist second.... It obliges him to adopt a therapeutic attitude that may entail abandoning the detached, morally neutral and emphatic stance that he has been taught. (Hassan, 1993, p 94)

However, a challenge to this kind of stance was previously set by a colleague and fellow Muslim, who in reference to this very point deplores curtailing the autonomy of clients, and with it opportunities to explore their options in full, through 'moral preaching and defining the right path for the client. Such practices create an authoritarian image of counselling that may be hard to get rid of' (Soliman, 1988, p 9).

The argument of what constitute the correct obligations of the Muslim professional towards a Muslim clientele will no doubt continue, particularly as the label 'Muslim' encompasses a veritable diversity of individual opinions and intellectual perspectives. However, what is needed in the meantime is a more critical evaluation of social work values, which could usefully revolve around at least two particular points: first, that of respect for persons and, second, non-judgemental acceptance. Regardless of cultural and religious context, some students find these values difficult to relate to in any case. They question whether one really can respect people who commit offensive acts, whether towards others, the community or themselves. This kind of dilemma in fact disguises a basic misconception, in that it is not the action that commands the social worker's respect, but rather the moral agency of the client to make decisions for themselves, as an autonomous human being, according to the value of self-determination.

The Rogerian person-centred approach clarifies the issue to some extent by positing that all living organisms strive towards self-actualisation. Clients often make decisions, as do we all, that may on the surface appear unwise. Yet these actions are often steps that wend progressively towards a more complete wholeness, if only through increasing insight into self-motivation and needs. While this actualising process may not lead to a complete achievement of defined goals, social work by its very nature remains optimistic that the self-determined path undertaken towards this end is one well travelled.

For Muslim social workers working with clients who do not necessarily share their beliefs or adhere closely to their practices, this does not need to be a bar to effective work. It does not, however, mitigate the need to extend respect towards clients and suspend negative judgements of them. Judgement in social work is a necessary component, but should be employed only in the evaluation of intervention and outcomes, not personal condemnation (Banks, 2006).

The equivalent of non-judgemental acceptance is tolerance, and this is a quality that is much demanded in social work practice. Tolerance is also a quality that is not highlighted in the media as being a notable strength in the wider Islamic community; in fact the usual depiction is quite the reverse. These corrosive messages are consequently filtered down through society at all levels, including schools, creating suspicion and dread of the Muslim 'other' (Richardson, 2004).

The accusation of rampant intolerance by Muslim groups, however, is a blanket stereotype that is unfair. Interesting ethnographic evidence contradicts this derogatory assumption, where tolerance is shown to be a most important attribute in the conservative Arab Muslim communities of Oman in the Arab Gulf, where commendable pains are taken to avoid labelling others as sinful (Wikan, 1991).

In conclusion, however, the threat of a clash of values between the profession and faith groups is not going to instantly dematerialise, but may well come increasingly to the fore. There are two reasons for this: Islam is one of the fastest-growing religions in the West, and other religious groups also share these same prescriptions. There is a need for more open and sensitive discussion in the classroom setting regarding social work ethics and values, and the potential conflict for practitioners of faith, as well as others. A sound justification for this educational strategy is that the ethical base of social work is the cornerstone of the profession, and therefore merits as much critical discussion as do intervention strategies.

Finally, the entire dimension of spirituality and religion is increasingly being emphasised in social work literature as a neglected aspect of life that should be adequately taken into account, not only for the benefit of practitioners, but, more importantly, for those of their clients.

Spirituality, epistemology and cosmology

As indicated, attempting to draw a distinction between the spiritual aspects of Islam and secular considerations is a futile task, since Islam offers a unified ideology that permeates all aspects of daily life seamlessly. This will be a somewhat difficult concept to grasp for many readers, given that for historical and political reasons such divisions are embedded in the very fabric of societal institutions in Britain. Social work here has long since shed those roots that were originally located in charitable or state-run organisations with religious affiliations (Fowler, 1984; Payne, 2006).

Dissent, however, is growing, particularly in the US, which experiences a far higher adherence to religion in the general population than is the case in Britain, despite the number of faith groups in this country. Nonetheless, the General Social Care Council, formerly CCETSW, has duly turned its attention to this matter in considering how the religious and spiritual needs of clients can be best catered for within social work provision (Furman et al, 2005).

This is no mean task, bearing in mind the point that while religion of necessity encompasses spirituality, the reverse is not necessarily the case, and therefore this area becomes a formidably large terrain to coherently address in social work. In addition, assessment procedures do not cover this dimension of the human experience in much detail, and therefore adaptations may be needed for assessment protocols.

Yet it should be emphasised that such protocols should not be rigid in conception or application since faith, as manifested through institutionalised religion and ritualised practice, varies significantly within and between communities and families, and indeed individuals in families. To be 'Muslim' is as fluid a concept as for any of the other major religions.

David Hodge (2006) strongly endorses this move in considering the body of research indicating that spirituality forms an important source of strength for clients, who see no reason why their beliefs cannot be integrated with social work intervention. He goes on to offer some useful open-ended questions that social workers might use in assessing clients (Table 5).

Table 5: Assessing for spirituality
1. I was wondering if spirituality or religion is important to you?
2. Are there certain spiritual beliefs or practices that you find particularly helpful in dealing with problems?
3. Are there any spiritual needs or concerns I can help you with?

Source: Hodge (2006, p 319)

For Muslims, as Al-Krenawi and Graham (2000) explain, the ritualised observance of prayers five times a day enables the devotee to adhere all the more closely to the pillars of faith. Group prayer is deemed to be more effective than solitary prayer in consolidating a sense of being part of the universal community of believers, and is subject to the same rules. They also maintain that prayer acts as a safeguard against 'anxiety and depression' (Al-Krenawi and Graham, 2000, p 297). This point is more obliquely made in a cross-cultural study of Pakistanis in the UK and Pakistan, in relation to a correlation of prayer with mental health – a finding that tallies with Christian faith groups, and presumably others as well (Khan et al, 2005).

However, as Barise comments, 'Anyone can face hardships, but Islam allows practicing Muslims to perceive and respond to problems through the teachings of Islam and by God's help' (Barise, 2005, p 8). Since in Islam it is accepted that nothing can happen against God's will, this enables Muslims to view hardships as having some intrinsic meaning and purpose. The following extract highlights this points well, and is taken from an ethnographic study of family care-giving of children with disabilities in the United Arab Emirates:

> Acceptance of Allah's will in this regard brings not merely compensations but actual blessings upon the home; and thereby piety, as construed in this positive way, represented dominant forms of strength and resilience in such families. Thus three of the families described themselves as reaping the rewards of their compliant conduct through dramatic changes of luck or continued prosperity and tranquillity. One child with severe disabilities was described by her mother as: 'A gift from Allah. He is testing us. Allah gives everyone problems. Sometimes they are financial and sometimes to do with health. He gives us these problems to see how we will overcome them. Since we always look after X [child] and love her too, Allah will protect us. He gave us a lot when he gave X to us.' (Ashencaen Crabtree, 2007b, p 56)

In attempting to comprehend the scale of the Islamic framework, and its interaction with social work, it is important to acquire a basic understanding of two important areas influential in the perceptions of many Muslims. The first is, how do people know what they accept to be true (epistemology)? The second, what agencies or forces exist in the universe that in turn may assist or subvert human endeavours to live a principled life as a Muslim (ontology)?

Education, according to Islamic principle, should not only be accessible to both sexes, but is considered a demonstration of *Imaan* (religious faith) (Haw et al, 1998). However, as Barise (2003) explains, in the Muslim faith knowledge is acquired from God (Allah) as the true source, and is divided into two distinct areas: that of revealed and acquired knowledge respectively. This knowledge may be certain or speculative from the mortal point of view; however, there is no basic contradiction between revealed and acquired knowledge at the level of ultimate authority: Allah. But where contradictions are perceived this is due to human ignorance and frailty only. These would be resolved by consulting the revealed knowledge contained in the holy Qur'an and the sayings of the Prophet Mohammed (Barise, 2003).

In terms of ontology, there are once again two main areas: *shahadah*, which corresponds to the Western notions of sensory data, and which can be known via acquired knowledge, and *gayb*: that which cannot be known through the senses and is only known through revealed knowledge. As Barise explains:

> The human environment includes both the seen and the unseen creatures such as jinn and the angels. From the Islamic perspective, all creatures exist in compliance with God's will. All creatures, from the tiny atoms to the mighty galaxies, worship God and thus co-exist harmoniously according to God's will. When one accepts Islam, one becomes part of this harmonious co-existence *willingly*. Being a Muslim thus necessitates revolving on an assigned course (just like the electrons and celestial bodies do) without transgressing boundaries and infringing on the rights of the self, the environment, and God. (Barise, 2003, p 8, emphasis in original)

The goal that Muslims are meant to strive towards, according to Barise, is 'all-encompassing peace' and to this end, he says, they are guided by the pillars of faith and of ritual practice, with God as the 'ultimate Helper' (Barise, 2003, pp 8-10).

In seeking to live a life that will keep them 'on the straight path' to Heaven and in Allah's good grace, Muslims seek guidance from multiple sources. Apart from the Qur'an, which is considered the literal word of Allah and offers guidance on a range of everyday issues including marriage and divorce, many Muslims also refer to the *hadith*. The *hadith* are the sayings and actions of the Prophet Mohammed, considered to be authenticated as the chain of transmission is verified and documented under the authority of recognised Islamic scholars. These *hadith* offer practical guidance on a range of issues and assist many Muslims in interpreting contemporary issues and in reaching decisions on how to behave and act in a particular situation. Accordingly *hadith* are referred to by most Muslims but not all, while some scholars might question the authenticity of many.

Straying from the straight and narrow path of piety is, however, a hazard for all humans. For Muslims, as for conservative Christians, Satan's influence is at the basis of wrongdoing, and it is he 'who capitalizes on human weaknesses as lassitude, desire for immediate gratification, tendency to forget etc.' (Barise, 2003, p 10).

If God empowers Muslims, Satan in turn attempts to enfeeble them. Barise goes so far as to claim that clients' help-seeking, and the subsequent development of a good professional, working relationship between social worker and client, comes about through the omniscience and omnipotent agency of God. This insight by the Muslim client can be used therapeutically to reinforce the intervention process. While presumably this positive motivator is not cancelled out if the social worker is not themselves a Muslim, for they are nonetheless providentially sent during a time of need.

Assessments and cultural diversity

Returning to Hodge's point regarding the need to assess for spirituality, it would be unfair to assert that social work in Britain has not been conscious of this important aspect and does not make any allowance for it. However, it would certainly be correct to say that this holds a lesser priority than, say, assessing for cognitive and physical functioning. In her comprehensive book on social work assessment Laura Middleton (1997) offers a checklist for consideration, which places religion in an ecosystems context, as shown in the summarised list in Table 6.

Table 6: Assessing resources	
Practical	**Personal**
• Financial	• Health
• Housing	• Spiritual beliefs
• Shops	• Self-help techniques
• Voluntary organisations	• Sense of humour
• Family	• Education
• Neighbours	• Strength of character/outlook
• Mosque/church/synagogue	• Physical strength
• Peer or support group	• Mental strength

Source: Middleton (1997, p 56)

However, in keeping with the unitary perspective of Islam, Barise (2005) offers an even more complex, indigenised Islamic social work model (Figure 1). This addresses the metaphysical transformations of Islam, as well as the procedural mechanisms of the profession. This unique model is therefore rooted in Islamic concepts, which are admittedly not always easily accessible to non-Muslims. Barise, however, is at pains to demonstrate how compatible the essential framework of social work is with Islamic perspectives. From the initial help-seeking stage by the client, to the assessment process, to goal-setting procedures, then on to outcome and, finally, evaluation – each step is commensurate and compatible with both the context of Islam and that of social work. This

Figure 1: Islamic social work model

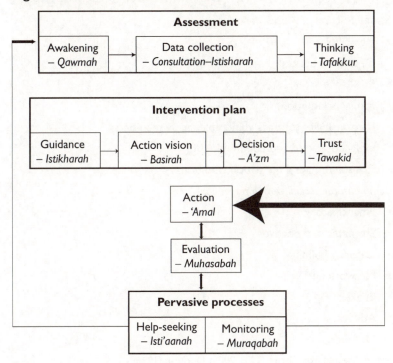

Source: Barise (2005, p 13)

alliance holds in relation to shared values, mutually agreed intervention and a successful outcome.

Finally, Barise's vision highlights certain attributes and attitudes, typical of Muslims, that are acquired through virtue of their religious conditioning. These, as collated in Table 7, can be usefully exploited by social workers, in their various roles as change agents, in formulating intervention strategies.

Despite providing food for thought, we might query how far Barise's model is germane in relating to the Muslim experience as a whole. Furthermore, it could be argued that the esoteric nature of the model does not easily provide a practical basis for task-centred social work intervention. One telling critique that can be levied against the model is that it does not address one of the more important issues in the UK, which revolves around a sufficient understanding and awareness of the help-seeking behaviour of minority ethnic individuals. For while a Somali refugee and a British Pakistani might have a faith in common, their experiences of migration, housing, settlement, skills, employment

Table 7: Complementary social work strategies
Some attributes of Muslim families
• Flexibility
• Optimistic outlook
• Resilience
• Family orientation
• Responsibility towards vulnerable family members
• Neighbourhood and community ties
• Consultation and mediation traditions
Commensurate social work intervention
• Emancipatory
• Strengths perspective
• Capacity building
• Networking
• Broker
• Advocate
• Mediator

Source: Adapted from Barise (2003, 2005); Dorfman (1996)

and class distinctions are more likely to play a greater role in terms of access to appropriate service provision.

In conclusion, it would seem that there are more commonalities to be discovered between the professional canon of social work and the Islamic faith, than actual points of difference. Although certain areas between the two remain open to debate, and are duly treated as problematic in this book, they do not negate those more numerous areas of compatibility. Nor do they divert from the essential message that social work is much enriched by taking on board some of the unique visions of Islam, particularly where these beneficially influence debates on social well-being and individual welfare. These have been social issues of great import in the historical and traditional Muslim world, and retain their relevance as much as ever in the contemporary multicultural, global community.

FOUR

Gender relations and the centrality of the family

Family morphology

The family in the Muslim world is the central institution in society, in being the primary one where social, cultural and religious values will be communicated to the growing child. In common with Christianity and Judaism, the Muslim family is predominantly patrilineal, where family membership and descent are followed down the male line (Warnock Fernea, 1995). This almost invariably indicates that, in common with the other major monotheistic religions in their traditional guise, Muslim families tend to be patriarchal. Yet it should be noted that patriarchal traditions pre-date the major religions and are grounded in factors other than religion solely. The greatest authority is consequently vested in the oldest male, be that father, husband, brother or son, on whom also lies the main responsibility for earning the family's living.

The morphology of Muslim families globally is diverse, with many different permutations, some of which are likely to be unfamiliar to many readers. A wide diversity of family structures can be found in the Middle East and some parts of the Indian subcontinent where families may adopt nuclear, extended or polygamous arrangements. This very much depends on the cultural context of that particular society, as well as the prevailing socioeconomic climate, since these domestic arrangements may often be dependent on the financial standing and means of livelihood open to members.

Wealthy, industrialised societies like those of the Arab Gulf, for instance, embrace a variety of domestic models: from those perceived to be traditional, extended networks, to nuclear and urbanised cohabiting units, typical of the West.

The archetypal family arrangement in many Muslim societies has been that of the extended family. Such an arrangement may be extremely large, in which several generations of both married and unmarried children live in the parental home along with grandparents. Ideally this ensures that the young, the old and the infirm receive support at all times from a pool of available adults. However, it should be noted that this has not always been the case in some parts of the Middle East where sometimes a married woman's role has been to serve her husband's parents while attending to her own family unassisted.

Equally, the family income might be swelled by a concentration of wage-earning members; yet, alternatively, individual incomes might be retained for personal use without the necessity of duly providing for the communal pot. Finally, although the extended family system seems to vary widely, the ultimate rationale behind such arrangements is obviously to provide sufficient and necessary care for family members in societies with a weak, or indeed non-existent, formal welfare system.

It is true to say, however, that such models are being replaced by smaller, nuclear families due to the forces of modernisation and urbanisation, which militate against the building of very large, expensive properties capable of housing a number of interconnected families. The lack of privacy inherent in the extended family system is also seen as a good reason to maintain discrete households in communities where there have been wide-reaching social changes accompanied by exposure to Western lifestyle models.

However, as Marwan Dwairy (2003) points out, a nuclear arrangement does not necessarily indicate greater privacy or independence for reproductive families, since often such groups live in very close proximity to relatives, in which patriarchal norms may still exert a powerful influence on the shaping of the normative behaviour of individuals.

The extended or nuclear division, therefore, is not one that can be viewed as clear-cut as families may remain very tightly-knit, whether they live beneath the same roof or not. An interesting example is one raised by Jørgen Nielsen (1999) in discussing the issue of *purdah*, referring to the practice of keeping women secluded from non-related men, as occurs in villages in Northern India, Pakistan and Bangladesh. This is regarded as a form of protection, and thereby, as the author suggests, is consequently not one that imposes hardship on women where they are surrounded by a large network of helpful relatives. Nevertheless, in the event of migration to the West, *purdah* can be transformed into a deeply isolating experience where women are placed in urban housing with unknown neighbours and removed from the interwoven matrix of extended family (Nielsen, 1999).

The issue of isolation obviously carries implications for social work, particularly as this can have a significant impact on mental health. In their qualitative study of Pakistani and Bangladeshi women, Ravinder Barn and Kalwant Sidhu (2004) identify social isolation as a contributory factor in the problems female participants experience in relation to daily coping, as well as in the process of adjustment to British society. The civic space is often perceived as foreign, threatening and largely inaccessible to the women in the study, not least due to language problems (Barn and Sidhu, 2004).

Social isolation carries other risks as well: it is, for example, a factor in domestic violence, an issue discussed further in the next chapter. On a wider scale, isolation can become part of a minority community's protective response, where neighbourhoods may become ghettoised due to the perception that the inhabitants' ethnic and religious differences are incongruent with the values and conduct of the wider society. A perception of being besieged by bigotry and racist attacks is likely to lead to the erection of social barriers, which serve to segregate individuals still further, making access to educational and employment opportunities even harder to achieve.

To return to the subject of family morphology, under Islam a man is permitted to take up to four wives on the condition that he can provide for them and their offspring equally, in terms of material goods, time and attention. Polygamy is of course viewed as acceptable in religious terms in having been practised by the Prophet Mohammed in his lifetime.

Polygamous marriages are for the most part not recognised as legal in the West, with a few exceptions; however, they are practised in a different form among the Mormons in the US. The right for Muslims to practise polygamy in Britain has been argued for at times, but to date there has been no accommodation of this practice in law. In addition, without wishing to appear facetious, even if polygamy were legal in Britain, the high cost of living would almost certainly tend to strongly militate against such practices, given the responsibilities of the husband as sole provider of equal resources to his wives under Islam.

The reasons for polygamy in Muslim societies have been put variously forward as, first, constituting a safeguard for women during times when the male–female ratio may be imbalanced in society due to war and widowhood. In addition, polygamy is seen to be acceptable in a barren union (on the wife's part) where children are desired, as is invariably the case, which we discuss later in the chapter on page 76. Polygamy is also viewed as acceptable where the first wife is too infirm to be able to participate in normal sexual relations within marriage. In these cases, polygamy is viewed as a better alternative for women than that of divorce, or celibacy on the part of the husband. Furthermore, it has been asserted that polygamy preserves the moral order of Muslim society, since it is commonly regarded as instinctual for men to desire women other than their wives (Mernissi, 1975). However, Fatima Mernissi goes on to indignantly argue, polygamy may have a very different effect on the self-esteem of men and women respectively, in that it tends to boost that of men, but has the reverse outcome for women:

> Polygamy is a way for the man to humiliate the woman as a sexual being; it expresses her inability to satisfy him. (Mernissi, 1975, p 16)

Mernissi goes on to point out that while polygamy is acceptable under Islam, polyandry (the taking of more than one husband) is forbidden. This has interesting and contradictory ramifications in relation to the perception of female sexuality from the Islamic perspective, as will be discussed further.

Some Muslim women would disagree that polygamy represents a disrespectful move on the part of men towards women, as Moxley Rouse (2004) makes clear:

> Islam requires the drafting of a marriage contract prior to legalizing the union, and this contract can specify that polygyny [polygamy] is unacceptable. Therefore, it is claimed that Muslim women view polygyny as the choice of both the man and the woman, and if a husband breaks a contract forbidding polygyny, a woman has a legitimate reason for divorce. (Moxley Rouse, 2004, p 68)

It could nonetheless be argued that many women are unaware of their rights to make such stipulations or would be hesitant to demand specific provisions in a contract. However, whether this constitutes a genuinely free choice on the part of all women of polygamous unions, the research evidence does appear to indicate that polygamy involves some negative outcomes for wives and families, particularly in relation to the first wife.

In Arab communities it is a common experience for the first family to feel supplanted by subsequent wives and their offspring, if not in terms of material needs, in terms of time and affection devoted by the husband (Al-Shamsi and Fulcher, 2005). Although there is little research into this phenomenon, polygamy has been associated with poor mental health outcomes for first wives and their adolescent sons (the situation for daughters remains unknown) (Al-Krenawi et al, 2002). Additionally, polygamy, as practised by Muslim families in the US, is also associated with spousal abuse when this is seen as a means to marginalise and tyrannise wives in these unions (Hassouneh-Phillips, 2001).

It would be misleading to suggest that the three main forms of domestic arrangements discussed here constitute the only morphology that Muslim families may conform to. The patrilineal model associated with Islam is not one that is universally embraced when it is juxtaposed with long-standing traditions that accept bilateral kinship, such as is the norm in many multicultural communities in Southeast Asia, where a child is regarded as descended equally from the mother, as well as the father, irrespective of Islamic precepts (Errington, 1990).

Uxorilocality is the final form of family morphology we consider in detail here, and is a feature found in some communities in Southeast Asia, including Muslim ones. To summarise, on marriage a man will go to live with his wife and her family in their home and will supply labour to his wife's kin. This is an interesting reversal of patriarchal systems where almost invariably a woman must leave her kin to join her husband and his family. The advantage of this kind of matrilineal system for women is that they are held in high esteem through the strengthening of mother and daughter ties (Rousseau, 1991, p 404).

Adult sons, therefore, as opposed to daughters, are transient in such communities in passing from one household to another. This refreshing difference serves to challenge dominant patriarchal notions of gender norms. As such, the relocation of a man from his mother's home to that of his wife's, has been somewhat caustically described as 'trafficking in men' (Peletz, 1995, p 85).

Indeed, in many Southeast Asian communities matrilineal lines of descent coexist with patriarchy, creating interesting areas of ambiguity and paradox. Among the Muslim Minangkabau of West Sumatra, Indonesia, inheritance is traced through the mother's line, along with lineage (Blackwood, 1995). The issue of inheritance appears to be closely correlated to the norms that govern cohabitation within communities. Consequently this provides an intriguing variation in relation to the inheritance rules of Islam, which permits daughters to inherit, but only half the portion allotted to their brothers (Al-Khateeb, 1998).

By contrast, among the Minangkabau, although married sons have rights to inherited lands for cultivation, their portion will return to their mother and sisters on their death (Blackwood, 1995). A similar system exists among the Malay communities in the Malaysian Peninsular State of Negeri Sembilan, in which the rights of daughters to inheritance of property are emphasised *over* those of sons, due to their greater parental responsibilities and the perceived limits of their ability to exploit an alternative livelihood (Peletz, 1995). As in the practice of uxorilocality, such inheritance rules ensure that a woman and her female descendants are the true guardians of ancestral lands.

Thus, unlike in the Indian subcontinent, in Southeast Asia the birth of a daughter does not necessarily imply the ruinous allocation of scarce resources through the entrenched dowry system. A daughter is not likely to be viewed as being a commodity that will be taken over solely by the family she marries into, as may occur for many women in Pakistan and China, for instance (Mohammad, 2005). For communities in Southeast Asia, the birth of daughters is not likely to be seen as a regrettable or lesser event than that of the birth of sons, but one which views the female child as a significant asset to her family and community.

These examples provide a most empowering notion of the role and status of daughters in contrast, for example, to the cultural preference for boys, which remains unabated in families of Arab heritage (Minces, 1992). A study of Muslim women's perceptions of equality in Saudi Arabia notes the inferior status of Muslim women compared with that of men:

> Having a baby boy is a source of pride and honor, while having a baby girl is a source of sympathy and consolation. If a woman has many boys, she feels happy and proud. But when she has many girls, people look at her with pity and sympathy. (Al-Khateeb, 1998, p 118)

Under Islam, however, the rights and value of Muslim women, however, are said to be affirmed. To highlight this point comparisons have often been drawn with the apparent lowly status of females in pre-Islamic Arab societies, that are said to have practised wide-scale infanticide of female infants by burying them alive. Yet other scholars contest this version and claim that pre-Islamic societies were much more accommodating than have been portrayed (Mernissi, 1975):

> Pre-Islamic marriage customs were flexible and some of them gave women considerable independence and control over their own lives. In such cases, women tended to remain within their kin family circles after marriage. The husband, if not related to the wife, visited her at her home. Sometimes there were several husbands at the same time, for polyandry existed. When the wife bore a child, she summoned her husbands and announced which of them she believed to be the father, and her word was law. (Karmi, 1996, p 77)

Such accounts obviously tend to diminish the liberating and life-saving effect of Islam on females and are therefore somewhat controversial. The accepted Islamic version is, however, that with the acceptance of Islam, the value of daughters was asserted by the Prophet Mohammed and the rights of women were duly elevated and infanticide consequently condemned (Jawad, 1998).

The rights of women over those of men, as illustrated in some Southeast Asian communities, are explained through the dichotomous but intertwined relationship of *adat* ideology (as it is uniquely manifested in Malaysia and Indonesia) and Islamic interpretations. *Adat*, or traditional, indigenous practice, is viewed as upholding women's autonomy and authority in societies where Islamic ideology asserts the prerogatives of men (Ong, 1995). Consequently, the dominance of Islam through state control in Indonesia creates 'contradiction' for the Minangkabau who both seek to retain their cultural matrilinear beliefs, while as 'devout' Muslims attempt to adhere to the prevailing attitudes towards women as primarily subordinate to husbands in the domestic and civil spheres (Blackwood, 1995, p 140).

The diversity of family structures in the Muslim world and their underlying rationale can be seen to be very wide, where the influences of culture and religion create some intriguing permutations. The dominance of each is often dependent on the forces of state and law, as well as the dynamic ties of tradition and social change. In relation to gender norms, these create patterns of interesting variation that add to the heterogeneity of the experiences of the *ummah*.

Marriage

Regardless of the adaptation of the family, there are values for Muslims that remain unchanged across social contexts. Marriage is considered very important, as the legitimate means of channelling sexuality, since chastity is considered highly important (Moxley Rouse, 2004). Muslim women are generally committed to marrying within the faith, but Muslim men may choose wives from other religions, although often they will convert to Islam on marriage. The Qur'an states that a Muslim can marry someone who is of 'the people of the book': namely, Christians and Jews, who are not required to convert, although conversion is required for all other faiths.

Among the Pakistani community in Britain, marriage is assumed as an expected outcome in a person's life, and unions may have been planned by parents from a daughter's infancy:

Often, women are prepared for their roles as wives and mothers from birth. Farah, aged 16, whose engagement for marriage was decided by her parents on birth, comments, 'Women are sold at an early age'. (Mohammad, 2005, p 188)

According to Lyon (1995, p 53) 'arranged marriages' continue to be regarded as the 'community ideal' among Muslim Asians. However, this concept itself is subject to wide permutations in terms of the form of the arrangement. Young people may be permitted to get to know each other first before consenting, or they may be brought together for the first time during the wedding. Furthermore, families may negotiate an agreed union through local contacts in Britain. Otherwise British-born children, most frequently daughters, may be sent to the parental land of origin to contract a marriage with someone from a known community, usually that of the family itself. The assumption behind such unions is that spouses will then be entitled to be brought into Britain to facilitate the marriage and to maintain transnational kinship ties. But this is a practice that, as Lyon says, the immigration authorities view with deep suspicion (Lyon, 1995). In some instances, however, parents may accept that their children will find their own partners, much along the Western pattern.

According to the African-American Muslim participants in Moxley Rouse's study (2004), the ideal husband, in common with notions elsewhere in the Muslim world, is pious, responsible and financially able to support a wife and family. However, in her similar study, McCloud states that the favoured 'Muslima' African-American bride is apparently one who has never been married before and has no children; McCloud goes on to say that well-educated women and those with prominent careers may have difficulties finding a husband, regardless of their right to employed work under Islam (McCloud, 1995). This indicates therefore that such personal competencies are not considered to be particularly attractive to prospective partners, who are evidently seeking other attributes in brides.

Moxley Rouse in turn quotes a participant who clarifies the rights of wives in relation to husbands:

The right to know where his wife is going every time she leaves the house (but not the ability to restrain her) and the right to sex when he so desires. She has other rights, including the right to distribute her husband's income how she sees fit, the right to work, to keep all her earnings for herself, to own property, to inherit, to educate and raise the children the way she wants. (Moxley Rouse, 2004, pp 152-3)

With the exception of the sexual access a man may enjoy with regards to his wife, which is in keeping with Islamic rules, this, on the whole, is a liberal interpretation within the milieu of a particular Westernised cultural context. Research into Arab families indicates that wives, of all ages, may be expected to seek permission from their husbands in order to go out and if this is denied, she has little choice but to submit to his decision (Ashencaen Crabtree, 2007c). The same situation is true of employment outside of the home, in which no automatic right is conferred on them regardless of their spouse's wishes.

In traditional Arab society (as well as for many South Asian communities), marriages were arranged by parents or by the child's male guardian in a practice that continues even today. Although a girl has a right to refuse a suitor under the principles of Islam, generally she was expected to waive her objections. Such filial submission was expected as an indicator of a daughter's respect for her parents' judgement, as well as her owing to her perceived ignorance of what was best for her, in addition to her unfamiliarity with men.

The ideal suitor was a cousin, and he was tacitly assumed to have greater rights than other men to make an offer of marriage to a girl. Moreover, he often had had a strong obligation to propose such a marriage, unless there were good reasons against it. The reasons behind this were that consanguineous unions tended to retain the bride within her own community and certainly within her own extended family, and this was viewed as a wise safeguard. A bride, it was felt, would be less likely to be maltreated by her husband were he to be related to her by blood and subject to the influence of two parental households who had known the couple since infancy. This notion, however, is challenged by Fikree (2005), who claims that in fact domestic abuse is very likely to be perpetuated in unions where a generational cycle of violence has occurred within the broader family context.

It had other benefits as well, in safeguarding the future care of elderly parents and ensuring that wealth remained within the family network (Dhami and Sheikh, 2000). In the UK, unions between first cousins are still common in families that originate from certain parts of the Indian subcontinent, for instance, and probably for very similar reasons.

Parenthood and child-rearing

Islam regards wedlock as the only acceptable route to parenthood, and a natural and pleasurable consequence of this relationship. Marriage and parenthood remain important objectives for Muslim couples. The marital union is a crucial step in a young adult's life; however, it is, in fact, the birth of children that confers adult status, as procreation is considered a very important religious obligation (Warnock Fernea, 1995; Sharifzadeh, 1998).

For Muslims, therefore, children are highly prized and practically universally wanted in a marriage. This is unlike the situation in the West where couples may decide to remain child-free, and these days with reduced social disapprobation attached to these decisions. Consequently Muslim families have traditionally been large, and often remain so globally, despite the progress of industrialisation, education and career opportunities for both sexes (but particularly for women), and improved mortality rates in many Muslim nations.

Commonly in many Muslim families, men and women hold clearly defined and often immutable parental roles in the raising of children. In Arab families infants and young children are cared for predominantly, and often solely, by the mother and other female relatives, including the child's sisters. Furthermore, the husband is not normally expected to be present during his wife's postnatal visits or during the birthing process itself. Birth and child-rearing are seen as essentially the domain of women where a man's presence is generally not considered necessary or appropriate (Bouhdiba, 1977).

As Tove Stang Dahl (1997) points out, Islam regards men and women as standing in a complementary position to each other. This, however, should not be understood to mean that the sexes are identical or even similar, as is the perception among many in the West, as well as several ethnic groups in Southeast Asia, for example (Monnig Atkinson, 1990). Rather, the essential natures of men and women mean that each holds qualities that make them particularly fitting for specific duties and responsibilities. Thus the sexes are regarded as occupying a polarised, as well as hierarchical, position in the continuum of human nature (Stang Dahl, 1997).

This view stands in some contrast to that which sustains the struggle of non-Muslim women in the West to share childcare and domestic burdens more equally with men, in view of women's greater participation in paid employment and civic society. Instead, although Muslim women in many regions of the world are increasingly undertaking successful careers in competition with men, this is often seen as an addition to, and of less consequence than, their domestic duties (Al-Khateeb, 1998). Although, it has to be said, in the UK participation in the labour market remains very low for Pakistani and Bangladeshi women, not least due to discrimination and the few opportunities they may enjoy for advancing in their chosen profession (EOC, 2007). This situation notwithstanding, the obligations demanded by maternity and wifedom are viewed as the primary function of Muslim women and commensurate with their natural abilities.

Young Muslim children therefore inhabit a world dominated by women. All their physical needs, as well as their educational needs, will ideally be met within this maternal milieu. For nurture, along with social training and gender norms, the implanting of knowledge together with religious values and conduct, is seen as primarily the mother's role and will be extended towards her children throughout their childhood (McCloud, 1995). An ideal of Muslim motherhood has been put forward by a participant from a study into Swedish and American converts to Islam:

> I think in Islam it is strongly recommended for women to be home with the children, it is not a law or a rule but it is promoted. There are so many blessings and *hadiths* saying that it is beneficial for everyone to have roles that are designated. That the man is the head of the household. . . . (Mansson McGinty, 2006, p 122)

For these particular converts the attractions of being affirmed in their wish to stay at home and immerse themselves in motherhood is a very important aspect of their Muslim marriage. It is also a point of view that stands at odds with many of the Western feminist dialogues they are familiar with. Theirs is a stance that is considered radical, particularly in Sweden, for running counter to Western discourses on the nature of equality in marriage and wider society.

The values that are promulgated within Muslim families may be very different from a child's or adolescent's non-Muslim peer group, as well as being seen as oppositional to those of society in general. Such contrasts can provide further areas of contention within the family setting and typically may occur across generations. Although, as has also been noted, a commitment to conservative and politically extreme interpretations of Islam has also been seen as a feature of Muslim youth living in Western societies, regardless of parental influence, and is consequently one that is often viewed in many quarters as problematic and threatening.

Returning to Arab society, while a young girl will always remain within this predominantly female world, her brother will be absorbed increasingly into the world of men through his father's influence from the age of five or so onwards (Bouhdiba, 1997). Eventually he will be expected to take on a fully fledged male role at a relatively young age, in which he will anticipate adopting an authoritarian and protective stance towards his sisters and women kin, regardless of seniority in age. Increasingly and inexorably the young person will separate himself from the exclusive feminine company in which he was reared (Minces, 1992, p 33).

Sexuality

Here we discuss sexuality in terms of heterosexuality, while homosexuality is considered in the next chapter. Bouhdiba (1997) remarks that psychologically the domain of the secluded feminine is one certain Muslim men may yearn for as representing the lost Eden of their innocent infancy. Unlike their sisters, men are unable to return to this comforting female environment, which later takes on a level of mystique. The physical separation of male from female is followed by a masculine psychological rejection of attributes regarded as belonging to the feminine: the soft, emotional, irrational, dependent and physically weak (Bouhdiba 1977; Al-Khateeb, 1998).

The Arab male's nostalgia for a delicious haven of feminine pampering, for instance, is not dissimilar in some ways to that which corresponds to the male Westerner's idea of the harem. This notion has historically captured the imagination of the West, having been reproduced in erotic and erroneous detail many times in paintings and films. However, historically the harem carried different connotations in the Middle East, in which it was a very real, forcibly enclosed establishment in which incursions from outside or escape were prevented. The very name originates from the word *haram*: that which is forbidden by sacred law (Mernissi, 2001).

The Westerner's sexual fantasy is effectively debunked by Mernissi, who throws cold water over the fiction for, having been born in a harem herself, she regards it as 'synonymous with prison' (2001, p 2). Far from being a bower of orgiastic delight filled with beautiful and sexually submissive women, she states that 'In Muslim harems, men expect their enslaved women to fight back ferociously and abort their schemes for pleasure' (Mernissi, 2001, p 14).

Mernissi (1975, 2001) has long been interested in the topic of sexuality in the Muslim world, and uses the conceptualisation of the harem to engage the reader in a learned discussion on gender. She points out that the idea of female sexual passivity, which in the West is quintessentially manifested through the notion of the harem, is a castrating concept towards women, and is furthermore one that is not recognised by Muslims. In fact, Muslims view female sexuality as a powerful and dynamic instinctual force and therefore place much importance on the mutual sexual satisfaction of couples within the boundaries of a lawful married relationship.

Sexual frustration is seen as mischievous and contributes to social disorder, a belief that stands in stark contrast to early Christian ideals in regarding the celibate life as the noblest path that can be followed, since sexual urges are viewed as inherently sinful.

Mernissi (1975) accordingly takes issue with the Christian concept of sexuality and states that Islam takes a stance similar to that of psychoanalysis in viewing raw instincts (libido) as neutral energy, neither good nor bad, but subject to, defined and channelled by the restraints of laws. Consequently she puts forward a powerful argument that female sexuality from the Muslim perspective is seen as in need of curbing through social and physical restrictions. Thus an active female sexuality, as comprehended in Islam, can result in the patriarchal strategies of seclusion and surveillance. This is further indicated in the term *fitna*, which refers to feared chaos, as well as meaning a beautiful woman (Mernissi, 1975, p 4).

In the West, the presumed disinterest and sexual passivity of women, as it has been historically framed in sexist discourses, requires no such coercive measures as the harem. This traditional view is constantly challenged by an increasing Western emphasis on female sexuality as dynamic and multifaceted. Yet, the madonna–whore, good girl–bad girl dichotomy is not yet dead and buried, for as any British female teenager knows, to be labelled 'a slag' remains the ultimate insult to a girl's or woman's reputation. Even for those who regard themselves as sexually liberated, they have yet to win a total and enviable freedom. For, as Mernissi argues, contemporary Western women are subject to the tyranny of merciless standards of accepted feminine beauty as devised by the male-dominated fashion and beauty industries. This is a domination that shackles women at least as much as the harem system in Mernissi's view, but is not one that Muslim women need be oppressed by (Mernissi, 1975).

Conforming to gender norms

The Western convert to Islam is in a unique position to be able to consider gender norms from a Western and a Muslim perspective, particularly those from secularised nations, like those of northern Europe. First, it should be pointed out that in the Islamic perspective the label of 'convert' is a misnomer, in that such individuals are seen instead as having 'reverted' to Islam, since it is posited that all people are born Muslims, but that social and cultural influences can divert the development of people from becoming proper Muslims (Mansson McGinty, 2006). Consequently for those who convert (or revert) to Islam, this symbolises a return to the correct and original spiritual path.

The greatest majority of people who convert to Islam are women, and they often find that the acceptance of a Muslim identity and lifestyle creates problems, in that families and friends may overtly reject their choice to a lesser or greater extent (Mansson McGinty, 2006). Equally, their new lifestyle will require adopting many new forms of socialisation in which, for instance, platonic male friendships will not be sustained on a one-to-one basis due to gender propriety. This carries ramifications for male social workers who are apt to discomfit or cause offence to Muslim clients if their encounters invade the space of propriety. Since such contact between the sexes, albeit seen as perfectly innocent by social workers, is also likely to inhibit effective professional intervention, it cannot therefore be regarded as helpful to the professional relationship. Such considerations, furthermore, may apply to Muslim males in relation to female social workers. Religio-cultural sensitivities obviously demand a more congruent accommodation in terms of the matching of worker to client wherever possible. However, professionals should not pander to cultural practices or individual prejudices that are discriminatory and contrary to the law of the land. A typical case, for example, relates to a Muslim family who refused to be allocated a Hindu social worker.

To return to the topic of conversion, entertainment such as clubbing and social drinking will usually be abandoned entirely in favour of appropriate, female-only gatherings (Rehman and Dziegielewski, 2003). Such converts will usually be obliged to seek friendships and relationships that are compatible with their faith, and logically these are most likely to be found among those who share their beliefs. Yet, converts may also have to struggle to find their place within the Muslim community and to be accepted as genuine, and can therefore find their identity and integrity questioned on both sides of the religious divide.

Modesty and propriety

The approach to adolescence is a time of great change for daughters in many Muslim families. Accordingly she will usually be expected to suspend friendships with boys other than her brothers, if indeed she had been allowed such playmates in the first instance. As we have seen, these forms of restriction will often extend throughout her adult life. Her close contact with males should now be confined to her *mahram*: those males who are not lawfully able to contract marriage with her due to consanguinity or marital bonds (Rehman and Dziegielewski, 2003).

The dress of a child will be transformed to the garb of adult, although in some societies even very young girls will have begun to adopt a form of adult female dress by adopting loose, long clothing and covering their hair. We learn that in the presence of her *mahram* a female 'does not need to cover her hair, neck or chest area' (Rehman and Dziegielewski, 2003, p 35). Although, as elsewhere, there are variations to this practice in which covering the head as a daily ritual is not prescribed by all denominations.

Modesty in dress is promoted for both sexes but the enveloping robes of some Muslim women, and in particular the use of veils, are the most conspicuous elements of certain kinds of Muslim dress. Depending on ethnicity and how conservative a family is, women may cover most of their hair with merely a fashionable scarf. Or veiling may involve a complex arrangement of materials (including cloth and even leather and wood) that completely covers the head and all of the face with the exception of the eyes. In the case of Afghani women the *burqua* incorporates even the concealment of a person's eyes where women are only permitted to squint through a small, restrictive window of crochet.

These concealing outer garments will be worn outside of the home or in the presence of strange men. In some Arab societies this outer robe and veil will be ubiquitous even in university settings, especially when there are male members of faculty present. However, it should not be assumed that this is a general practice in all Muslim countries, for some, like Malaysia, tend to place much more emphasis on student security issues that are not best served by facial concealment.

In European countries with established Muslim communities the issue of secular school uniform and the demands from Muslim girls to replace these with customary robes continues to be controversial. In defence of its particular secular tradition, France has banned the wearing of *all* religious symbols by pupils, including veils, crucifixes and skullcaps. Since the ban several French Muslim students have transferred to British educational establishments, although these too have been involved in controversy. This was highlighted by a recent court case, in which it was argued that a British schoolgirl had the right to attend school wearing Arab dress (the *jilbab*) instead of a school uniform modified to meet the requirements of culture and religion. In another case, a school assistant was sacked for refusing to remove the *niqab* (her full veil) after pupils claimed they had difficulty understanding her. It has since been leaked that education secretary Alan Johnson has stated that he expects schools to ban the wearing of full veils on 'safety, security and teaching' grounds (Wintour, 2007).

Few items of clothing proclaim a stronger commitment to a set of values than the veil for Muslim women. Such values may be regarded as antithetical to those of the dominant culture in Western societies, and often arouse strong and very negative emotions in the general public. These circumstances have been duly considered by Lord Ahmed of Rotherham, the first Muslim peer in Britain. His comments were quoted by *The Guardian* newspaper as, 'The veil is now a mark of separation, segregation and defiance against mainstream British culture' (Press Association, 20 February 2007).

In the same article, Lord Ahmed goes on to say that although the original purpose was to prevent the harassment of women, the wearing of the veil is viewed as antagonistic, and concludes that the veil is a 'physical barrier to integration'.

In the West, in general the complexities of appropriate clothing for Muslim people, and women in particular, have yet to be fully comprehended. Indeed, the veil has become a contested symbol, in which it is seen as both oppressive to women and as empowering; as a strategy of segregation of women from civil society, and as a means by which women may safely negotiate it. Given these great contradictions it is hardly surprising that the issue of the veil arouses such strong emotions between Muslims and non–Muslims, and where, to confuse matters still further, in each camp may be found both ardent Muslim proponents of the veil and its fierce opponents.

The origins of the veil (the *hijab*) come from a literal reference to the Arabic word for a 'curtain'. This relates to a verse in the Qur'an when the Prophet Mohammed wished to separate himself and his bride from the presence of a male visitor (Mernissi, 1991). To clarify this account Anna Mansson McGinty (2006) explains the huge significance of this event and the later extrapolation to the veil, in which it provides not only physical privacy from the eyes of men, but in addition creates the necessary distance between the sexes for propriety.

The verse presents, in Mernissi's view, a division between public and private, between the profane and the sacred, but was later turned into an understanding of gender segregation (Mansson McGinty, 2006, p 112).

The veil acts as a form of *purdah*, in that it is worn in public areas, which, as Mernissi argues, 'is a male space. The veil means that the woman is present in the men's world, but is invisible' (Mernissi, 1975, p 84).

It is interesting to note that Robina Mohammad states that *purdah*, in terms of the wearing of a veil, is practised in a more extreme way in Bradford than in Bangladesh, as women presumably are regarded as in need of more protection (Mohammad, 2005). Furthermore, in a direct challenge to Western views on the issue of the veil as oppressive, it is put forward as a means of preserving the chastity of females. Indeed, Haideh Moghissi quotes one male Pakistani commentator as saying that the veil constitutes one of the 'basic principles of human rights in the Islamic world' (Moghissi, 1999, p 27).

So it has been argued that the veil permits a Muslim woman to conduct her business in the external world in a literal and metaphysical space that represents decorum as well as personal safety. To illustrate this point, in relation to Islamic resurgence in Malaysia, it has been asserted that the veil should not be dismissed as merely a cultural anachronism. Instead by wearing it contemporary Muslim women are enabled to benefit from and participate in the 'social milieu' of the upwardly mobile and professional classes, without insult to their morality, or overtly offering a challenge to male authority (Ong, 1995, p 180).

This situation is equally true for young Muslim women in the Middle East in seeking educational and career opportunities that were often denied their mothers, but without offending cultural, gender-related mores.

However, the political implications of the veil are also made apparent, particularly in relation to its modern usage. Mansson McGinty (2006) refers to studies of Javanese women who in donning the veil consciously use this as a strategy of self-transformation demonstrating their outward commitment to Islam. The wearing of the veil in this Indonesian context is also regarded as a crucial means towards a remaking of the social order in the closer image of Islam. In this vein Haleh Afshar (1996) clarifies the use of the veil as a political statement:

Islamist women are particularly defensive of the veil.…
[Nevertheless], many Muslim women have chosen the veil as
the symbol of Islamisation and have accepted it as the public
face of their revivalist position. (Afshar, 1996, p 201)

This, however, is precisely the point that has been raised by politicians
in Britain who claim that the wearing of the veil in this fashion is
designed to imply a separatist stance in society. Predictably, this may
then be regarded as not only a gesture of alienation towards Western
values, but as actively hostile towards those of the prevailing culture.
Under these circumstances it is hardly surprising that moderate Muslim
voices in Britain, such as Lord Ahmed, raise concerns regarding the
wearing of the veil, and the safety of the wearer.

Afshar (1996, p 201) alternatively argues that for many Muslim
women the veil is seen as liberating in that women become 'the
observers and not the observed'. They thereby become freed from
being regarded as sexual objects by men. It is also, she states, a form of
protection from sexual harassment and a means of gaining respect.

In her study of female converts to Islam, Mansson McGinty describes
the physical and metaphysical liberation that participants feel in
adopting conservative Muslim dress:

Fatima understands the veil as something that keeps the
spiritual energy inside. An image of veiled power emerges;
the experienced space of safety implies a sense of control
and power. The power of being 'invisible' but observing,
the power of controlling sexual energy from both outside
and inside. Understanding the veil as 'protection' from 'guys
eyeing you' instead of as oppression, she thus reverses the
power perspective. By donning the veil she disciplines her
own body and sexuality as well as strengthens her Muslim
sense of self. (Mansson McGinty, 2006, p 121)

Revealing, Western-style clothing is frequently castigated by the
participants in this study, as are the wearers of such items in being
perceived as demeaned through being exposed to the sexual
gratification of men (Mansson McGinty, 2006). Nevertheless it is also
noted that the converts in particular have also been verbally attacked
by Muslim women for acceding to a form of dress that these fellow
Muslims regarded as anachronistic and decidedly oppressive, based on
their cultural experiences in Iran, for example (Mansson McGinty,
2006).

This is not an isolated controversy, but is one that is analysed by Haideh Moghissi (1999) who powerfully refutes the idea that veiling forms a protection of women from rape, assault and murder within Muslim societies. Instead, following El Sadaawi, she points out that:

> Women in Islamic societies are caught between the globalized image of femininity or female beauty as a commodity in the West and the Islamic notion of femininity 'protected' by men and hidden behind the veil. In fact, 'veiling and nakedness are two sides of the same coin,' in which women are manipulated into serving agendas of control by others. (Moghissi, 1999, p 46)

Feminism and Islam

The issue of conservative Islamic dress raises a host of implications for social workers to consider, since one sole interpretation is clearly not tenuous, given the multiple meanings that may be attached to the wearing of the veil (Moghissi, 1999). The enforced imposition of facial concealment on the women of Iran and Afghanistan, for example, may have little in common with the willing adoption of this dress for second-generation Muslim immigrants to Britain or for converts to Islam.

The clash in values that is nonetheless felt in relation to the wearing of the full veil in British society is one that does require sensitivity, since such proponents may consequently become the visible targets of Islamophobic intolerance and abuse. Evidently this represents a somewhat ironical situation given the understanding that the veil is meant to both conceal and protect the wearer, but which in fact may create quite the opposite effect.

The self-habituation to concealing female dress is obviously a matter that has ramifications for feminism. Many feminists in the West would find such cloistering and segregatory practices in conflict with their personal values, as indicating the inferior status of women. In addition for some, such strategies could be regarded as conflicting with the transformative and emancipatory values of social work. The recent media images, for instance, of Able Seaman Faye Turney being forced into female dress during her captivity by the Iranian Public Republican Guards was widely seen as a simple but devastatingly effective strategy in divesting Turney of her equal status with men in general, including in relation to her male crew, thereby totally eclipsing her gender-neutral, professional competence as a sailor:

> One minute, there Faye Turney had been, in naval uniform steering a small boat, on patrol in the waters that divide Iran from Iraq. The next thing we knew, she was dressed in shapeless garments and a headscarf, and appearing on television as a nobody, a vulnerable, defenceless little woman. (Jardine, 2007)

However, where dress is adopted as a matter of choice rather than coercion this should not conflict with social work values. Nevertheless it is a moot point how far a pubescent schoolchild, for example, is able to make an informed and free decision without having been subjected to influence and pressure. Yet, it could equally be argued that social and peer pressure are brought to bear on other teenagers seen parading in cropped tops and miniskirts. Nonetheless if concealing, enveloping dress codes were thought to create obstacles to the normal personal development of children in terms of their physical, emotional, social or behavioural well-being then social workers and educators would be obliged to address these concerns. In this event dilemmas would emerge in relation to a conflict of social work values: those which recognise and respect the religious and cultural observance of individuals, and those that uphold the rights of children. Although, as the law makes clear in the 1989 Children Act, the welfare and protection of children is of paramount consideration. To date, however, this question of whether conservative dress codes do inhibit a child's development in all these spheres has yet to be fully considered and discussed.

As feminist epistemology makes clear in terms of the political relationships between men and women, there is not one single path that should be followed, but rather there is a plurality of feminisms, in which the perspective of white, middle-class feminists has been dramatically challenged by women from alternative ethnic, cultural and class identities.

Similarly, Moghissi (1999) claims that there does not exist a unified, coherent feminist philosophy in the Muslim world, nor do women label themselves 'feminists' as such. Yet, as Mir-Hosseini (1996) remarks, women's issues abound in the literature on Muslims and Islam. Furthermore, women's contributions to social development are now more fully recognised in the Muslim world than ever before, and concertedly harnessed in many regions.

According to Moghissi (1999), concerns for greater equality between the sexes and the representation of Muslim women in public life do exist and have done since the 19th century. Muslim female leadership in global politics is accordingly a force to be reckoned with. Consequently these arguments and considerations serve to create lively and contemporary debates among women and men in the Muslim world.

Moghissi takes care to delineate one crucial point in reference to Fatima Mernissi. She comments that there is a difference between 'Islam as a belief and personal choice, and Islam as law, as state religion' (Moghissi, 1999, p 139). There exist political activists and scholars who promote a secularised Muslim vision of equality between the sexes. Accordingly, the identification of self as Muslim is seen in a cultural and spiritual sense, but without necessarily embracing state religion that imposes legislated sexual discrimination.

To comprehend this point better, Fatima Mernissi offers the following clarification:

> To understand the dynamics in the Muslim world today, one has to remember that no one contests the principle of equality, which is considered to be a divine precept. What is debated is whether Shari'a law inspired by the Koran, can or cannot be changed. (Mernissi, 2001, p 22)

Etin Anwar (2006, p 221) draws out the 'metaphysical, social, ethical and eschatological grounds' for equality between the sexes, in an examination of relevant verses of the Qur'an (Table 8).

However, there is a prominent stance in which the state law is not opposed, but that the interpretation of *shari'a* law is, as it currently stands. Malaysia's Sisters in Islam, for example, focus their efforts on

Table 8: An Islamic egalitarian gender system
• Both men and women, by virtue of their being in the world, are God's creatures
• Men and women as persons (selves), partners, members of society, and servants of God are obliged to respect each other
• Men and women will receive rewards according to their actions and behaviour
• Men and women are jointly responsible for preventing evil and promoting good
• Men and women as persons, partners, members of society, and God's creatures and servants are, therefore, equally expected to maintain each other's rights in order to be recompensed in the hereafter

Source: Anwar (2006, p 21)

introducing a different interpretation of the Qur'an, which they would argue has been wrongly understood by male theologians, in reducing women's status under Islam to that of inferiors. Such views have been articulated by prominent female theologians like Dr Amina Wadud, who is reported by a Malaysian newspaper as saying that:

> What we have seen are fourteen centuries of traditional exegetical works that were exclusively written by males. This historical legacy established a male advantage…. It tends to marginalize or deny outright women a first-hand representation in discussions of basic paradigms on which much of the Islamic perspective rests. (Hamzah, 1996)

Much more puzzling to Western feminists, however, is the claim that Islamic 'fundamentalism', as it is viewed in the West, attracts many Muslim women. This is particularly so because such movements are usually otherwise seen as instrumental in victimising women religiously and culturally. The stereotype of women living under deeply conservative Muslim regimes is, to quote Moghissi, that of 'veiled, secluded, ever-passive … mute, immobile and obedient creatures' (Moghissi, 1999, p 138).

However, as Haleh Afshar points out, in Islamic terms so-called fundamentalism is seen by the zealous as 'revivalism' and symbolises a return to a purer and 'golden age' of Islam – and thus this vision is framed as empowering to women:

> They argue that Islam demands respect for women and offers them opportunities, to be learned, educated and trained, while at the same time providing an honoured space for them to become mothers, wives and home-makers. (Afshar, 1996, p 200)

Afshar goes on to claim that these female advocates of revivalism apparently despise feminism as manifested in the West, because feminism is associated with foreign colonialism, as well as offering spurious freedoms to women in the West that are themselves dubious and illusory. The argument therefore runs that feminism has ultimately failed in its mission to alter the labour inequities between the sexes, but is instead culpable in having contributed to the devaluing of the benefits of matrimony for women (Afshar, 1996).

A full investigation of the paths Muslim women may take towards self-actualisation in terms of the politics of gender, as well as those of religion obviously lies outside the scope of this book. However, social workers working with female Muslim clients would be well advised to realise that the issue of sex equality is a highly complex one, as well as being deeply contested terrain. Muslim women who oppose conservative interpretations of Islam need empathy, and should not be subject to the undermining of their personal identification as Muslim, in a cultural and spiritual sense.

Muslim critics of conservatism may or may not include those who embrace the principle of living under Islamic *shari'a* law. Those moderates who accept the principle may instead seek a reinterpretation that is not perceived to be coloured by fallible and male-orientated discriminatory attitudes towards females. However, this does not mean that the former secularist group should necessarily be regarded as apostates, even if, as in Moghissi's words, 'The ultimate goal of the secular reformers is not to modify *Shari'a*, but to do away with it altogether' (Moghissi, 1999, p 130).

In conclusion, what does become clear is that the Islamophobic stereotype that Muslim women live in bondage under a universal and culturally oppressive regime is unfounded. Abusive circumstances for individuals undeniably exist, as will be discussed later. However, what is apparent is the complexity and heterogeneity of the Muslim world, where symbols, such as the veil, for example, carry a multiplicity of meanings and defy a simplistic definition. Likewise the convoluted and esoteric conceptualisations of gender and equality span numerous interwoven discourses that do not lend themselves to a brief summary. While social workers cannot be expected to appreciate all the subtleties of the distinctions of the Muslim perspective, as has been introduced briefly here, it is important to avoid assumptions that reduce the multiple dimensions of human experience in the Muslim world to that of a single, misinformed and therefore misleading one.

FIVE

Working with families

Here we cover issues relating to conflict within a Muslim family, including divorce and spousal abuse, as well as more extreme forms of domestic violence towards other family members. Later, we also consider child welfare issues with respect to child protection procedures and the accommodation of children. Throughout this chapter we seek to examine the assumptions and beliefs that underpin family behaviour and responses in conflict situations, as well as highlighting the implications for social work practice.

In discussing traditional means of resolving family conflict, we must differentiate between that which is promoted in the Qur'an, and other methods which have evolved across cultural groups. In Chapter Three we saw how the use of mediation by a respected, senior male authority figure can help to resolve an otherwise entrenched and deteriorating inter-family war of attrition within an extended Arab family (the *hamula*) (Al-Krenawi and Graham, 2003). In Arab Muslim societies there are many other forms of peaceful resolution, including one of the most important, the concept of *sulh*: a form of reconciliation using mediation (Al-Krenawi and Graham, 2003). According to Süleyman Derin (2005-06) *sulh* is associated with Sufism, whose mysticism, in common with many other spiritual philosophies, is fundamentally non-violent, and was in turn inspired by the accounts of the Prophet Mohammed:

> The Prophet (pbuh) displayed the greatest examples of this clemency and compassion. For instance, when the people of Taif stoned him, instead of asking for their punishment, he asked for their forgiveness. In fact, he never prayed to God for the destruction of the people who harmed him: even when he was pressed to do so he replied: 'I was not sent to this world for condemnation; I was sent as the Prophet of Mercy.' (Derin, 2005-06, p 2)

Although essentially a religion of reconciliation, Islam, however, also accepts the concept of vengeance, and it is said that this signifies a restoring of the status quo, rather than being moved by vindictiveness (Al-Krenawi and Graham, 2003). These authors refer specifically to 'blood vengeance', which is described as an 'obligation to kill in retribution for the death of a member of one's family or tribe', through which family pride (*Ar*) can be restored (Al-Krenawi and Graham, 2003, p 284). This is a practice which is commonly accepted throughout Arab Bedouin culture where it is regarded as an established guarantee of security that members of a *hamula* extend towards each other (Al-Krenawi and Graham, 2003). They go on to describe the distressing case of a Bedouin family who flee into the desert where they live under conditions of extreme stress, dire poverty and utter isolation in an attempt to avoid a death sentence at the hands of a neighbouring *hamula*. Whatever the purported motivation behind blood vengeance, the consequences appear very similar to the enactment of the 'blood feud' or vendetta of Southern Europe.

It is quite demoralising to learn that the author Al-Krenawi, a Bedouin social worker, is unable to offer any real protection to the adults or even the deprived and disturbed children in this family, when working within cultural parameters. The best that can be done is to supply them with some material goods to alleviate their present distress (Al-Krenawi and Graham, 2007).

Although it is evident that blood vengeance retains a hold in contemporary Bedouin culture, in the United Arab Emirates this has been replaced by 'blood money' (*diya*), in which a family may choose to be financially compensated for the killing of a relative. So prevalent is this arrangement that all motorists, Arab and non-Muslim expatriates alike, make sure that they are well insured for a substantial payout of *diya* in the event of a fatal road accident.

However, it seems fitting to conclude this section on traditional conflict resolution by returning to the Sufi approach in which sinfulness and crime are viewed as closely overlapping, and where for Sufis, at least, the criminal is viewed as a sick person who requires, above all, compassion and mercy (Derin, 2005-06).

Contemporary family conflicts: changing gender roles

As has been pointed out, there are many variations of family life among the *ummah* and therefore no single example can serve as typical of the whole. Muslim family life is often said to be rigorously hierarchical and with clearly defined, gender-specific roles. Particularly so in relation to wage-earning and child-rearing duties, yet even here this depends on a wide range of factors governing the needs of individual family units, as well as the influence of culture. Modernisation in turn is changing the face of the Muslim family internationally, and specific roles may become more permeable and flexible as opportunities in society widen for both men and women. Modern Emirati women, for example, appear to have little in common with female kin of previous generations due to a radical transformation of the social landscape and the need for nationalised education and skills in society. For a large number of Middle Eastern women, juggling careers and family commitments will become the predominant factor in their life that it is for many women in the West.

Although these changes are beneficial both to society and for women seeking greater empowerment both within and beyond the home context, change often involves a certain level of transitional tension; thus family conflict may emerge from within and across generations and gender divisions. Conflicts leading to domestic violence can therefore occur where migrant families attempt to impose transported cultural values to keep certain members of the family under tight control. Such strategies tend to have the hardest impact on the younger females of the family, for reasons that will be explored further in the section (p 98) on spousal abuse in the Muslim communities (Ammar, 2000).

Family crisis due to 'unlawful' sexuality

Threats to family cohesion leading to family conflict can be found in many ways. Sometimes these may manifest themselves through an individual demanding the right to choose a marriage partner of their own, irrespective of the choice of parents. Occasionally this may involve opting for a lifestyle and values that are regarded as very different from, and indeed even incompatible with and antagonistic to, the traditional culture in which the previous generation was raised. Such a case could typically revolve around the development of a gay or lesbian identity.

Homosexuality is an issue of huge controversy in the Muslim world for religious reasons. The political head of Iran currently denies that it exists in their society, while the international gay community monitors the numbers of gay men executed in Iran, which include teenagers.

However, in common with other life variations, attitudes towards a homosexual or transsexual identity vary across the Muslim world. These range from the outright condemnation and rejection found in the Islamic context in Somalia, and much of the Middle East, to partial acceptance in Malaysia, which, despite moving towards greater conservativeness, has to date been regarded as relatively liberal. In Malaysia the transsexual *pondan* ('boy-girl') can obtain a recognised and even respected niche in society (Ashencaen Crabtree and Baba, 2001; Mahamud-Hassan, 2004).

There are few data regarding the issue of sexual orientation among the Muslim *ummah* in the UK, but it is reasonable to speculate that this is very likely to be a highly problematic issue in relation to identity formation, and family and community acceptance for Muslim gays and lesbians. Given that Islamophobia is a problem in general, and that there are indications that this feeds into bullying in schools, a stigmatised sexual identity is likely to add to a deeply troubled dynamic leading to multiple oppression. This victimisation, however, is one which is not likely to be supported through feelings of empathy and solidarity in the immediate community, although there are a few support groups operating with this injunction in mind (www.naz.org.uk; www.safraproject.org).

Rejection at various strata of the ecological context of the individual, especially at the fundamental level of home and family, inevitably creates situations of high risk to mental and physical health, which can be particularly injurious in vulnerable youth.

The abhorrence and rejection from those with homophobic attitudes is not exclusive to Muslims alone, but can also be found among other sectors of society, particularly religious ones. In considering this issue in general, Mallon (2005) offers several useful nuggets of advice to social workers dealing with such situations; these are summarised below in Table 9, although they should be considered critically, alongside several caveats in relation to Muslim clients that are subsequently discussed.

Mallon (2005) offers some useful guidelines, which can be effective in relation to some minority ethnic groups. In relation to Muslim families, however, the attitude towards homosexuality is not only culturally based but also faith based, as well as being influenced by class and education. As such it may prove impervious to moderation towards the rejected individual. There are practical issues to consider as well. It is unlikely that social workers would be able to conduct much in the way of 'bibliotherapy' for Muslim families, since there is a dearth of specific and helpful information on the subject, apart from condemnatory, religious-based tracts, which regard the homosexual act as an abomination. Furthermore, it is also claimed that the very concept of a gay identity is nonsensical in the Muslim perspective, since it is only the homosexual act that counts, and not the inclination, which should be restrained (Halstead and Lewicka, 1998).

Halstead and Lewicka go on to say that it would be quite wrong to claim that homosexual eroticism is unknown in the Muslim world; for example, the faithful are assured that they will be served by young men

Table 9: Families in crisis: working with homophobia
• Defuse the crisis through relationship building and calming of family tension (particularly in relation to stigma)
• Identify and work with the most uncomfortable individual first
• Work on changing attitudes through discussion and the use of informative reading material ('bibliotherapy')
• Link the family into any appropriate, informal support groups
Additional and interrelated points to incorporate when working with Muslim clients are:
• Involve the most senior member of the family at the beginning, from whom the other relatives are likely to take their cue
• In Muslim families fathers should be listened to first, unless they are clearly indicating a deferment to another member of the family, e.g. the mother
• Rapid construction of supportive partnerships around vulnerable youth (of both sexes) using a coalition of social work networks, youth services, community-based advocates and teaching professionals
• Being aware of and prepared for extreme reactions in the family setting, in relation to the protection of minors and vulnerable youth. This risk factor relates to child protection and domestic violence procedures

Source: (Mallon, 2005)

as perfect as pearls in Paradise. Furthermore many Sufi texts are lyrically erotic in this regard, although this is viewed as a spiritual allegory rather than incitement to the gay lifestyle (Halstead and Lewicka, 1998). Furthermore it would be quite wrong to claim that homosexual love has not at times been practised and celebrated in Muslim societies historically (one thinks of the photographs taken of Taliban soldier lovers in this respect), as well of course as in pre-Islamic Arab culture. However, *hadiths* make it clear that this kind of carnal conduct is a form of *zina*[1] and is therefore unacceptable in Islam.

Clearly, the religious rejection of active homosexuality in Islam (which, incidentally, is similar to the views of many Christians), requires much caution in relation to social work intervention with families in crisis. It would be wise for social workers to bear in mind that the notion of a 'gay identity' is problematic for Muslims, who draw a neat distinction between the homosexual act and the inclination. The latter is much more likely to be acceptable to families, provided it does not translate into action, and this may provide the beginnings for constructive family negotiation where young gay and lesbian people continue to be dependent on the family support system.

Divorce

Divorce is permitted in Islam but is not encouraged; both men and women have the right to initiate a divorce but with different conditions attached. Muslim communities have developed differently in their attitude to divorce, and in some Muslim societies, such as certain Arab communities, it is more acceptable than among South Asian Muslim people. This may be a result of cultural influences from living alongside Hindu communities, which consider divorce to be impossible according to the Hindu Laws of Manu.

In Islam there are many different forms of divorce, the most common being *talaq bil tal*, which occurs when a man pronounces 'I divorce you' three times to his wife. The *shari'a* states that this has to be pronounced in front of two adult male witnesses, and between each pronouncement there has to be a gap of 30 days. This time lapse is to enable the husband to reflect and rethink his decision, as a divorce does not become final until the third pronouncement. The *talaq* therefore provides a 90–day respite in which discussion, mediation or resolution can take place.

This type of divorce has at times been distorted, with stories of a husband pronouncing 'I divorce you' in rapid succession without a time gap or witnesses present. Such a divorce does effectively dissolve the marriage but is termed a *bi'da*: an undesirable innovation but legally binding within Islamic law.

Women, on the other hand, have to either stipulate their right to divorce in their marriage contract, or otherwise they need consent from the husband to divorce. A stipulation in a marriage contract is often problematic as most women are unaware that they have this right, and some women even armed with this knowledge might be afraid to commence marriage with the request of the right to divorce.

When a woman requests a divorce it is called *khul*. A husband can refuse to consent, but is still free to remarry where polygamy is permitted. It is, however, more problematic for a woman whose husband refuses to consent to a divorce. Here legal action would need to be taken by the wife through a *shari'a* court or through the intervention of an *imam*.

A divorce, according to Islam, does not entail spousal support payments but the husband has to repay the *mehr* (a form of dowry, but one held in trust for the wife in the event of divorce) that was designated in the marriage contract to his ex-wife. In the case where there are children, the father is responsible for supporting the children. To reiterate, in patriarchal traditions children are considered to 'belong' to the father. This of course can differ greatly from one Muslim society to another and will depend on how embedded *shari'a* law is in any specific society. In the context of minority Muslim communities in the West most couples will register their marriage, as Muslim marriages may not be considered legally binding. Therefore, in the event of a marriage break-up the national family courts will be involved, and couples might have to obtain two divorces: one secular and the other religious. There have been publicised cases where some divorced Muslim women have not realised that they also need to obtain a *talaq* and have tried to remarry, only to find out they require this before they can contract another Muslim marriage.

Divorce carries deep stigma for women, particularly in South Asian communities. While divorced men may rapidly remarry, a divorced woman is considered a pariah and is often isolated from her family and community, and ultimately is blamed for the break-up. Some support groups have been set up in the UK, particularly in South Asian communities, to reduce the level of isolation experienced by divorced women. The social stigma attached to divorce means that women may often prefer to remain in an unhappy marriage. Divorce rates among Muslim communities are relatively low. However, very little research has been carried out in the UK to quantify the number of divorces and investigate the circumstances and experiences of divorced individuals, especially women.

Domestic violence: forms and features

Domestic violence is a shorthand term covering a wide range of abusive situations that includes some or all of the following factors: physical, psychological and emotional, sexual, neglect and financial abuse. The dominant feature, however, is the victimisation of one or more individuals by other members of the family, as opposed to abuse in other settings, such as residential institutions.

In the West, the general assumption is that domestic violence is synonymous with spousal (or partner) abuse. In other cultural contexts the victim may be the sibling, the child, the daughter-in-law or the parent of the abuser, to name but some relational variations.

With respect to domestic violence and Muslim families in general, there is a growing body of literature in relation to spousal abuse; although in terms of other forms, such as elder abuse, there is scant information. However, in the West it is older women, in common with their younger female counterparts, who are more likely to be abused in domestic settings than men.

Commensurately one of the few references emerging from the Middle East in relation to elder abuse relates to that of an older woman suffering from physical neglect and psychological abuse. Accelerated social modernisation is regarded as eroding the extended family network, leading to atomised family units where traditional respect for, and care of, elderly parents is on the wane (Barise, 2003).

Spousal abuse in the Muslim communities

In contrast with domestic violence, the issue of spousal abuse in Muslim societies has been more extensively studied. Douki et al (2003), for example, argue that domestic violence is endemic in Arab societies. Haj-Yahia (2003, p 203) goes on to sum up his research into 'wife beating' in Arab society in Israel by concluding that justification for spousal abuse in this region is 'considerably more prevalent than in Singapore, the USA, or Australia'. Wives are blamed for provoking the attack through 'careless' or 'provocative' behaviour as well as 'behaving in a way that is not appropriate for a woman' (which may include questioning and self-assertion) (Haj-Yahia, 2003, p 203).

Elsewhere, research data into domestic violence in Bangladesh reveal it as a common hazard for women living there (Koenig et al, 2003). Fikree and Bhatti (1999) ascribe domestic violence, with associative physical and mental health consequences, as affecting one third of their population sample of Pakistani women living in Karachi.

In relation to Arab Americans Nawal Ammar comments on how cultural stereotypes influence police procedures when investigating domestic violence. Accordingly Arab males are viewed as 'particularly violent, controlling, and exceptionally oppressive of women' (Ammar, 2000, p 58). In contrast, Arab women are viewed as conforming to the feminised image: 'submissive, veiled, helpless and accepting of all forms of oppression' (Ammar, 2000, p 58). It should be noted, however, that Ammar is not denying the extent of domestic violence in the Arab American community, which she regards as serious, but only the cultural caricatures that prevent the police from making the most appropriate judgements in attempting to help victims. Her plea is for a 'criminal-justice system … that is culturally sensitive and respectful of Arab-American cultures' (Ammar, 2000, p 66).

Two particular issues emerge from Ammar's paper. First, that the criminal act behind domestic violence is undermined by locating this abusive activity within the discourse of the 'sacred-religious', where 'both the Bible and the Qur'an condone the ownership and battering of women' (Ammar, 2000, p 61). Second, Ammar considers the way domestic violence is used by migrant families settling in the West as a means of distancing themselves and their female kin from the perceived negative ways of the new environment (Ammar, 2000).

In relation to Ammar's first point, it is interesting to note that in the majority of discussions touching on the issue of domestic violence in Muslim families or societies, the same Qur'anic verse will invariably be quoted with varying interpretations attached, as for example:

> As to those women on whose part ye fear disloyalty and ill conduct, admonish them (first), (Next), refuse to share their beds, (And lastly) beat them (lightly); but if they return to obedience, seek not again them Means (of annoyance): for Allah is Most High, great (above you all). (Kort, 2005, p 373)

It is, however, asserted by some that this should not involve leaving marks on a wife's face or her body (Doi, 1992). Kort also offers readers an interpretation given by a 'cyber-mufti' on an Islamic website that suggests that the beating should in fact involve no more than a symbolic tap (Kort, 2005, pp 376-80).

Yet this verse has for the most part been used to justify spousal abuse as a form of legitimate correction of women, to the extent that assault administered 'with good intentions', and provided it is not to the face or is fatal, cannot be punished under Egyptian criminal law (Ammar, 2000, p 62). Such religious justifications can equally be found in the UK, according to Fikree (2005) reporting a Bradford study of Muslim men and women, which found that Islam was used as justification for violence by male participants. By contrast the female participants referred to their faith as a source of strength to cope with domestic violence.

Obtaining help

The exact figures relating to domestic violence towards minority ethnic women in the UK are hard to quantify given the lack of comprehensive research in this area, but they are assumed to be large. Southall Black Sisters have long campaigned for women subject to domestic violence and living under stringent immigration rules to be better catered for. The success of this campaign can be seen in the new 2004 Domestic Violence, Crime and Victims Bill, which amends some of the former legislation to offer greater protection to such individuals; although it is argued that the uncertain immigration status of other victims leaves them vulnerable to further abuse since they have no access to refuges via public funds (www.southallblacksisters.org.uk).

For minority ethnic women fleeing domestic violence the issue of finding a suitable refuge is problematic, with insufficient mainstream provision to cater for religious and cultural needs (Pryke and Thomas, 1998). Back in 1988, Lena Dominelli pointed out in her now venerable tract *Anti-Racist Social Work* that Muslim women require refuges where they are not going to be subjected to racist discrimination or Islamophobia, as has been experienced at the hands of other residents, and even by some refuge workers (Dominelli, 1988).

In addition to pejorative attitudes by some, the need for a private space for prayers or to be able to follow dietary and cooking norms and habits, may not be sufficiently catered for in many non-specialised refuges (Bhatti-Sinclair, 1994). In one of the few papers that addresses the issue of places of safety for Muslim victims of domestic violence, Nooria Faizi (2001), writing from the context of the US, discusses refuge initiatives and their successes. She primarily compares two different forms of refuge, in which one based in Arlington, Texas remained open for only 18 months. During its short lifespan the 'shelter' imposed very strict Islamic-based guidelines on the conduct of its residents, which included enforced prayers and the coerced commitment that residents would not ultimately take up employment where they might encounter men from outside their immediate family *mahram*. This latter restriction in particular served to ensure that battered women would find yet another, and almost insurmountable, obstacle towards achieving financial independence away from their abusers (Faizi, 2001). In addition to this, the refuge felt obligated to report and seek the permission of the local mosque before admitting victims, thereby ensuring an open-door policy that was contingent on the approval of men. This also ensured that the women's right to confidentiality was effectively breached.

The latter issue is by no means trivial when one recalls two shocking cases where a couple of British South Asian women were murdered by their abusive spouses while supposedly being in places of safety. In 1985 Balvant Kaur's trail was traced to Brent Women's Refuge with tragic consequences, while in 1991 Verduna Patel was actually killed inside Stoke Newington police station (Pryke and Thomas, 1998).

Faizi (2001) then goes on to compare the draconian and ultimately futile regulations both underpinning and undermining the Arlington refuge, with a programme in Atlanta, Georgia. This refuge maintains its links with *imams* and conforms to basic Islamic rituals, but is not coercive and to date has had no security problems (Faizi, 2001).

Culturally sensitive or separatist refuges are likely to increase due to demographic and social needs over time, especially if they are supported by legislation that recognises the need for more inclusive services for women and their children. Yet, as those working in this field know well, leaving an abusive relationship is a huge and difficult decision for women to make, regardless of culture, ethnicity or faith. Because of the extremely disempowering nature of domestic violence, such a decision requires great desperation and determination on the part of victims, whose flight may finally be prompted by fear for their children, as much as, if not more than, for themselves.

However, research findings also show that women from minority ethnic groups, such as those of South Asian descent, may have particular problems accessing places of safety. The literature on this subject does not usually define research participants into faith classifications, but tends to subsume those of Indian, Pakistani, Bangladeshi backgrounds under one Asian category. Consequently, it is implied that the problems for women from these geographical regions may be very similar.

One specific issue that is highlighted by research is the difficulties women may have in being able to speak of their experiences in the first place. However, as Yoshioka et al (2003, p 171) point out, 'Certainly a battered woman's ability to disclose abuse, and thereby receive instrumental and emotional support, is critical to her survival'.

Back in Britain, Bhatti-Sinclair (1994) notes that many abused Asian women in her study had hardly ever voiced their experiences to anyone, not even to close members of their family. What, however, are the dynamics that lead to such remarkable reticence on the part of these participants? Bhatti-Sinclair notes in particular a lack of cultural community support in the discourses she records, to the extent that sharp criticism may be levied against abused women who speak out, and even towards the natal family if they attempt to intervene on their daughter's behalf.

Furthermore, Reavey et al confirm that South Asian participants face enormous challenges in terms of disclosure due to a sense of loyalty to family or cultural families, as well as a pronounced sense of shame:

> These dynamics give rise to issues such as whether to remain silent in order to maintain family honour (described as 'izzat' within some communities) which can subsequently act as a barrier to seeking help. (Reavey et al, 2006, p 174)

Writing from the US, in comparing South Asian, African and Hispanic women subject to domestic violence, Yoshioka et al (2003, p 172) comment on the shared ethos of 'familism and collectivism', in which the emphasis decentralises the individual over the unity of the family and the collective well-being of the whole. In specific reference to South Asian women, these authors comment that the severing of the connection with the abusive spouse through divorce is considered a very undesirable outcome by participants, a conclusion equally shared by Bhatti-Sinclair (1994), with Faizi (2001) commenting on how hateful in the eyes of God divorce is for Muslims.

The question of women's status is bound up with the existence and exercise of domestic violence, although this too remains a contested area, where research data worldwide provide an unclear picture. Koenig et al (2003), citing Jejeebhoy and Cook (1997), report that although in some Indian states high levels of autonomy among wives reduced the risk of domestic violence, in more conservative areas this proved not to be a protective factor. Furthermore, in the Philippines the risk for wives in this regard is higher where they dominate decision making in the home than where husbands enjoy the leadership role. In addition, these authors also cite findings that show that women's involvement in credit and group-based saving programmes in Bangladesh commensurately decreased the risk of abuse. However, in relation to their own study of women's status in rural Bangladesh the picture remains variable, dependent on whether the norms of the community concerned are conservative or liberal, with those living in the conservative end of the spectrum at a greater risk of violence (Koenig et al, 2003):

> More autonomous women, at least initially, are likely to violate established norms concerning gender roles and call into question the larger family's honor and prestige and, as a consequence, to incur a higher risk of domestic violence. (Koenig et al, 2003, p 10)

This has some clear implications in relation to Muslim families in Bangladesh, since the authors point out that, regrettably, religious membership is a further factor that influences domestic violence, whereby higher levels of violence existed in their study group among Muslim households than among Hindu families (Koenig et al, 2003).

The issue of religion is inextricably bound up in the unpalatable one of domestic violence, although it should be emphasised that many would argue that justification for abuse is based on a misinterpretation of religious principles. In this vein, Faizi (2001) offers the following chilling account of an American Muslim woman who, despite being subject to constant and extremely dangerous abuse, feels compelled to remain with her abuser:

> The woman was willing to jeopardize her own life, as well as the lives of her three children, because she believed that leaving her husband would damn her to hell. Usually, one of the major obstacles to leaving is not having anyone to turn to within the family. The irony in this situation was that the wife's family, including her father and brothers, had encouraged her to leave the abusive relationship and offered her refuge. Nevertheless, she was determined in her religious convictions and remains with her abusive partner to this day. (Faizi, 2001, p 18)

Sexual abuse of spouses

Although the above case is certainly extreme, one form of abuse that is particularly problematic is sexual abuse within marriage. Case study 3 exemplifies the deeply isolating position of such women in obtaining help due to religious and cultural beliefs that assert the male prerogative over the female's when viewed as a chattel. Although this case is taken from Ashencaen Crabtree's personal practice in Malaysia, in general the assumptions and circumstances surrounding domestic violence are usually applicable to conservative Muslim communities, whether living in a Muslim society like Malaysia or in the context of the West (Ashencaen Crabtree and Baba, 2001).

Case study 3: Spousal abuse in Malaysia

A Muslim Malay woman, Aini X, who worked in the Malaysian health system, was informally referred to one of the authors by a medical consultant who had become aware that she was a victim of domestic violence. Aini X was very reluctant to be interviewed at first, but after a considerable amount of reassurance regarding confidentiality agreed to discuss her concerns in a counselling session.

This lady presented as a very anxious, tearful individual who was evidently both depressed and fearful. She disclosed that she had been subject to many years of physical, psychological and sexual abuse by her husband. Although, she said, she had once been reasonably content in her marriage and had borne several children, matters had seriously deteriorated between the couple, to the extent that she claimed to be frequently raped by her husband. She claimed that he regarded sexual congress as his absolute right and would resort to violence if she attempted to avoid his advances. She also said that he regarded her reproductive organs as his by right in which to plant his seed (this couple already had six small children), and wished to keep her in a state of constant pregnancy and childbearing.

In desperation she had tried to talk to her relatives about the problem but this had led to no resolution. She then tried to get an *imam* to mediate on her behalf, but he had not appeared to be at all sympathetic to her, and had made it clear that he believed her husband was acting within his rights. Finally, and with considerable courage, she had surreptitiously gone to lodge a complaint with the local police. The results were catastrophic: two relatives of her husband worked in the police force, and had quickly become aware of her presence. Before having the chance to make her complaint, she had been forcefully escorted back home into her husband's keeping where the error of her ways was made clear to her.

After helping her to unburden herself over the course of a few sessions and exploring the available options with her, which indeed were not many, Aini X's case was finally referred to a fringe, Muslim, woman-oriented legal service who attempted to help her and her children escape from her abusive marriage.

Forced sexual relations in marriage are by no means confined to Muslim marriages, of course. This has only relatively recently been framed as marital rape and a form of domestic violence in the West, where once it was commonly viewed as the unspoken but accepted fate of many women. Islam, however, creates particular areas of ambiguity and difficulty in this respect, since a woman's submission to her husband's sexual demands is considered one of her marital duties. Etin Anwar makes this clear in quoting a part of the following Qur'anic verse al-Baqarah (Surah 2, Verse 223) going on to adjure men to purify themselves before sexual acts with their wives: 'Your wives are your tilth; go, then, unto your tilth as you may desire. . . .' (Anwar, 2006, p 73).

Although, as Fatima Mernissi points out, mutual sexual satisfaction is important in marriage, nevertheless the primary issue is that wives cannot refuse sexual intimacy without fear for their souls:

> If the wife refuses to have intercourse with her husband she is penalized both on earth and in heaven. The Prophet, according to Imam Bukhari, said a woman 'who is asked by her husband to join him in bed and refuses to do so is condemned by the angels who throw anathemas on her until daybreak'. (Mernissi, 1975, p 24)

According to these scholars, therefore, wives can be regarded as sexual objects within marriage, and are seemingly denied any legitimate right to refuse to be used in this way. Thus it not surprising that, according to British research findings (Reavey et al, 2006), it is extremely difficult for abused women in these circumstances to seek help in relation to sexual abuse, over and above physical violence.

Sexual abuse may not be identified therefore as a specific type of domestic violence, but only as a general exploitation of the disempowered self. The following quotation from an advocate working in a South Asian women's organisation illustrates the problems related to helping and protecting victims by prosecuting offenders:

> She [abused wife] didn't acknowledge it was rape but she said he forced her to have sex that she didn't want to. And they said ok, that's rape but she didn't understand the concept of rape so when it came to court, she couldn't go into court and ... talk about rape coz she didn't believe that it was ... she felt it would make her look bad as a wife, so she couldn't do it. (Reavey et al, 2006, p 177)

These authors go on to add that in their study the reluctance of South Asian women (including Muslim participants) to speak out on the topic of sexual abuse was related to the trivialisation, and even, in some cases, normalisation, of the female experience of coerced sex in marriage as rooted in cultural and faith-based interpretations. Participants had problems framing what was taking place within a Westernised concept of marital rape. But instead, the authors argue, due primarily to the intertwined dynamics of familism and collectivism, the women regarded their experiences as merely another manifestation of power play, where women living in strict hierarchical and patriarchal structures regarded themselves as effectively powerless to resist (Reavey et al, 2006). Once again the very act of speaking out was seen to damage the family *izzat* (honour) and cast a bad light over the women's reputation in consequence, rather than that of the perpetrator's (Reavey et al, 2006).

Some might argue that if a woman does not frame forced sexual intercourse within marriage *as* rape, then the psychological and emotional consequences, at least, would not be as severe as on those victims who define such acts precisely in this way. Research findings, however, show that domestic violence, including sexual abuse, is a factor in mental health problems affecting South Asian women, as is the case for other population groups (Dienemann et al, 2000; Chew-Graham et al, 2002).

Additionally, a review of research findings in Britain shows that among young South Asian women these forms of domestic violence contribute to self-harm and suicide, particularly among isolated individuals suspicious of mainstream services and those catering exclusively for minority ethnic groups (Chew-Graham et al, 2002; Reavey et al, 2006). Ominously, many of these women felt unable to approach health agencies and social services precisely because they felt that their referrals would come to the attention of people from their own community who worked in such settings and would betray them to their families.

For these women, much more work needs to be done by the mainstream services in relation to building trust through reliable, culturally competent and strictly confidential outreach work that targets vulnerable groups discreetly, creatively and, above all, effectively. A corollary is the need for streamlined, integrated services that can swiftly assess risk to offer support and appropriate places of safety to women and children at risk of domestic violence, without need for further, unnecessary delays and exposure to hazard wherever possible. Where professional assessments indicate a significant risk for clients the model of intervention needs to be one of rapid 24-hour, crisis management.

Forced marriage as domestic violence

Improved outcomes for clients are considerations that the British government and the police force also have to consider in relation to the more unfamiliar or extreme forms of domestic abuse. These refer to, first, the coerced marriages of young females, which is a matter of growing concern. Each year hundreds of South Asian Muslim girls are removed from school by their families for the purpose of marriage. The extent of forced marriages is unknown; however, it is feared that there are many. A survey carried out by Bradford City Council tracked 1,000 schoolboys and an equal number of schoolgirls from primary school to secondary, to find that only 860 schoolgirls were still on the school rolls in secondary school at the time of investigation. These missing youngsters had apparently been taken out of Britain back to Bangladesh and Pakistan for the purpose of marriage (Tickle, 2006).

Southall Black Sisters have no reservations about categorising forced marriages as a form of domestic violence. On their official website can be found contact numbers that possible victims, or those concerned about their welfare, can use to obtain advice and help. Furthermore, the same website refers to the Forced Marriage Unit, operating under the auspices of the Foreign and Commonwealth Office (FCO), which deals with around 250 cases a year. The Unit has produced guidelines for social workers, for instance when young people approach Social Services directly, as well as when they are repatriated by the FCO and need assistance. Regrettably, there has been concern expressed about the low uptake of these guidelines by social service departments and child protection services.

The Unit draws a clear distinction between arranged marriages, which have been freely consented to by both parties, and coerced unions where the victim is harassed, threatened and even beaten into accepting the situation. This is regarded as an unacceptable breach of human rights. Additionally the Unit liaises closely with British consulates overseas with a view to helping to rescue girls and women from deplorable domestic conditions where they may have been kidnapped, held captive and finally subject to rape by a stranger 'spouse'. Prevention, however, is considered the best way to tackle the problem of forced marriages, and therefore the Unit regularly engages in outreach work in targeted areas of the UK.

Encouragingly, support can also be found from some *shari'a* law experts, such as the Islamic Sharia Council in Leyton, where the council takes on the role of 'releasing' Muslim women from enforced and bad marriages in general. In addition to *shari'a*, their divorce rights are of course protected under British jurisprudence in any case. However, for concerned Muslims wishing to conform to Islamic family law, the *shari'a* ruling spiritually ratifies the situation under Islamic principles, in addition to the legal weight of British law. Satisfyingly, both civil and spiritual law are in mutual agreement with regard to enforced marriages being indefensible (Bell, 2007).

Murder, 'honour' and domestic violence

Finally, we consider perhaps the worst form of domestic violence, the so-called 'honour killings', which follows hard on the heels of two particularly harrowing cases highlighted in the media recently.

'Honour killings', as they are popularly called, refer to crimes in certain minority ethnic families where the real or imagined conduct of a family member, invariably female, is viewed as bringing the family's reputation into some disrepute. The conduct of the murder victim is almost always that which runs against the normative values of the indigenous culture of the family of origin, but which is not considered either illegal or particularly immoral (indeed, often the conduct is considered perfectly normal) in the adopted country of the West. The cultural belief governing a brutal family response to their relative's behaviour is that the killing of the offending individual somehow cancels out any supposed disrepute on the *izzat* of the family.

The very term 'honour killing' is descriptive of these transported cultural values, which are alien to the new societal context. But such a term may also tend to ameliorate the innocence of the victim in the minds of certain members of the public. Others will regard the phenomenon as a barbaric, cultural aberration in society that is impossible to relate to except by viewing it through the lens of cultural relativism. The phrase 'honour killing' does a serious disservice to victims in that it tends to disguise the brutal truth, which is, essentially, domestic violence taken to the extreme of murder.

The most recent example of this kind of crime hit the British headlines recently when the body of a 20-year-old Kurdish woman, Banaz Mahmod, was found in a suitcase after being strangled by her father and uncle. Her crime was to fall in love with a Kurdish Muslim boyfriend who was not from the same village. What was particularly appalling in the case of Banaz was that all her previous attempts to alert the police to her danger were effectively ignored since she was viewed by the interviewing officer as melodramatic and manipulative, despite the accused parties being notorious in the family for violent oppression (McVeigh, 2007b).

In 2004 Heshu Yones, a Kurdish girl aged 16, was savagely stabbed 11 times before having her throat slit by her father in the family bathroom. An anonymous letter by someone in the close-knit Kurdish community in West London had been sent to her father accusing her of behaving like a prostitute since she was going out with a boyfriend. His reaction was explosively and mercilessly terrible (Butalia, 2003; Bedell, 2004).

It has been estimated that many other murders in the UK can probably be classified as 'honour killings' and currently 117 murders are being investigated, and in many cases reinvestigated. Following Banaz Mahmod's tragically avoidable death the Crown Prosecution Service is now implementing changes in how suspected crimes of this nature will be investigated, with new police assessment models to evaluate risk to vulnerable women (McVeigh, 2007a).

Internationally these types of murder are common. Tripathi and Yadav (2004) assert that great numbers of females are murdered by male family members with most crimes taking place in the Middle East:

> Thousands of women and girls are stabbed, burned or maimed every year by husbands, fathers or brothers who believe they have brought dishonour by being unfaithful, seeking a divorce, eloping with a boyfriend or refusing to marry a man the family has chosen. When the victims do not survive, the crime becomes an 'honour killing', a term that has come to symbolize the cruel irony of a conservative Islamic society that purports to shelter women, yet often condones savage violence against them in the name of male and family honour. (Tripathi and Yadav, 2004, p 64)

In Britain, family conflict involving *izzat* may involve the lesser but still very serious crime of physical abuse of girls and women by fathers and brothers mostly, although horrifyingly mothers are also often implicated in both abuse and even murder. Increasingly, however, families are distancing themselves from murder, as well as covering their tracks, by hiring contract killers to carry out the deed. More fortunate girls may instead find themselves at the centre of a family plot to take them out of the country for forced marriage elsewhere with a view to controlling any attempts at independence.

Two main lessons can be gathered from these appalling forms of domestic violence, namely that social workers, teachers and the police need additional training to understand the risks involved for vulnerable girls and women from minority ethnic cultures. In addition to this, procedural guidelines need to be firmly in place to respond appropriately with a view to protecting those at risk. One concern that has been raised in relation to teachers, but can just as easily apply to social workers and the police, has been that they can actually instigate violent family responses. This may occur when taking the otherwise routine steps of contacting the family to discuss areas of concern they have in the care or management of the girl in question. Avoiding contacting the family tends to conflict with the professional outlook of both social workers and teachers who usually seek to involve families with a view to resolving problems. In the case, however, of schoolgirls at risk, caution and confidentiality must be the first professional response while proper risk assessments grounded in cultural awareness are rapidly undertaken, since this is another variation of child protection work.

The issue of cultural sensitivity, together with a focused person-centred approach, is therefore of paramount importance, since the client may have no other resource to fall back on except that of the abusive family itself. She may also feel that she is betraying the family by the very act of seeking help out of a need for self-protection. It is important therefore for both professionals and their clients to be able to distinguish family and cultural norms from that of faith, where one is decidedly not informed by the other. Yet there is also a tremendous need for concerted outreach work to bring the seriousness of the issue home to targeted communities, in order to enable them to take collective responsibility for the attitudes that generate violence. Particularly since according to a recent and alarming poll undertaken for the BBC's Asian Network one in 10 young British Asians believe that murders committed in the name of family honour can be justified (BBC, 2006). Table 10 offers some guidelines for intervention in domestic violence when working with Muslim families.

Abuse of children

Over the years there has been a wealth of research data written on the topic of child abuse and neglect, as well as a large quantity of material on professional protection procedures and guidelines. It is not our intention therefore to offer a lengthy explanation of child abuse as a phenomenon or its legal implications, since it is assumed that readers unfamiliar with this very important area of social work are best served by referring to texts dedicated to the subject.

Instead, our discussion here revolves around how social workers may consider these issues in relation to Muslim perspectives on the subject, as well as offering some examples from the global community of the *ummah* on how child abuse allegations have sometimes been dealt with internationally.

As with domestic violence, research data pertaining to child abuse tend to classify cases along broad ethnic lines rather than faith. This obviously tends to disguise evidence-based data that may be highly

Table 10: Working with domestic violence
• Improved multidisciplinary risk assessment procedures and rapid response protocols
• Effective, early collaboration between professionals involved in the care and protection of females at risk of all types of domestic violence
• Improved training of professionals to work more effectively in this area
• Ensuring the immediate safety of the possible victim before contacting the family
• Enlisting the help of culturally knowledgeable, faith-informed, community-respected mediators to advocate on the victim's behalf with the family of origin, if this is what the client wishes
• Obtaining legal advice and guidance for the victim via British jurisprudence and *shari'a* experts
• Working to prevent victims being taken out of the country until the client's wishes, circumstances and safety have been adequately investigated

relevant to Muslim families, as opposed to, say, Vietnamese Buddhist ones. It is difficult, therefore, to tease out specific examples of how social work assumptions may have had a negative impact on intervention with Muslim families specifically. That said, one case dating back to the late 1980s and cited by Ely and Denney (1987) discusses the strongly suspected physical abuse of a female toddler by her Muslim Asian mother, where the child presented as severely undernourished and with a fractured skull. As an example of poor practice the interpreter used, in the following interview, an eight-year-old cousin who was used to translate several different and incoherent accounts of how the injury occurred from the mother. The social worker's belief was that the girl was being abused since she was a middle child in a family where there were four daughters. Patriarchal sexism was assumed to be inherent in all Muslim families and therefore believed to be the reason behind this victimisation.

Although it is true that in many Asian societies boys are preferred over girls, it is not true of all, and even in relation to cultural norms, families differ in their attitudes towards daughters. Islam as a faith, regardless of cultural variation, openly disapproves of the devaluing of daughters, as *hadiths* extolling the virtue of being a father to daughters make clear.

The prevalence of Muslim families in UK child protection cases is therefore notoriously difficult to ascertain where data is scarce (Chand and Thoburn, 2006). However it is alleged that discrimination is a feature in relation to social work intervention with mixed Asian populations. Humphries et al (1999) take issue with the problems posed by language barriers and the use of interpreters when dealing with Asian families, as well as the appropriate accommodation of Muslim children by social services.

In a review of research literature Chand and Thoburn (2006) claim that white children and those of Asian origin are under-represented in the statistics for children receiving formal child protection work. Although the authors also state that by contrast the combined group of African Caribbean and African children were given an average representation in the same data.

Turning their attention to discipline issues among Bangladeshi parents, Chand and Thoburn cite research data that suggest that physical abuse is tied to punishment strategies, and these are once again used as means to curb Westernising tendencies in adolescents (Chand and Thoburn, 2006). By contrast, mothers from the Punjab appear to rarely use and even disapprove of corporal punishment (Chand and Thoburn, 2006). A further interesting piece of research from Irfan and Cowburn (2004) indicates that examples of harsh corporal punishment may be found among some Pakistani parents in the UK, where a sample group of Pakistani youngsters had experienced the following forms of discipline at the hands of siblings, mothers and fathers. A statistical proportion of 65% of young people in this study had experienced being slapped, and 50% had been punched. A further 42% had been hit with a shoe by their mother. In addition, some forms of rare and unusual punishment were indicated, which included cold water immersion, suffocation and Chinese burns.

Despite this, less than half of the respondents considered being spanked or hit with a shoe as constituting abuse, and regarded their parents as loving but occasionally driven to exasperation, or even a more serious loss of control. The authors, however, offer a caution against duly dismissing some forms of family discipline as relatively harmless. Rather they view corporal punishment as liable to spill over into serious abuse, as in the case of a 15-year-old Pakistani girl, beaten with an iron rod, whose offence was seen in terms of transgressions against culture, *izzat* and religion (Irfan and Cowburn, 2004):

> These causes are clearly linked with the concepts of honour
> and shame, which many Asian Muslim families are reluctant

to let slip and they will go to any length to keep intact; although such reticence apparently may extend to the community at large. The concern of honour and shame for the victims of abuse becomes nothing more than a form of social control designed to protect the abuser. (Irfan and Cowburn, 2004, p 96)

Chand and Thoburn (2006) report a survey undertaken in 1997, which found on social work casebooks that the majority of children suffering from neglect in Britain were white, standing at 32%. This was followed by children of African Caribbean descent with mixed parentage (26%) and finally Asian families taking up the rear end of the scale at 11%. In terms of sexual abuse Chand and Thoburn (2006) mention data in relation to Muslim children in Britain, where in 1991 several Bangladeshi boys came to the attention of social workers in Tower Hamlets. However, the overall picture of child sexual abuse in relation to Muslim children is far from clear, due partially to how the phenomenon is studied, whether in terms of points of referral for social work intervention or in relation to actual court proceedings dealing with child abuse. One study reviewed by Chand and Thoburn (2006) suggests that white children (the term is used as a category irrespective of faith) are more commonly referred with respect to sexual abuse than others. But in another study, this time reviewing court proceedings, a higher proportion of mixed heritage and South Asian children were seen than in the referral study (Chand and Thoburn, 2006).

One important issue highlighted by these authors refers to the inhibitions that families and communities may feel towards sexual abuse issues over and above those felt by the general public. Related to this point is that terms used to describe and define sexual abuse may not easily translate into the language or the conceptual framework of certain minority ethnic groups. In this vein Chand points out that phrases relating to masturbation, sexual fantasies and anal intercourse are not easily translated into Punjabi, for example (Chand, 2000, p 71).

Furthermore there may well be huge reservations relating to any reference to the topic altogether, for both cultural and religious reasons, and this is particularly evident throughout much of the Muslim world. It is true to say that there is only a minute amount of research literature that refers to sexual abuse among Muslim populations at all. We would argue that this is closely associated with the perceived distastefulness of the subject altogether, to the extent that nations may be in total denial that such social problems exist in their particular society (Crabtree, 2006).

One of the rare exceptions to this general silence is a paper written by Abu Baker and Dwairy (2003), where they discuss cases of incest in a Palestinian community in Israel. Accordingly they note that a recent survey found that 20% of 12-year-old Palestinian boys and 11% of girls had made reports of sexual abuse, in which 40% were perpetrated by relatives and neighbours (Baker and Dwairy, 2003). It is interesting to note that the issue of the gender disparity of the victims is not discussed in their paper, which raises speculation regarding whether boys are at considerably greater risk of sexual abuse in Palestinian society, or whether the abuse of girls is less likely to come to light for whatever reason.

These authors go on to critique the social work intervention strategies used in one particular case study: that of a 12-year-old female victim of sexual abuse perpetrated by her paternal grandfather, who was imprisoned for the crime. Baker and Dwairy describe how this outcome created huge conflict between the opposing sides of the paternal and maternal extended family network. But one where the child is regarded as tainted and her suffering ignored (Abu Baker and Dwairy, 2003). The subsequent rejection of the child by her family in this account is viewed by the authors as a fundamentally punitive means of displaying the collective anger at the dishonour brought on the family reputation, as well as being a form of disassociation. The authors then go on to offer the following warning:

> In the case of incest, institutional (state) intervention threatens the family structure and therefore the family members are enlisted to protect the family unity and reputation, even at the cost of sacrificing the victim. In some cases, the family may even go so far as to kill the victim as an attempt to 'save' the family honor.... Arab society blames females for not being able to protect themselves from sexual intercourse out of wedlock, even it happens as a result of brutal rape. (Abu Baker and Dwairy, 2003, p 113)

Despite having critiqued the way the child protection procedure attempted to prevent further abuse, the authors are nevertheless unable to find an alternative, effective way of protecting Arab children, like this girl, without affronting the family's fierce sense of honour and privacy. Thus, although instructive in many ways, this cannot provide guidelines towards culturally sensitive social work that takes as its mandate the primary need to ensure the physical protection of children at risk, before considering the lesser needs of others, particularly adult family members.

In other parts of the Middle East the procedures for child protection remain at a more rudimentary level than that shown in the Israeli–Palestinian context. Tentative research into child abuse in the United Arab Emirates has revealed that children at risk remain highly vulnerable to continuing abuse due to a combination of factors. First, although steps are being made to attempt to rectify the situation, deeply inadequate child protection protocols have yet to be replaced. Second, to compound the problem, tertiary education uniformly offers a highly censored social work curriculum, which is absolutely allergic to any topic that pertains to sexuality, other than that of heterosexuality within wedlock (Crabtree, 2006; Ashencaen Crabtree, 2008, forthcoming). Crippled by completely inadequate training in this respect, future social workers in the United Arab Emirates are completely unprepared for work in child abuse. The consequences are that it remains very largely undetected, as well as publicly unacknowledged, as Case study 4 graphically illustrates.

Case study 4: Child sexual abuse in the Arabian Gulf

A 14-year-old Emirati girl with genital injuries was brought to a United Arab Emirates hospital by her mother. In private the girl informed a social worker that she was being repeatedly raped by her brother. She asked the social worker not to disclose this to her family as she was terrified of their reaction, saying that they would kill her if they knew of her plight. The social worker called the police and informed the mother of the girl's allegation. The mother angrily denied her daughter's claim and instead accused their gardener, a disposable Asian migrant labourer. The daughter persisted with her allegations against her brother, but the police were powerless to act unless the mother pressed charges. This she adamantly refused to do. After treatment the daughter was sent back home into the abusive family situation without any charges being pressed or her safety guaranteed in any way. No further information is known regarding her fate. (Crabtree, 2006, p 234)

Such depths of denial can also be found in other Muslim nations, such as Pakistan, whose child protection policies only extend to the 1986 Child Labour Act (Munir, 1993; Miles, 1996). The largest Muslim nation of all, Indonesia, has attempted to promote child welfare through its Ten Years Movement for Children, but how effective this is at tackling child abuse is unknown. Yet, although there is clearly a long way to go, the picture is not completely depressing, and once again Malaysia offers a useful example. Here, modern social work is properly engaged in tackling child abuse in collaboration with the health and the police authorities and where professional work is supported by the 1991 Malaysian Child Protection Act (Munir, 1993).

Family responses to allegations

The allegation of sexual abuse of children in the family is always a very emotive issue for families to contend with. The challenges for social workers are often compounded where there are cultural and ethnic differences to take into account in relation to the nature of the alleged abuse, the intention of those involved and the psychosocial context for the victim and its family.

In considering good social work practice in the Western context, the cultural context of the child is frequently emphasised, and professionals involved in child protection cases are urged in the first instance to closely consider the context of the allegation. For example, it is considered important to differentiate between traditional, cultural practices that are actively harmful, and those that are merely different and innocuous, like co-sleeping with babies and children (Gough and Lynch, 2002).

Harran (2002) follows Chand's definition in urging practitioners to understand the motivation behind the use of certain cultural practices. This then permits practitioners to be able to discern whether such practices are actually considered harmful to the child's well-being within that cultural context. As Chand explains:

> [C]ultural differences in the way families rear their children
> should be ... respected, but where child abuse does occur
> it should be understood that this particular family has gone
> beyond what is acceptable not only in the British culture,
> but in their own. (Chand, 2000, p 75)

Yet this suggestion is also problematic. Chand's advice appears to take a firmly relativistic view of child abuse: that is, whether something can be viewed as abusive is dependent on whether it is viewed as such in the originating culture of the family (Webb et al, 2002). On the other hand, child abuse could also be argued to be subject to more universal definitions regardless of culture, since, as some critics have pointed out, certain cultural practices, whether well intentioned or not, are evidently harmful to children, such as female genital mutilation (Webb et al, 2002). Or, to give another example, the unusual and very unpleasant punishment, apparently practised among some West African families, of placing hot peppers or ginger root in the anus or vagina of older children to deliberately inflict suffering (Koramoa et al, 2002).

Consequently, there are a number of hazards facing social workers dealing with child abuse issues among minority ethnic groups. Chand (2000) highlights two main areas in relation to cultural deficits: hesitancy to intervene due to fears of insufficient cultural knowledge to evaluate the home situation accurately; alternatively, anxieties may be felt that there could be unnecessary intervention, based once again on the practitioner's cultural ignorance.

The first concern is illustrated in reference to two cited cases of Muslim children in the UK, the first relating to the physical abuse of a five-year-old boy by his mother, who had previously been subject to concern in connection with neglect of her older children. The case conference was hampered by the liaising link worker, who shared the family's cultural background, and refused to believe that the mother could be capable of the offences committed. This view appears to be based less on the mother's personal attributes but rather on some generalised cultural notions of idealised motherhood (Webb et al, 2002).

The second case considers the case of 'EF', a child of Arab heritage with multiple disabilities, who was seriously neglected by her mother. This neglect was consistently overlooked by social work practitioners, despite clear indications that the child's health and well-being obviously were in jeopardy in the home situation, and that the young mother herself was coping poorly due to an ongoing history of mental illness:

> EF's name was not entered on the child protection register. She was seen by social services as a child in need rather than a child in need of protection; health staff argued that both applied. Instead of a protection plan, an assessment was resolved on. Five years on, there has been little change. The family continue to live in conditions of extreme socioeconomic deprivation. EF is intermittently excluded from school for health and safety reasons because of recurrent cockroach infestation of her wheelchairs, clothes and hair. (Webb et al, 2002, p 401)

Case study 5 is equally instructive on the topic of cultural deficits. Here practitioners conspicuously depart from normal child protection procedures in the evaluation of outcome for a child from a minority ethnic group. Although the family involved in the next case are not fully identified in terms of either ethnicity or faith, this case is eerily similar to that of the 14-year-old Emirati girl previously mentioned.

Case study 5: Cultural collusion in child abuse

AB, an 11-year-old girl is found to be heavily pregnant, but no child protection investigation commences, either at this time or after the baby is born and accommodated by social services. It is decided not to investigate the case since the mother's reasoning is accepted at face value: that a police investigation would jeopardise her daughter's future chances of marriage. A year later, AB bumps into her former social worker just after the girl has had another pregnancy terminated. This procedure was quietly arranged by her GP (of the same cultural background as the family) and the obstetrician, neither of whom raised alarms over her continuing sexual abuse. At this point AB is accommodated and reveals that her brother was her abuser, a fact she claims was known to her family all along.
Source: (Webb et al, 2002)

Finally, it is inevitable that social workers will sometimes be unjustly accused of discrimination when carrying out their legitimate duties in relation to child protection. Understandably most people would wish to shy away from such accusations, and instead would like to show that they are culturally sensitive individuals. However, where practice involves double standards for minority ethnic families, leading to some children receiving less statutory protection than the norm (such as in the cases of AB and EF), practitioners need to rethink their priorities. As Table 11 indicates, cultural competence does not only mean sensitivity towards difference, but also disallowing inconsistencies to infiltrate vital assessment and intervention processes for fear of appearing Islamophobic or racist.

Adoption and fostering

Child abuse and neglect is one of the foremost reasons for the accommodation of children in long-term care, be it residential, foster care or, for the fortunate minority, through adoption. There is a serious need for more research into the whole topic of accommodation and the subsequent adjustment process in relation to Asian children, which would generally include many, but obviously not all, Muslim children who require such services. Specific issues that pertain to Muslim children under these circumstances have still not received any dedicated

Table 11: Anti-oppressive practice versus cultural deficit attitudes
• Reflecting on faith-based and/or cultural stereotypes that militate against a non-judgemental, objective professional attitude
• Avoiding poor practice e.g. the failure to evaluate the needs of minority ethnic children and families using similar risk assessment strategies as used for children from more familiar cultural/ethnic backgrounds
• Distinguishing between culturally relative practices, which may be regarded by perpetrators as non-abusive, and any actual harm to children, which should be evaluated on broader definitions of abuse
• Addressing any possible collusion impeding effective practice where practitioners (including all members of the multidisciplinary network) share similar cultural assumptions and beliefs to that of the family under investigation

investigation. However, it is generally acknowledged that the need for black, Asian and mixed-race foster and adoptive parents far outweighs supply. There has been much speculation about the reasons for these shortages, since social workers are keen to place children in families that share a common ethnic and cultural background. A pragmatic, often heard riposte is that this strategy relegates children to long-term residential care unnecessarily.

Intriguingly, some significant research data suggest that there are marked gender differences in how well boys and girls fare in long-term foster care with foster parents of a similar cultural background. These indicate that while minority ethnic girls, as might be expected, do well, counter-intuitively boys did not do as well and tended to deprioritise the topics of 'race' and ethnicity over the everyday practicalities of getting on with life in their new family (Moffatt and Thoburn, 2001). The authors speculate whether the attitude of the boys might actually fit in better with white foster parents, who in general, being largely unaffected by them, were also likely to minimise 'race' politics. They also wondered if perhaps the behaviour of these boys was for some reason more threatening within minority ethnic families than it would seem in white families (Moffatt and Thoburn, 2001).

Frazer and Selwyn (2005) consider adoption from cultural and faith perspectives and consider both areas to be important issues for consideration by social workers. This is clearly an important point, bearing in mind that shared culture does not necessarily mean shared faith, and the converse is equally true. Humphries et al (1999) use this very point to explore the appropriateness of one particular long-term placement where a Muslim child was placed with Muslim parents. Unfortunately there was no common cultural heritage between the child and his foster parents, which created a mismatch despite good professional intentions.

Selwyn and Frazer (2005) argue that the population demographics of Britain explain why Muslim and Sikh families may be ultimately deterred from adoption. They argue that such families usually have a large number of young children to care for already. Moreover, Pakistani and Bangladeshi families often live in overcrowded homes, which suffer from a lack of basic amenities, and obviously this does not militate in favour of adoption in the view of either prospective parents or for placing agencies.

There are, however, two further very significant points to be made that are generally overlooked by non-Muslim academics considering the topic of appropriate long-term placement of Muslim children in need. First, in many Muslim societies the adoption of Muslim children by non-Muslims is totally unacceptable, even in the case of national crises, such as the thousands of Indonesian children left orphaned and unprotected after the Southeast Asian Tsunami of 2004.

Second, it is not uncommon to be told that adoption for Muslims is *haram* (forbidden), as there is no explicit guidance regarding it within the Qur'an. However, it has been said that it is open to discretion (Goonesekere, 1994), and consequently adoptions do take place in several Asian and Southeast Asian countries. Furthermore, some popular Islamic cyber sites point out that Mohammed Himself was an orphan and adopted orphans later in life. The rules for adoption under Islam are unusual in Western societies, since the patriarchal prerogative appears to carry greater emphasis than the rights of the child to be parented (see Table 12). These stipulations strongly emphasise the outsider status of the adopted child in relation to lineage, property and marriage, and where a melding of identity between adopted child and family is not considered to be either desirable or acceptable in this interpretation. This has been stated in the following way: 'It is not possible for someone to assume parentage on the basis of a simple declaration; adoption then is considered an attempt to deny reality' (Gatrad and Sheikh, 2000, p 68).

Furthermore, Goonesekere (1994) points out that adopted Muslim children are disadvantaged under Islamic law in relation to inheritance, citing a case in Sri Lanka where an adopted child's right to inherit was legally challenged.

Table 12: Adoption in Islam
• The adopted child retains the biological father's surname.
• The adopted child inherits from the biological family not the adoptive one.
• When the adopted child is grown the adoptive family are not considered blood relatives and therefore marriages can be contracted with one of them.
• If the adopted child is provided with property/wealth from the biological family, the adoptive parents must not intermingle that with their own.

Source: About.com:Islam

The ambiguities surrounding adoption from the Islamic perspective, coupled with the legal anomalies across societies, are likely to hold implications for Muslim families in the West. The assumptions underpinning adoption by social work agencies may not be mutually shared or understood by those minority ethnic families. The problem of low uptake in the adoption of Muslim children may be far more fundamental than the otherwise important points raised regarding demographics and socioeconomics. If so, it could well be that appropriate long-term foster care is a more feasible proposition for many Muslim families, who are currently discouraged from formal adoption.

Note
[1] The term *zina* refers to 'unlawful' sexuality and encompasses adultery, fornication, rape, prostitution and homosexuality.

SIX

Health issues and Muslim families

Medicine in historical Islam

Historically the Muslim world has enjoyed a very long and enlightened attitude towards health and healing, in which Persian and Hellenic medical knowledge provided a useful foundation for Muslim scholarship to build on and develop into a rich repository of learning. The great Islamic cities of Baghdad and Cordoba were the sites of many hospitals, which boasted a system of interns as well as teaching and library facilities. They supplied rudimentary nursing care, held well-stocked pharmacies and even ran outpatient services (Udwadia, 2001).

Furthermore, Rassool (2000) mentions how some hospitals' wards were divided into those catering for specific maladies, such as infectious diseases and mental illness. Consequently, during the early mediaeval period, these centres of medical excellence were unparalleled throughout the civilised world.

This great focus on medicine can be viewed as deriving from the Islamic emphasis on the interrelation between health, sickness and spiritual growth. Illness is seen as a testing ground for spiritual soundness, whereby the faithful are rewarded for enduring these trials with patience (Sheikh and Gatrad, 2000). However, as the Prophet Mohammed affirmed, the stricken should nevertheless seek help for their illness, since 'There is a cure for every malady save one – that of old age' (Sheikh and Gatrad, 2000, p 34).

Faith, culture and health

The health status of Muslims in Britain is not possible to quantify completely given that statistical data are not gathered on faith groups. However, what is known is that there are higher rates of certain kinds of heart disease and diabetes among people of South Asian origin, which would encompass those who adhere to Islam (Swerdlow et al, 2004). Due to religious prohibitions some health issues such as alcohol abuse may be carefully concealed within Muslim populations, preventing the user from obtaining the help that they need. Although research suggests that while smoking is considered a lesser offence among young Asian Muslims, it nonetheless flies in the face of 'religious obligations to guard one's health and steward one's finances', which may lead to avoidance of revealing addiction (Bradby, 2007, p 664).

Regardless of faith everyone is heir to the possibility of serious illness throughout their life, something that Islam fully acknowledges, and obviously, the health afflictions of Muslims are shared across 'race' and creed. Some might well argue that an emphasis on faith is far less relevant to our understanding of the needs of patients than that of cultural background. Furthermore the body of literature devoted to medical anthropology tends to focus primarily on cultural interpretations of health and disease as primary signifiers dictating behaviour and cognition, whereas other forms of analysis would focus on ethnicity and socioeconomic status as offering more significant insights into health. Faith, however, becomes particularly relevant to practitioners when these come into conflict with medical models, nursing and administrative protocols that make few or no allowances for individual needs. This could be in relation to understanding the needs for religious observance in Muslim stoma patients, whose involuntary production of faeces (or gas) during prayers is regarded as nullifying their observance – a deeply demoralising situation (Kuzu et al, 2001). Or, for instance, by assisting Muslim women to access breast screening services (Millon Underwood et al, 1999).

In this chapter we outline some of the issues that social work practitioners, when dealing with health provision, may need to consider in work with Muslims (although some issues may pertain equally to other groups); bearing in mind, once again, the need to avoid essentialising clients into an undifferentiated mass. Here then we draw some lifespan parameters around the topic, in so far as they are loosely framed by the boundaries of birth and death.

Social workers working in multidisciplinary health-based teams are likely to share some professional values with other professionals, in which nursing is increasingly taking a more transcultural approach (Andrews, 2006). Hopefully, this means that the reductive attitude of biomedicine is mediated by a focus that takes greater account of the personal background of patients and clients, together with the interwoven and complex factors of 'politics, economics and values' (Andrews, 2006, p 84). Transcultural nursing indicates transferring skills to the care of people from many diverse backgrounds. Thus this approach is compatible with both ecological social work perspectives of individuals and a person-centred approach.

The variety of health issues pertaining to Muslim individuals and families is obviously vast and cannot be contained within the scope of one relatively brief chapter. It is our aim therefore to discuss some of the more conspicuous or serious needs of Muslim patients in multidisciplinary health settings, while adding the qualification that this is an area that demands further research and investigation as a whole.

Reproduction

As has already been mentioned, Muslim families value children, and indeed reproduction is considered an essential rite of passage in the achievement of fully adult status. In many regions of the world, Muslim families are often bigger than the European norm; and although this has been linked to agrarian, subsidence-based societies, even in wealthy, urbanised countries the trend towards larger families remains evident.

Part of the reason for this high fertility rate is based on faith, as well as cultural values and socioeconomic realities. Additionally, where women are valued primarily in a biological role, and where there is a cultural preference for sons, there is likely to be a high ratio of children per union (bearing in mind also the additional factor of polygamy) (Obermeyer, 1994).

However, this is not to assume that every pregnancy will be welcome, although whether or how conception is avoided is an issue that varies widely across the Muslim world. Although there are those who believe that the use of contraceptives is unacceptable on the grounds of faith, others will resort to coitus interruptus (withdrawal) as being the one method that receives sanction under Islam, based on the words of the Prophet (Bahar et al, 2005). Naturally, however, there will be many Muslims who quietly or overtly practise a variety of methods that are considered more reliable than this, but among many of the faithful and those in developing nations coitus interruptus is likely to be the preferred, and often indeed sole, method of family planning.

In the UK setting high fertility rates in women have not been viewed in a positive way, and probably this is particularly the case for those of Asian descent. Accordingly, Schott and Henley (1996) give an account of some offensive remarks offered to Asian women in antenatal settings:

> When an Asian woman comes in to have her fifth of sixth
> baby they are so rude to her, especially if she doesn't speak
> English. They say terrible things right to her face, like 'I'd do

something to your husband if I could' or 'This one should be sterilised' and she often just smiles politely because she doesn't understand. (Schott and Henley, 1996, p 183)

Racist attitudes like these connect with underlying fears that minority groups threaten majority populations through perceived over-breeding, and evidently elicit hostile responses. This can be exacerbated if health professionals believe that minority families have larger than average families on sexist grounds, in which parents favour sons over daughters. Social workers have an important role to play in health-based settings to support particularly vulnerable women, while addressing some of these concerns and prejudices among health professionals, as these are likely to have a negative impact on the well-being and treatment of hospital patients.

Pregnancy and birth are periods in a woman's life when she will be increasingly exposed to contact with health professionals, many of whom will be men. For women, regardless of culture and faith, this is an anxiety-provoking time, particularly when subjected to medical procedures that can be worrying, uncomfortable or even degrading, as internal examinations are often felt to be by many women. Respect for modesty and dignity is often overlooked in busy antenatal settings, where it is easy for any patient to feel merely processed and dehumanised.

An unthinking obedience seems to be expected by medical staff. It is not surprising therefore that some women from minority groups will not always cooperate fully with staff, leading to a hardening of existing prejudice towards an assumed state of benighted ignorance among such patients.

This issue becomes all the more important in relation to foetal screening procedures, where the purposes behind this should be carefully considered with patients. It is particularly important to weigh up the value of such procedures, particularly if dealing with patients whose religious convictions would not permit them to abort a malformed foetus in any event. This caveat is one that applies not only to Muslim women, but also to some other religious groups.

It is a common belief among Muslims that 'ensoulment' of the foetus occurs 120 days after conception, corresponding roughly with the 'quickening' or feeling of the foetal movements by the mother (Obermeyer, 1994; Gatrad and Sheikh, 2001). After this point termination (abortion) is considered inadmissible under Islam, although it should be said that for many Muslims termination may not be considered an option at any point, through personal belief or simply because it is not available in their society. Yet it is also reported that it would not be incompatible with Islam to carry out these procedures provided that it is medically necessary due to serious risk to the mother's life (Yeprem, 2007).

Given these restrictions, extending foetal screening to all pregnant women without considering the implications on an individual basis could be regarded as unhelpful, paternalistic and wasteful of resources. However, equally it should not be assumed that a screening will not be helpful to Muslim women, as some would opt for termination even at a later stage of pregnancy, while for others advance warning of any potential problems might be welcomed for those wishing to plan ahead. In each case, couples should be given the facts as well as the options open to them to make an informed decision by having access not only to medical and genetic advice, but also to counselling support that once again takes into account faith and cultural issues.

Ahmad points out that there is a high level of perinatal mortality and congenital malformations by the Pakistani community resident in the UK, an issue that has often been picked up among health and social care providers working with Pakistani communities (Ahmad, 1994). The reasons for this, Ahmad argues, are not clear-cut, although consanguinity has frequently been viewed as the dominant cause. It is the case that some couples will have a higher risk of producing an abnormal foetus because of their genetic heritage. However, it is debatable how far first-cousin marriages, common in some minority communities, are to blame. Ahmad et al (2000, p 49) state that there is increased risk in such unions where there is a family history with 'an autosomal recessive pattern of inheritance', which leads to heart conditions, metabolic disorders and limb disorders. However, Ahmad argues that other factors may also come into play, particularly racist inequalities in health service provision, which have an impact on the delivery of high quality antenatal care supportive of minority group women. He goes on to mount scepticism against messages preventing the marriage of cousins, as likely to be viewed by targeted communities as nothing more than cultural imperialism. Furthermore, he adds, this also indulges in victim blaming by locating poor birth outcomes as based purely on inadvisable cultural practices (Ahmad, 1994).

Clearly then, the issue of consanguinity in relation to reproduction represents a contentious issue where the stakes are high for minority ethnic communities, and until more is known an accurate assessment of risk cannot be properly ascertained. Nevertheless it is important for social workers to be aware of the issues, particularly when working with minority group families where consanguineous unions are common, for often these kinds of families will be aware of the weight of Western medical disapproval surrounding traditions that have long been adopted as the norm in many societies. This is particularly the case when working with families caring for disabled children, where knee-jerk assumptions relating to culturally-based marriage practices and their tragic outcomes are best avoided.

Even normal pregnancies for women from minority ethnic communities are unlikely to reach the post-birth period without some collision with health staff. One area for Muslim women revolves around fasting at Ramadan. Although certain sectors of Muslim society are exempted for a time from fasting due to frailty, illness or pregnancy, some women will choose to fast. Their reasons may be pious, or communal – in wishing to join the rest of the family, or they may be aware that the fast will be postponed until a less convenient time. Medical staff are often unsupportive of this idea, and although there is little medical evidence to show that this is actively harmful to women and their unborn babies, the medical advice is likely to be disapproving without considering any options that would help pregnant Muslim women deal with the Ramadan expectations more effectively (Fowler et al, 1990).

Childbirth is a particularly vulnerable time in a woman's life when the unfamiliar, the insensitive or the coercive is particularly harmful to the labouring woman and her unborn baby, both psychologically and physiologically. It is not possible to make generalisations regarding good birthing practice for Muslim women, since this is so clearly tied to personal expectation, education and culture rather than faith alone. Nonetheless, some worrying research data show that South Asian women, many of whom may be Muslim, are offered less pain relief in labour than white women (Schott and Henley, 1996). The authors go on to say that the reasons for this distinction are unclear but may be tied to language barriers and the belief among midwives that Asian women make an exaggerated fuss during labour. On the other hand, women across cultures often derive relief from being able to express pain without necessarily indicating a wish for pain relief, while some will go through the labour process virtually in silence. These different ways of managing pain are indicative of personal coping strategies, personal values and cultural conditioning, as well as how well women are supported by family and staff during labour.

In a number of cultures the placenta carries important symbolism and there are many different ways of dealing with it. However, for Muslims it is considered to be polluted (as is menstrual blood) and should be disposed of as soon as possible (Schott and Henley, 1996). Finally, these authors advise that Muslim women are not expected to say formal prayers, which involve bodily movements, during menstruation and 40 days after giving birth. They are also exempt from the 36th week of pregnancy due to the physical exertions required.

The newborn baby may become the subject of several important Islamic rituals that welcome her or him into the world. The first proper word that the baby should hear is that of *Adhan*, the call to prayer where the baby will hear the name of Allah, followed by the declaration of faith (Gatrad and Sheikh, 2000).

The authors go on to describe other rituals, such as the *tahneek*, where softened date (or honey) may be rubbed on the baby's upper palate preferably by a respected family member. A *taweez* is often tied around the infant's neck or wrist: this pouch contains a prayer designed to protect the baby and should only be removed during an emergency. Finally if the baby is a boy he will be circumcised. 'Circumcision' of female infants can also occur, although this is often a much more serious event and is discussed later in the chapter. Islam encourages women to breastfeed their babies up to the second year. Although this practice ties in well with World Health Organization recommendations, breastfeeding beyond a few months is still regarded as rather dubious and self-indulgent in British society, despite the benefits to the baby and mother. It is unknown how far this excellent practice is being maintained in Muslim communities in the UK.

Social work practitioners are unlikely to be involved in the birthing and postnatal processes normally; however, they do have an important role to play in relation to infertility issues. This, as is generally appreciated, is a deeply traumatic condition, where a huge sense of grief, bereavement, personal inadequacy and guilt can be experienced. More than being solely a personal tragedy this is one that also extends to the wider family, where a break in the generational chain can cause a significant and resounding sense of failure and loss.

In some communities where the status of women is linked to childbearing the inability to produce a child is likely to seriously jeopardise her standing in the family and community. Furthermore, in some Muslim countries the failure to produce a child may well lead to repudiation by the husband or being obliged to accept the minor role in a polygamous union.

The search for a solution that most couples will consider when a normal conception fails to occur carries important implications and restrictions within the Muslim world. As we have seen, fostering rather than adoption may be more acceptable for Muslims and assisted conception is only acceptable under certain conditions. Donor sperm is never acceptable since progeny should only be the product of the sacred union of husband and wife (Aboulgar, 2006). By contrast, provided that donor eggs are used within polygamous unions this may be a legitimate way forward; however, such resorts are not viable in the Western world where polygamy is illegal. Thus the choices before a Muslim couple may be more restricted than for others in the same position. This may lead to a reduced chance of producing offspring and a greater risk of spousal rejection of wives, as well as that of domestic abuse in certain cases.

Genital mutilation

The term 'genital mutilation' is one that the majority of people will immediately associate with females in Muslim societies, as in reference to 'female genital mutilation' (FGM). This, however, not only entertains some inaccuracies in relation to faith issues, but could equally be applied to any practice that interferes with or amputates part of the genitals in either sex. This, for instance, is an issue that some Jews are now revisiting as being outdated, traumatic and harmful in relation to the circumcision of sons. The question has been raised whether baby boys are entitled to protection from sexual mutilation as much as are girls, since, it is argued, circumcision is not compatible with either human rights or the Hippocratic Oath (Baer, 1997; Svoboda, 1997).

The religious mandates that prescribe the removal of the foreskin of baby boys on the grounds of hygiene have also been raised in conjunction with similar practices under Islam. However, it is true to say that this is a highly controversial topic that has not received much serious consideration by Muslims, who continue to advocate the circumcision of males as obligatory. Abu-Salieh is one of the few Muslim writers who outwardly condemns male circumcision, commenting wryly:

> [I]nternational organizations have generally refused to involve themselves in the issue of male circumcision. It is likely, they are afraid of being considered anti-Semitic.[2] This is notably the case with the World Health Organization, the United Nations Fund for Population Activities, UNICEF, and Amnesty International. These organizations, responsible for overseeing the protection of human rights, are always ready to criticize – and correctly so – female sexual mutilation but have become accomplices in the violation of the fundamental human right of male infants to an intact

body. The fear of anti-Semitism paralyses them. (Abu-Salieh,
1997, pp 54-5)

Consequently, as Sheikh and Gatrad (2000, p 61) briefly comment, the
attempts of 'Muslim apologists' to argue against the practice are unlikely
to be successful. Instead, to minimise injury to infants they support
the idea of carrying out male circumcision under the NHS – which
being medically unnecessary is itself a controversial notion. However,
by contrast, current research recommends promoting circumcision
among sub-Saharan males as a cost-effective protective factor in the
spread of HIV/AIDS (van Dam and Anastasi, 2000).

Female genital mutilation

If the circumcision of boys from faith communities is still contentious
in many Western countries, interference in the genitals of girls and
women is increasingly being regarded as an outrage. The reason for
this is that female 'circumcision' is frequently a far more traumatic,
life-threatening event with serious lifelong repercussions.

The World Health Organization has estimated that FGM has been
practised on between 100 and 132 million girls and women worldwide
(WHO: www.forwarduk.org.uk/what.htm) and not exclusively in
Muslim communities. There are a number of forms practised with
varying degrees of trauma attached (Table 13).

Feminist analysis points to female genital mutilation as a practice
that is rooted in the control of women's sexuality. The repercussions
of FGM destroy female physio-psycho-sexual integrity leading to
lifelong problems connected to normal development, sexual activities
and childbirth and can even result in long-term damage to bladder
and bowels. The massive physical and psychological trauma of such
crude, violent assaults on the female anatomy hardly bears thinking
about, particularly when considering that these procedures are often
inflicted on infants and small girls usually without any anaesthetic or
medical knowledge, equipment or back-up whatsoever.

The origins of FGM are unclear, although it is practised in
many African countries. It is interesting to note that some form of
circumcision has been found on ancient Egyptian female mummies, and
is thought to mark a class distinction. Furthermore, it was apparently
practised in the fifth century BCE, among the Phoenicians and Hittites
for example (Ras-Work, 1997). Since then it has been found as far
afield as modern-day Ethiopia, Somalia, Egypt, Sudan, Saudi Arabia,
Yemen and Iraq, and is also present to a lesser extent in Jordan and

Table 13: Forms of female genital mutilation
• *Sunnah* Removal of the prepuce of the clitoris. Sometimes involving incisions or abrasions made with a needle, as found in Indonesia and Malaysia
• *Clitoridectomy* Total amputation of the clitoris
• *Excision* Removal of the clitoris and labia minora
• *Infibulation* Amputation of the clitoris, the labia minora, parts of the labia majora and stitching both sides of the vulva, leaving a small opening for urination and menstruation
• *Defibulation* Is performed to allow sexual intercourse or childbirth
• *Refibulation* Following childbirth or if the husband is absent for a long period of time
• *Gishiri cut* Performed by traditional midwifes during childbirth, cutting open the soft tissues to enlarge the opening
• *Angurya cut* Traditional surgery to remove the hymen loop on female infants in Nigeria

Source: Ras-Work (1997)

Syria (Minces, 1992) and in some South Asian and Southeast Asian Muslim communities (Dorkenoo et al, 2007). Until fairly recently it could even be found among certain tribes in the Buraimi Oasis in the United Arab Emirates (Brooks, 1995).

FGM is not confined to these regions alone but is also practised in certain minority ethnic communities in Europe, Australia, New Zealand, the US and Canada as well. Children may often be removed from the country of residence for a holiday in the family's country of origin only to return with genital mutilations (Grassivaro Gallo, et al, 1997; Müller, 1997). FGM is considered a form of child abuse and accordingly this implies serious implications for social workers internationally (Taylor, 2003).

The connection of FGM to Islam is hotly contested by a number of scholars who rightly point out that it is a pre-Islamic tradition and found among some animist and Christian communities as well. A typical situation can be found in Ethiopia where approximately 90% of females, including Christians, Muslims and Jews, have experienced sexual mutilation. It is further stated that it is not condoned in the Qur'an, although equally a mythical debate is often quoted between Mohammed and a female practitioner of FGM, in which Mohammed does not prohibit the practice but advises her not to cut too deeply (Abu-Salieh, 1997). Furthermore, circumcision (for males) is described as a *sunnah*: meaning that it conforms to tradition commensurate with Islam; however in relation to women it is described as *makrumah*: meaning a religiously non-mandatory, but nevertheless *meritorious*, action (Abu–Salieh, 1997).

Whether this was a factual or mythical conversation on the part of Mohammed, it is undoubtedly the case that many Muslims across the globe regard FGM as sanctioned under Islam. Thus in quite a few Muslim-dominated regions the practice continues as being essential for female Muslims as an identity marker and to ensure a respectable future within the community:

> A common strategy used by various agencies around the world to eradicate female circumcision has been to argue that the practice pre-dates Islam and therefore is cultural and not religious. ... However, this kind of argument does not acknowledge the complexity of contemporary identities and the way that practices may be appropriated into tradition and become authentic to that tradition. (Newland, 2006, p 396)

The challenge for health and social work in the UK (and in other Western countries) is to know how FGM should be dealt with in relation to women and children who have experienced this practice or who are in danger of it. It is something of a concern to see that apart from community education programmes under the international non-governmental organisation, FORWARD (Foundation for Women's Health, Research and Development; www.forwarduk.org. uk/about), there is little research undertaken or commentary made on this particular subject in the social work literature, especially as it is currently estimated that there are 21,000 girls aged under 15 at risk of FGM in Britain (Dorkenoo et al, 2007). It is additionally thought that around 66,000 girls and women may have already undergone the procedure (Williams, 2007).

Children at risk of FGM are nominally protected by law under the 1985 Prohibition of Female Circumcision Act and the 2003 Female Genital Mutilation Act (Williams, 2007). They can furthermore be prevented from being taken out of the country for this express purpose under the 1989 Children Act: Section 8 (Hopkins, 1999). Nonetheless, it is obvious that it is exceedingly difficult for social services to be sufficiently proactive in preventing such situations without prior warning. Once the child has been subjected to FGM, there may seem little point in prosecuting parents, although some similar cases have been prosecuted in France. However, younger siblings at risk can benefit in then being put on the child protection register.

Parents who are complicit in subjecting their daughters to FGM do not regard this as a form of abuse, but as safeguarding their child's future by the standards of their own cultural norms. Social workers may in turn be duly anxious about challenging practices that are regarded as cultural and even faith-based. To avoid alienating parents altogether, while protecting children in their care, requires a sensitive but persevering and pedagogical approach by social workers. One such account is briefly cited by Hopkins in reference to Sone (1992) of an Asian social worker practising in Ealing, West London, working on a case where two children are at risk of FGM and are duly placed on the child protection register:

> The social worker used persuasion and education to dissuade the family from undertaking the practice, although the family were new refugees, and after 6 months the girls were removed from the register. There are obvious lessons to be learned from the strategies employed in that case. (Hopkins, 1999, p 929)

FGM often comes to light during routine health assessments and antenatal care. Commendable initiatives like that of the African Well Woman Clinic at Northwick Park Hospital are being developed to meet the gynaecological and antenatal needs of infibulated women (McCaffrey et al, 1995). However, clearly there is scope for a multidisciplinary approach, and the assistance of health-based social workers should be utilised when such cases are presented.

Arguably there may be little practical assistance that can be offered by social workers under these circumstances. Nevertheless, given the trauma of the initial experience, in addition to the client's growing awareness that FGM is generally considered abnormal and horrifying in the new cultural setting, there may well be a wealth of psychosocial, psychotherapeutic supports that can be provided. To reiterate, a key role will revolve around education in order to break the generational chain of abuse that may otherwise be inflicted on younger members of the family. To this end, a strong argument can be made for the recruitment of specialised social workers who are able to work across cultural boundaries to address the inevitable cultural and language barriers that will otherwise frequently arise.

Disability and Islam

Islamic principles do not discriminate against people with disabilities; instead Muslims are encouraged to extend care to those in need (El Naggar Gaad, 2001). An example of this can be found in Section 25 of the Constitution of the United Arab Emirates, where people with disabilities are regarded as being subject to care by primarily their families or other caregivers, as well as equal in status to others (Alghazo et al, 2003). Furthermore, historically disability has sometimes been very successfully incorporated into mainstream society, as in the case of blind public reciters of the Qur'an, whose popularity was based on their ability to permeate the segregated worlds of men and women without offence (Abdel Haleem, 2001).

Nevertheless, although Islamic precepts are liberal and progressive in this regard, it is a culture that largely dictates responses towards disability, including exposure to human right concepts and discourses of empowerment. Additionally, in many developing, impoverished countries infants born with disabilities are far less likely to survive than those in more affluent regions. However, in the UK the situation may be reversed, in which:

> Deprivation, consanguinity and the general reluctance of Muslims to abort foetuses with congenital abnormalities are key reasons for the high levels of handicap found amongst the Muslim community. (Sheikh and Gatrad, 2000, p 67)

Thus, as these authors comment, the experience of dealing with disabilities in the family on a long-term basis may be a new one for many Muslim families in Britain, but one which is by no means uncommon. This said, it is important to differentiate between physical and intellectual disabilities, in which according to one study set in Leicestershire the latter rate is comparable between people of South Asian origin and white people (McGrowther et al, 2002). However, multiple disabilities can affect many individuals, in addition to mental health problems. This clearly represents a considerable challenge for informal and formal care providers.

It has been found that families of Middle-Eastern origin tend on the whole to harbour negative attitudes towards disability in progeny. For example, one study of families residing in the US observed that the birth of children with disabilities is accompanied by feelings of shame (Sharifzadeh, 1998). This is very similar to the attitudes that can be found in Lebanon and Jordan, while in Palestine disability is viewed as a blight on family honour, and even as supernatural and maleficent (Ashencaen Crabtree, 2006). In addition, the same author (2006) comments on the interweaving of multiple forms of oppression in relation to gender, 'race' and disability, reporting that in these regions while males may be assisted with education and employment, girls and women are often subject to neglect and physical as well as sexual abuse. This is by no means unknown in the UK where some argue that in general 'child abuse and neglect are inextricably interwoven with disability' (Cohen and Warren, 1990, p 253).

A few studies have been carried out in the UK on Pakistani and Bangladeshi families caring for a child or children with disabilities. One study by Fazil et al (2002) notes the social and economic deprivation of participating families, in which, contrary to the stereotypes, there was little support from the extended family. Furthermore it was found that mothers were burdened with the majority of care, and were sometimes regarded as culpable for the birth of a disabled offspring, and even subject to abuse. These findings are commensurate with similar observations of attitudes towards mothers in the Middle East, in which women tainted by these kinds of births may be rejected or displaced (Ashencaen Crabtree, 2007b).

In Britain, Bywaters et al (2003) comment on the supranormal explanations given by parents to account for their child's disability, in which they may regard themselves as being punished by divine will. These authors also go on to say that in their understanding such interpretations are not congruent with Islamic beliefs. Yet in some Muslim cultures supernatural entities such as *jinns* may be regarded as responsible for disabilities in children, rather than attributed solely to the will of God (Atshan, 1997).

In relation to the paper by Bywaters et al (2003) these views also emerged in Ashencaen Crabtree's (2007b) study of family responses towards disability in the United Arab Emirates. However, this attitude was a minority one. Instead, a much more positive message of affirmation of the child and their faith was given by most families in the study that was more compatible with the Islamic view in regarding illness and disability as a test of piety set for the faithful. Where the Islamic view is upheld then it is likely that this will lead to a more positive attitude towards disability itself and the value of people with disabilities, than where this is regarded negatively.

An additional concern raised in the paper by Bywaters et al (2003) relates to shame as a factor preventing parents from accessing health and social care services. This is held in conjunction with a sense of powerlessness felt by parents towards the idea that either they or professionals can alter circumstances or alleviate them in any meaningful way. In this vein, Fazil et al (2002) comment on the low uptake of services by Asian families that is related to a negative perception of what can be achieved:

> Finally, such attitudes are said to lead to low expectations of their children's future as adults and to reduced willingness by parents to encourage their children to achieve maximum independence. (Bywaters et al, 2003, p 503)

Case study 6 is taken from Ashencaen Crabtree's practice and illustrates some of these dilemmas.

Case study 6: Disability, care and a collision of values

A young Pakistani man with significant learning disabilities living with his caregiving family was referred to an Adults with Learning Disabilities Team for an assessment of need. The social worker involved found that he spent most of his day doing little and usually sitting in the family's parked car outside the house for hours on end. Because the car was parked within the locked compound surrounding the house this was considered by his family to be an appropriately safe environment for him.

Having assessed his needs the social worker suggested day care, which the mother as main carer showed some interest in receiving. The social worker started searching for an appropriate placement for her client where he could receive more stimulation and enhance his daily living skills. The client was duly placed and soon the day care staff reported that he was beginning to make good progress: he was interacting well with staff and other service users, and particularly enjoyed the specialist music sessions at the centre. The family who had yet to visit the resource personally was told the good news.

One month after starting at day care the young man was abruptly withdrawn from the centre by his family who claimed that all the stimulation he was receiving was having a bad effect on his character. They disclosed that their son was now less content to sit passively at home but was more excitable, and had started becoming noisy, using both verbal articulations as well as trying to recreate percussion rhythms with household items. All this the family found to be entirely unacceptable. Earnest attempts made to persuade them to return their son to the centre were rejected, as were invitations to visit the centre and see for themselves how well the youth was doing. On consultation with the team manager the social worker followed their directives, although with misgivings, in which she eventually had no choice but to accept the family decision and close the case. After several tantrums the youth's behaviour at home returned to its former passive, inactive state.

This particular case highlights several important points. The first is a clash of values found in the attitude of the family towards the issue of disability, contrasting with that of the social worker. What was made abundantly clear in the meetings between the two parties was that the family were unused to the idea of care taking place outside of the family setting, where predominantly the mother and female kin would be the main caregivers. The ethos and environment of day care was therefore entirely unfamiliar to them, which unfortunately they declined to acquaint themselves with further for personal reasons. Furthermore, the family did not regard any progress by their son as a real possibility; his personal development was permanently static, so far as they were concerned. The only wish made by the family was that the youth was taken care of in a suitably protective environment for a few hours a week to give the family some respite. All attempts to educate the family into a greater understanding of what could be achieved for their son was treated with much doubt.

In addition to this, the social worker's value-based argument that their son had the right to achieve his optimum development was also one that was effectively dismissed by the family. Unfortunately, since their son was not competent to express his own wishes on the subject, and his feelings could only be inferred from his behaviour (arguably a subjective evaluation), it was not ultimately possible to override the family's decision, since in other respects they were sufficiently observant of his basic needs.

The removal of their son from his day centre was thus framed by the family as dissatisfaction with the service judging from the outcome at home, rather than one based on the input given by staff and the youth's positive responses to their care. The greater animation that the youth was now displaying at home was viewed as disruptive and pointless, since he was obviously unable to achieve normal independence now or in the future. The caregiving role, from the family's point of view, was one restricted to prevention of harm solely, rather than maximising learning opportunities and normalising this young man's otherwise stunted human potential.

A sad and frustrating case, then, by social work standards, and one that connects with the concepts of social disability and disabling environments. It is also instructive as an example of the mismatch of values, attitudes and expectations as they were played out between the social worker and the client's family. It is worth reminding ourselves, however, that although the professional position today is that every client is capable of personal growth, this was not always the case. The warehousing of people with disabilities in Britain was the norm until relatively recently.

Probably the faculty of speech and appropriate social behaviour, more than physical ability, is the common yardstick that most people globally have used to measure how far people with disabilities merit the care and courtesy extended to others. The following extract taken from a research interview with an Arab guardian of a severely autistic child in the United Arab Emirates offers some further insights into this hypothesis. Here the participant conveys deep dissatisfaction that the early intervention service involved had yet to teach the child to speak:

> If people don't understand or talk they cannot greet people
> properly. Then people won't respect them. If he [grandson]
> doesn't live in this world [verbal communication], he will
> be like an animal. (Ashencaen Crabtree, 2007b, p 253)

What is of interest is, first, that this graphically illustrates the guardian's lack of realism regarding his grandson's abilities. Second, and more to the point, it conveys a very real and understandable fear regarding the boundaries that were felt to mark the human (with all that that implies) from the non-human.

In relation to the situation in the UK, it has emerged from research that families caring for relatives with disabilities are not as well supported by the extended family as professionals often assume (Fazil et al, 2002). Yet, it has to be said, anecdotal experience from our practice does not necessarily support the idea that Muslim families are particularly concerned about faith issues over and above other more specific concerns.

However, undoubtedly there is a cultural deficit dynamic operating in relation to contact with social services and provision that is deterring minority ethnic families from taking up services more frequently. Our findings suggest that this is in large part due to a lack of suitable information regarding the purpose and value of services available in the area and how these can meet the needs of families.

Consequently, it would seem that many of the problems of uptake relate to inadequate service provision and structural barriers, as well as an insufficient number of professionals able to communicate with minority ethnic families in their own native tongue. An equally important role congruent with this situation would be that of constructing a cultural and conceptual framework that works towards shaping family attitudes and expectations to a more beneficial and positive outcome for the client.

Mental health issues

Much has been written on the topic of 'race'/ethnicity and mental health issues and close consideration has been given to racial preponderance of psychiatric hospital admissions; less commonly to the uptake of mental health services among minority ethnic groups (see Bhugra, 1997; Nazroo, 1997; Fernando et al, 1998). In this book we will not revisit these areas in detail, as essentially this is a broad and complex area falling outside of our remit here.

Mental illness, however, is an important issue for Muslim communities, which, as we have seen, have historically held an abiding interest in this topic in relation to humane care and healing (Rassool, 2000). Shahrom Hatta (2001) asserts that the legal aspects of forensic psychiatry have always been present in the care of people with mental illness in Islam. Thus the 'insane' person (*majnun*) was seen as suffering an abnormality in terms of emotion, cognition and behaviour from which a benign course of therapy could hopefully return him to a state of health (Hatta, 2001):

> For more than thirteen hundred years, Muslim physicians have recorded the various ways of treating the insane; including prayers, social manipulation, music therapy and pharmaco-therapy. (Hatta, 2001, p 183)

Melancholia was one such abnormal state that received scholarly attention from these physicians (Hatta, 2001). Today we would refer to this state as clinical depression, an affective disorder that the World Health Organization classifies as one of the foremost conditions that affects people worldwide.

Depression, as is commonly known, is particularly prevalent among women, commensurate with the estimation that women are at the highest risk of mental illness (Wood Wetzel, 2000). This has been linked to the multiple forms of oppression whose impact falls more heavily on females throughout their lives, and includes all manner of abuses under the broad headings of sexism and patriarchy, sexual exploitation and violence, poverty and capitalist exploitation. It is therefore not particularly surprising to learn that, although South Asians as a group are estimated to have the same or lower rates of depression and anxiety than the general population, depression has been estimated as twice as high among 'Asian and Oriental' women, compared with white women (Burr and Chapman, 2004). There is clearly a discrepancy operating here, in which the authors differentiate between depression that is *treated*, and that which remains medically undetected. The hypothesis tested is that women of South Asian origin tend to somatise their depression, in which mental distress is translated into physical symptoms. The findings suggest that while these participants are aware of their emotional distress, they are much more likely to seek medical help from GPs for headaches and flu, for instance (Burr and Chapman, 2004). These symptoms are considered *legitimate* reasons for seeking help, whereas depression is regarded as '"moaning, worrying" and being upset' (Burr and Chapman, 2004, p 444). This finding is supported in another study into the expression of mental illness where Muslim women of Asian origin formed the majority of the participants (Fenton and Sadiq-Sangster, 1996). This is echoed in yet another study in which only one third of South Asian participants, primarily Pakistani, are male (Husain et al, 1997).

Issues of embodiment or somatisation of mental distress apart, the question remains why women of South Asian origin are more likely to suffer from depression than South Asian men? There can be no definitive answer, yet some factors will immediately resonate with a social work understanding of the psychosocial impact of oppression, together with the impact of loss and bereavement.

Fenton and Sadiq (1996) have laid out some of the factors that eroded the mental health of the female Asian participants in their study. These include relationship problems, which commanded enormous anxiety for participants, as the family is usually far more central to the well-being of its members than it is for non-Asians.

Racial hostility was another factor that was regarded as contributory to the women's mental distress (Fenton and Sadiq, 1996; Fenton and Sadiq-Sangster, 1996). The extent of the racism experienced by British Muslims, together with its trivialisation by the media, is the topic of an impassioned article by Seamus Milne writing in *The Guardian* newspaper, in which we hear the following indictment:

> Britons are now more suspicious of Muslims than are Americans or citizens of any other major Western country, including France. According to an international Harris poll last month, nearly 30% of British people believe it's

> impossible to be both a Muslim and a Briton. (Milne, 2007)

The effects of such antagonism, which, according to Milne, are largely uninformed by any personal acquaintance with real (as opposed to mythologised and demonised) Muslims, are more completely explored in Chapter Seven of this volume. However, it is clear that the present climate of hostility towards Muslims in Britain is likely to engender great anxiety and stress among many, and may affect the mental health of individuals (Kai and Hedges, 1999).

Other areas of risk relate to poverty and deprivation, which have long been linked to mental health problems, and, as the demographic evidence shows, many Muslim Asian families in Britain are forced to live under circumstances of privation, with few employment prospects to alleviate their distress.

The extended Asian family is often regarded as a source of practical and emotional support to the extent that formal service providers may assume that their input is not necessary. However, such assumptions are by no means always correct in the case of the caregiving of children and other relatives with disabilities (Katbamna et al, 2004). Research findings into family care indicate that this is often given with devotion and can be a very enriching experience leading to personal growth in carers (Hastings and Taunt, 2002). At the same time it is often demanding, socially isolating, physically and emotionally exhausting, and imposes heavy financial penalties on families as well (Read, 2003). These are all factors that once again have an impact on the mental health of carers, cutting across ethnic and faith divides in the UK and usually falling to the lot of mothers. In line with this observation, the study by Husain et al (1997) suggests that it is mostly marital difficulties, burdens of care and housing problems that predominate as stressors in the lives of South Asian women.

Although most Asian families in the UK do not live in extended families, when this structure is in place this in itself can be another source of stress and anxiety. Sonuga-Barke and Mistry (2000) contribute their findings to a small but growing body of research literature regarding the psychological benefit to mothers and children in extended Hindu or Muslim families that specifically include a grandmother. The results are interesting: while children were shown to fare well, as did grandmothers, the mental health of mothers, and particularly Pakistani Muslim mothers, suffered in consequence. The majority of mothers, with an emphasis of Muslims over Hindu mothers, was shown to experience higher rates of depression and anxiety compared with counterparts living in nuclear families. The authors suggest that this may be due to the feelings of a loss of agency and control in situations where grandmothers are overly intrusive. However, it is also noted that Muslim mothers tended to be younger than the Hindu participants in the study, with the inference that they therefore lack authority and self-confidence (Sonuga-Barke and Mistry, 2000).

As previously discussed, South-Asian Muslim girls and women may feel oppressed by patriarchal socio-sexual control within the family setting, relating to the honour concept of *izzat* (Chew-Graham et al, 2002). Furthermore, and connected to *izzat*, a more obvious causation lies in the phenomenon of domestic violence, which is itself associated with poor mental health outcomes for victims.

Extreme distress may ultimately be enacted in suicide, which for Muslim, as in Christianity, is forbidden. It is often regarded as a criminal act in some Muslim countries, and in general is treated as a taboo subject in Muslim regions (Sarfraz and Castle, 2002; Pritchard and Amanullah, 2006). Suicide statistics may be camouflaged under the category of 'other violent accidents', which are duly much inflated compared with minimal figures for suicide (Pritchard and Amanullah, 2006, p 422). With respect to the UK, these authors warn practitioners against overlooking possible collusion between interpreters, the patient and family with the aim of minimising the extent of the mental distress, and hence the risk of stigmatised suicide.

A further point worth considering relates to the issue of migration. In relation to the preponderance of African Caribbean men in psychiatric care, studies have considered the impact of cultural dislocation, the removal from supportive networks and the effects of racism on migrants in terms of mental health issues (Rack, 1982; Acharyya, 1996; Barnes and Bowl, 2001). Similar dynamics exist in the West for other migrant groups who experience racism and assimilation problems, in which they too are often at risk of mental health problems (Noh et al, 1999). However, the picture is less clear in the UK, in that although depression and anxiety do not appear to rank highly in the South Asian population, it is more than likely that much lies medically undetected. Mental health problems may be internalised or somatised, for reasons of *izzat*, or due to language and cultural barriers these may be disguised or simply remain hidden.

However, it is by no means unlikely that vulnerable individuals who have recently migrated into Britain may find it hard to adjust to norms and values that are in conflict with those in their country of origin. Case study 7 is once again taken from direct practice and illustrates some of these points.

Case study 7: Migration, cultural norms and mental health

An elderly Yemeni lady with moderate dementia was sent from the Yemen by relatives to live with her married nephew in London, since it was thought that formal health and social care services in this country would be more appropriate to meet her needs. After a short time the nephew contacted social services to request assistance as his aunt was proving to be more dependent on himself and his wife than he had anticipated. On visiting the family the social worker found the lady in question to be a frail individual with no English language abilities. The assessment suggested that the client was feeling very insecure by her relocation to an entirely new cultural setting, being a move that had not been of her choosing. Her ensuing wandering behaviour at home had resulted in the family locking her into her bedroom at night, which had greatly aggravated her anxiety. On consultation, the family stated they wished to continue caring for her but were keen to opt for day care during the week.

Day-care provision was arranged at a centre where there were a significant number of Asian clients, with whom it was hoped she would eventually make friends. Here she seemed subdued, but that was considered to be an understandable adjustment to her new setting. Unfortunately after a few days the placement was jeopardised by a sudden deterioration in her mental health status, when she was found to be very distressed on arrival at the centre. The nephew confided that he and his wife were finding it very difficult to get his aunt onto transport in the morning due to her hysterical behaviour, but had no idea why she was so reluctant to go.

On investigation the social worker uncovered the reason for the client's distress. Although once at the day centre this lady was segregated from males in an all-female Asian clique, compatible with her cultural norms, no such division was in place on the transport used, where males and females were placed together according to logistics. This close proximity to unrelated men had created a huge conflict in the client, exacerbating her distress and, consequently, her dementia. Once her nephew's wife took over the role of driving her to the centre in the family car, she returned to her previous levels of functioning and no further incidents of psychotic-type behaviour were reported.

Anthropologists have long been fascinated by the accounts of 'culture-bound syndromes' emerging from far-flung regions of the world. These show a diversity of behaviours together with accompanying interpretations to perceived abnormality and disorder that on the face of it are unfamiliar to Western observers. In association with these has been an interest in the range of healing methods used to combat dis-*ease* in the specific cultural setting. Spirit possession is one typical interpretation of behaviour that would in another cultural setting be classified as mental illness. Such interpretations remain common in a number of communities, as exemplified by the notion of possession among Bangladeshi families in Britain (Bose, 1997).

Among many Muslims worldwide the concept of possession is fully accepted, indeed the very word *majnun* means a person possessed by a *jinn* (Hatta, 2001). *Iblis*, the fallen angel (the Islamic counterpart of Lucifer), is thought to be 'the source of much mental, physical and psychosocial suffering' (Al-Krenawi and Graham, 1999, p 55).

Sometimes, therefore, the biomedical and psychoanalytical model that social workers understand and operate within in this country may have little relevance to an individual whose frames of reference come from a very different perspective, as the account in Case study 8 illustrates.

Case study 8: The possessed Arab student

An Arab social work student was anticipating her forthcoming wedding that had been traditionally arranged by her parents. The ceremony took place during the academic semester, but following the honeymoon period she failed to return to class due to an unspecified but serious illness. This sickness was attributed to a possession of a *jinn*, which had entered her body during the wedding. Every time her husband approached her for sexual congress she would show florid signs of demonic possession. No blame was attributed to either party by family or friends. It was merely accepted as an unfortunate event that would hopefully be cured in due course, eventually enabling her to return to normal functioning in relation to her duties as a newly married woman and student. (Ashencaen Crabtree, 2008, forthcoming)

The power of prayer is often emphasised as vital to healing in the Islamic framework. Thus, Al-Krenawi and Graham (1999, p 53) discuss the role of the Arab 'Koranic mental health' healer who, through combining prayer with traditional healing, is not dissimilar to other traditional Muslim healers: the Malay shaman – the *bomoh* – or the *bak* of Uzbekistan (Rasanayagam, 2006). The role of such individuals is to provide a culturally informed healing ceremony that is also regarded as compatible with the Muslim faith. This is despite the fact that such practitioners are often as much disapproved of in Islam as spiritualists are by the Catholic Church, being fundamentally rooted in paganism. Yet Muslim cosmology is rich in supernatural entities, both benevolent and malign, and their agency is viewed as the means to either elevate human nature or divert it to degradation and ruin.

The more immediate concern, however, is that these frames of reference may seem to be yet further examples of delusion and psychosis by practitioners ignorant of cultural and cosmological variation. This feeds into the criticism by Fernando et al (1998) that diagnosis contains a strong element of racial bias, and Chakraborty's (1991) point that psychiatry has yet to grasp the implications of ethnicity and cultural diversity.

End of life

Death and bereavement, once everyday community events, are now issues that have become topicalised in being part of the academic, theoretical discourse. Furthermore, although death in infancy and young adulthood (particularly in relation to childbearing) is still commonplace in developing nations, very few in the developed world will have had personal involvement in this kind of untimely death. The modern-day experience of death is often that of the demise of grandparents, who die quietly out of sight in hospitals and hospices rather than at home. Consequently death has become a remote and unlikely contingent; and, as has often been pointed out, some people feel so awkwardly embarrassed in the face of someone's bereavement they feel powerless to respond appropriately.

In a multicultural, multi-faith environment, medical and social care staff will need to deal with the realities of death across ethnic and religious divides; however, unfamiliarity with faith, ethnicity and culture can intensify feelings of ineptness.

In the Muslim *ummah* bereavement reactions vary, as they do for all people, according to individual temperament, family conditioning and cultural norms. For example, death in Ethiopia is generally accompanied by a shrill, heart-rending ululation, while Bedouin women fall into a keening lament that may continue for days (Abu-Lughod, 1993). It is claimed, however, that Muslims are prepared for the issue of death from an early age as it is mentioned many times in the Qur'an (Raad, 1998). Islam, regardless of cultural variation, lays down some very clear guidance regarding how the faithful should grieve, its duration and how the bereaved should be supported in a return to adjusted living.

The academic view of death and dying, as taught to social work students among others, is largely informed by a critical analysis of

Elisabeth Kübler-Ross's (1970) seminal work. This continues to provide a useful framework, despite a critique of the linear approach of the stages she outlines, as well as an ethnocentric bias. However, some Muslim social work and medical students may regard this as largely irrelevant to them, as reflected in the following quotation relating to the teaching of death and dying issues to Malaysian Muslim students:

> The discussion of denial, anger, bargaining and guilt has frequently been seen by some students to be irrelevant in discussing the needs of dying Muslim clients. Such clients, through virtue of their religion and culture, are usually seen to have transcended these base emotions. What may be a frequent process among other races cross-culturally would not be expected to present emotional and psychological difficulties for Muslims. (Ashencaen Crabtree and Baba, 2001, p 479)

What, then, is the unique perspective given to Muslims on this difficult issue? We learn that most Muslims would prefer to die at home, although this is a preference that is not relegated to Muslims alone but is in fact one shared by most people. In discussing a study examining the palliative care issues of Bangladeshi patients in Tower Hamlets, Odette Spruyt (1999) notes that the majority of such patients chose to be cared for and die at home, with many wishing to die in their country of origin. She comments that the existing research literature links death in hospital with people of lower socioeconomic status than those who experience 'home deaths'. However, in the case of many minority groups, and Muslims in particular, such a correlation does not hold fast. These families are more likely to be influenced by traditions which view family care of the dying as both an extension of normal care and a sacred trust (Spruyt, 1999; Gatrad and Sheikh, 2002a).

Individuals facing the end of life whose needs cannot be met entirely in the home are likely to need every reassurance that their cultural, faith-based needs will be respected within the new caring environment. Working constructively with the patient and their family to define and meet their needs is likely to alleviate the great anxieties some will feel about moving to unfamiliar, potentially frightening new surroundings, at an extremely vulnerable stage in life. Factors that are likely to be highly significant are those that relate to prayers, diet, pain relief[1] and of what kind (for some faiths, such as in Buddhism, maintaining mental acuity is spiritually important up to the last conscious moments of life). In addition, that they will have access to an appropriate spiritual adviser;

that their family will be welcome to keep them company during their care and at whatever time of day or night; and, finally, that their bodies will be treated according to time-honoured custom in due course. Such stipulations will require commitment by the relevant health authorities and the staff serving them; however, much suffering may be alleviated by this kind of sensitive, inclusive approach.

Even in the event of good planning not all eventualities can be covered. Furthermore, despite any evident need some families will find the move towards formal care very hard. For when end-of-life care cannot be administered at home family members may feel public shame and private guilt, which can greatly exacerbate natural grief reactions and lead to conflict with service providers, as Case study 9 indicates.

Case study 9: Family perception of abandoned responsibilities

A 72-year-old Pakistani man with cardiac and renal failure was referred to the community palliative care team to discuss respite care in the hospice. His family, with whom this gentleman lived, were anxious about other relatives viewing his admission to the hospice as an abandonment of their responsibility of care, especially as the hospice was seen as a white, middle-class, Christian environment.

The eldest son agreed to stay with his father during his time at the hospice. On admission he explained how upset his father was to leave his wife and home. The hospice doctor raised the issue of the resuscitation policy; this shocked the son, as he had expected his father to be resuscitated without question. The patient soon suffered a cardiac arrest, was resuscitated and transferred back to hospital where he later died. The death occurred at the weekend and within 24 hours of admission, leading to the involvement of the coroner with a consequent delay in releasing the body for burial. This caused further grief and distress for the family, who felt that if the patient had not gone to the hospice these problems would not have arisen.

Source: Adapted from Jack et al (2001, p 380)

It should be pointed out that, while euthanasia is forbidden under Islam, the artificial prolongation of the lives of all terminally ill Muslim patients is not being implied. Instead, the withdrawing of treatment in some cases where the prognosis is inevitably that of imminent death is considered religiously acceptable (Sarhill et al, 2001; Da Costa et al, 2002; Gatrad and Sheikh, 2002a). Nonetheless, Gatrad and Sheikh

(2002a) advise that such decisions are more easily reached where a Muslim physician is available to deal with Muslim families and support them in their decision making. In turn, families may require the additional advice of senior male members of the family and religious advisers.

Because the spiritual dimension of death is predominantly emphasised in Islam the dying person will be helped to pray for as long as they are able (having first carried out the necessary ablutions); as well as listening to recitations of the Qur'an (Gatrad and Sheikh, 2002a). Ideally, their bed should be placed facing Mecca, which in Britain lies towards a south-east direction (Sheikh and Gatrad, 2000). One issue that may cause concern to medical staff in relation to hospital policies is the number of visitors the dying person may receive. This may be far in excess of the numbers usually visiting the bedside of dying patients in Britain, for this is a time when people will seek forgiveness from the dying person for any trespasses they may have committed in the past (Sheikh and Gatrad, 2000).

Islam stresses the importance of accepting the reality of death by the dying, as well as the bereaved, where ultimately the dead are viewed as embarking on a journey to their true home 'returning to the Highest Company' (Sheikh and Gatrad, 2000, p 101). It would not therefore be proper for a devout Muslim to rail against divine judgement, as indicated in Kübler-Ross's stages, although Abu-Lughod (1993) mentions the conflict between that which faith dictates and culture (and even maybe instinct) urges. Moreover, as Ashencaen Crabtree and Baba (2001) point out, this assumption is to conflate *is* with *ought*, where many dying Muslims may well feel emotions that they are discouraged from expressing. Working across faiths, social workers may need to reflect on how to support the needs of clients, as well as those of families, particularly when these needs are not simultaneously congruent. This would apply to the situation of the individual's strongly felt, emotional needs and what is prescribed by faith and culture. This is especially important for Muslim clients when what is being felt at that moment is perhaps the need and space to openly grieve with the thought of impending death.

After death has occurred, there are some immediate tasks that need to be accomplished by the family and their followers, and medical staff should accordingly liaise closely with them to avoid family distress. Most of the funeral preparations will take place at home and often families will use the services of a 'local Muslim funeral committee' to arrange for death certificates and the funeral (Schott and Henley, 1996).

According to Yasien-Esmael and Rubin (2005, p 497) under *shari'a* law on hearing of a bereavement one should utter thanks to God, reciting 'We are all to God and we shall return to him. God, I ask you to provide the appropriate recompense for me for this tragedy/accident and leave me only the good from what has occurred.'

The body of Muslims must be washed by one or two respectable and pious fellow Muslims of the same sex who can be entrusted with the office, for even in death the proprieties of gender segregation and physical proximity should be observed (Yasien-Esmael and Rubin, 2005). The body will be wrapped in a simple white shroud, Sheikh and Gatrad (2000) adding that this shroud would be the cloth that had been worn on the *hajj* pilgrimage in life.

Prayers will be said over the body at the mosque or at the grave site, which will not be marked by engraved gravestones but may carry some other marker. It is very important that the body is buried as quickly as possible, its face turned towards Mecca. Under Islam the burial should take place within 24 hours of death; connected, no doubt, to the historical sanitary concerns regarding the effects of a hot desert climate on corpses. Consequently, any delays will cause distress to families as being disrespectful to the deceased and bringing fears that decomposition will commence, for embalming is not permitted (Schott and Henley, 1996).

Funerals mark further gender distinctions, for women are prohibited from attending funerals, even that of their own child. This relates to Islamic precepts regarding attitudes of acceptance and decorum, which women are not considered to be able to uphold due to the perception that they are more emotional than men.

Mohammed made it very clear that grief should not be expressed with voluble weeping and lamentations (and it is particularly forbidden at the graveside), as causing pain to the deceased, who, based on a further saying by the Prophet, may be regarded as sentient to the point of being able to feel actual physical pain (Sheikh and Gatrad, 2000). For this reason, as well, post-mortems are a highly problematic issue for Muslims (Gatrad and Sheikh, 2002b).

Islam emphasises the desirability of a rapid return to normality following loss, where bereavement is structured across a strict timeframe. According to Yasien-Esmael and Rubin (2005), official mourning (*hidad*) takes place three days after the announcement of the death, where patience and forbearance are the hallmarks of a pious demeanour. Unlike the often overwhelming ritual for Christian families, where although beset by grief they are often expected to provide food and drink for attendees to the funeral, in Islam visitors instead bring the food to the home of the bereaved in order to ensure that they eat properly. After seven days mourning is concluded; ablutions and a cleaning of the house mark the return to normal life, although the death may be officially marked 40 days later and again on the anniversary (Yasien-Esmael and Rubin, 2005).

However, bereaved Muslims experience relief through being able to take a proactive stand to assist their deceased relatives in the next life by praying for them and performing meritorious deeds on their behalf, such as going on a *hajj*. For in death there are stages for the dead to pass through, which the living can ease by such good deeds in their name. Table 14 outlines these stages.

Table 14: The Islamic schema of existence
• Life before conception
• The lower world (life on earth)
• The intermediate realm
• Judgement Day
• The Garden and the Fire

Source: (Sheikh and Gatrad, 2000)

The souls of the dead attain their place in the celestial hierarchy according to their deeds in life. The highest place, it is said, is allotted to the prophets, while the souls of martyrs are free to choose their place in Paradise; some may not enter into heaven itself, and the souls of non-believers will simply rot in their graves (Yasien-Esmael and Rubin, 2005).

In terms of practice, ordinary bereavement counselling services are likely to be problematic in relation to assisting potential Muslim clients. They in turn may regard the idea of seeking professional help for grief as being essentially irreligious, and therefore likely to induce or exacerbate guilt. The response of some service providers will probably be that assistance with such needs are best left to the family concerned and to their religious adviser. Consequently, there remain further questions to be answered about what kind of social work practice would be appropriate for dying Muslims, apart from close liaison with the latter into their expressed wishes. Certainly for some Muslims there will be unmet needs regarding prolonged, suppressed or complicated grief. However, what kind of support practitioners can offer will remain unclear until the research gap into this challenging area is at least partially bridged. This could usefully highlight any outstanding issues of concern relating to the psychological and emotional adjustment of the dying and bereaved individuals, especially those who require more support than can be found in the existing framework of religious, cultural, family and community expectations. Such services could conceivably be particularly beneficial to those whose loss relates to stigmatised or specifically difficult circumstances. HIV/AIDS, suicide, domestic violence or death under traumatic or notorious circumstances are those that immediately come to mind as likely to require professional help. Nor should we forget the needs of those who are simply unable to come to terms with dying and death in conformity with faith-based and socially sanctioned values and conduct.

Notes

[1] Pain is a highly subjective state and varies across gender and ethnicity. It is claimed that some patients (women and certain ethnic groups) suffering from chronic and even terminal illness often have their experience of pain discredited by medical staff, who assume that the level of pain felt is in fact lower than is being reported by the patient (Werth et al, 2002; Croissant, 2005).

[2] Meaning in relation to Arabs as well as Jews.

SEVEN

Muslim communities, crime, victimisation and criminal justice

Introduction

This chapter examines criminal justice issues in relation to Muslim communities, particularly drawing on research undertaken in the UK, but also involving a broader international dimension by including other countries, notably France, Germany and Australia. Muslim communities as the victims of crime, Muslims as perpetrators of crime and criminal justice responses to victimisation are areas that are explored here. An underlying theme to this chapter is that whereas, traditionally, identities in relation to 'race'/ethnicity have generated substantial research and policy attention within a criminal justice context, in the post-9/11 era religion as an identity marker is taking on greater significance, with attention being placed particularly, although not exclusively, on Muslim communities.

'Race'/ethnicity and criminal justice

In the UK, equality and diversity issues within the criminal justice system have traditionally been considered through a predominantly secular framework in relation to 'race'/ethnicity rather than religious identity. This means that 'racial'/ethnic groupings have been identified and used to guide service delivery and provision, and religion has tended to be overlooked. For example, agencies of the criminal justice system record suspects', offenders', victims' and employees' identities according to 'racial' and/or ethnic categories, not religious categories. Thus, statistics in relation to stop and searches conducted by police under counter-terrorism legislation use racial rather than religious categories. This means that although statistics may suggest an increase in the number of Asians stopped and searched, it is not possible to gauge the circumstances of such events in these statistics (Garland et al, 2006). While direct and institutional racism by the police, the courts and the penal system has been extensively documented (Hood, 1992; Kalunta-Crumpton, 1999; Bowling and Phillips, 2002; Shute et al, 2005), and policies have been implemented to tackle these issues, discrimination on the grounds of religion has rarely been addressed. Whereas the Home Office regularly publishes statistical information about minority ethnic groups under the publication *Race and the Criminal Justice System: Statistics under Section 95 of the Criminal Justice Act*, no similar publications are to be found in relation to faith. The 2006 Equality Act has established a new single Commission for Equality and Human Rights (CEHR) that brings together all six strands of discrimination – 'race', age, gender, disability, religion and sexual orientation – into one unified organisation. Interestingly, when exercising its powers relating to its community functions, the CEHR will be required to have 'particular regard' to 'race', religion or belief, suggesting that faith identities will increasingly be monitored and used for policy development and analysis.

Notably, the Prison Service in England and Wales has been monitoring the religious identity of inmates for a number of years. Prison statistics show that Islam is currently the second fastest-growing religion in British prisons, and Muslims appear to be over-represented in prisons by over threefold. Prison statistics show that on 30 June 2005 10% of the prison population was Muslim, 17% Roman Catholic and 32% Anglican (Home Office, 2006, p 105). Since Muslims comprise 3.1% of the general population (National Census, 2001), they are clearly over-represented in prison, an issue returned to later in this chapter. In France, since the second half of the 1990s, it has been illegal to ask someone to declare their religious faith, and so there are no official data about the religious or ethnic identity of French prisoners (Beckford et al, 2005). These authors argue that, in contrast to England and Wales (where religious identity is categorised by the prison authorities), French prisons give rise to highly individualised expressions of Islam, and opportunities for collective prayer are scarce in French jails (Beckford et al, 2005).

Muslim communities and victimisation

When focusing on victimisation, it is important to consider Muslim communities as members of 'race'/ethnic communities, as well as being members of a religious grouping. This is because Muslims might be at a higher risk of certain types of crime due to their 'race'/ethnicity as well as their religious affiliation. At the same time, the ways in which the process of victimisation is experienced may be influenced by individuals' identities in relation to their 'race'/ethnicity as well as their religion.

National crime surveys suggest that people belonging to minority ethnic groups experience high levels of victimisation. For example, findings from the British Crime Survey show that Pakistanis and Bangladeshis (who are likely to be Muslims) are significantly more likely than white people to be the victims of household crime. They are also significantly more likely to be the victims of racially motivated attacks than Indians, black or white people (Clancy et al, 2001, p 2). Findings from the British Crime Survey also indicate that more than one third of assaults directed against Asians and blacks are considered to be racially motivated by respondents (Bowling and Phillips, 2003). The impact of racist crime is particularly severe. Findings from the 2000 British Crime Survey indicate that a much larger proportion of victims of racial incidents said that they had been very much affected by the incident (42%) than victims of other sorts of incidents (19%) (Clancy et al, 2001, p 37).

In relation to Muslims being victims of crime on the basis of their faith identity, data are accumulating that measure the extent of faith communities' victimisation. It has to be emphasised, however, that any measures of victimisation are likely to be significant underestimations because individuals often do not report their experiences to the authorities.

The Home Office Citizenship Survey, which does include faith identities and looks at perceptions and experiences of prejudice and discrimination (though not experiences of criminal victimisation), reveals that Hindus, Muslims and Sikhs are substantially more likely to say that they feel very worried about being attacked due to their skin colour, ethnic origin or religion than Christians, those of other religions and those of no religion (DCLG, 2006, p 28). According to a Home Office report published in 2001, *Religious Discrimination in England and Wales*, while in theory it is difficult to disentangle discrimination based on religious grounds from discrimination based on ethnicity, in practice some of the persons who were questioned in this study did appear to be the targets of discrimination and violence as a result of their religious beliefs and practices (Weller et al, 2001). In a survey looking at the effects of the events of 9/11 on discrimination and implicit racism in five religious and seven ethnic groups, religion was found to be more important than ethnicity in indicating which groups were most likely to experience racism and discrimination.

Implicit religious discrimination refers to daily life situations in which covert religious prejudice, such as being treated rudely or not being taken seriously, can be experienced. British white people also reported a rise in post-9/11 discrimination, and of those in the study who said they faced religious discrimination, almost half were Muslim (Sheridan et al, 2003, p 19). It is important to note that since 2005/06 the British Crime Survey has been monitoring the faith identities of respondents and so statistics in relation to the crimes that faith communities experience are likely to become available here.

In a post-9/11 environment, religious hate crime is increasingly featuring in the policies and practices of agencies of the criminal justice system. In Britain, under the 2001 Anti-Terrorism Crime and Security Act, a religiously aggravated element to crime was introduced, which involves imposing higher penalties on offenders who are motivated by religious hatred. So far, there have been relatively few religiously aggravated prosecutions; nonetheless, the majority of victims who have been involved have been Muslim. Between 2005 and 2006, out of 43 cases of religiously aggravated crime, 18 incidents involved Muslims as victims, three involved Christians as victims, and one involved a Sikh victim, with 21 victims' religious identities being unknown or not stated (Crown Prosecution Service, 2006, p 45). Of course, the number of hate crimes that are prosecuted is tiny in comparison to the number of hate crimes that are actually committed, particularly as most victims do not report their experiences to the police.

Muslim community groups, often working in partnership with local police services, play an important role in monitoring and documenting instances of hate crime. For example, the Forum Against Islamophobia and Racism (FAIR), the Islamic Human Rights Commission (IHRC) and the Muslim Council of Britain are three organisations that monitor hate crimes committed against Muslim communities. According to the IHRC, there was a rise in the number of anti-Muslim attacks during the holy month of Ramadan (IHRC, 2006). This illustrates that cultural/religious events can influence the incidence of faith hate crimes. Other events, at both national and international levels, can also influence the number of religious hate crimes that are committed. For example, following the bombings in London on 7 July 2005, the Metropolitan Police Service recorded a sharp increase in faith-related hate crimes, including verbal and physical assaults (EUMC, 2005). In some parts of Germany, violent attacks on fast-food outlets owned by Muslims are a regular occurrence, and mosques and other Muslim-owned establishments have also been attacked. Attacks on Muslim-owned establishments in France and other countries of the European Union have also been documented (for more details see EUMC, 2006).

As well as monitoring and documenting instances of hate crime, Muslim groups offer help and support to the victims of crime. For example, in Britain, some Victim Support schemes have developed good links with locally-based Muslim charities so that the volunteers who run these charities have the opportunity to be trained on how to provide support to victims by Victim Support (Spalek, 2006). The former Muslim Women's Helpline provided support to Muslim women over a wide range of issues including divorce, domestic violence, arranged marriages, sexual abuse and incest. Mushkil Aasaan (Community Care for Asian Families in Crisis) develops religious and cultural primary care packages that service providers can purchase; and the An-Nisa Society offers numerous services which include accredited training in Islamic Counselling. The Muslim Youth Helpline (MYH) is a national faith and culturally sensitive support service for Muslim youth in Britain, developed from a realisation that young Muslim men were not accessing support services from within their own communities or from mainstream service providers. The MYH offers long-term support to clients, including befriending and faith/culturally sensitive service provision (Malik et al, 2007). Muslim welfare organisations have found that the fact that they cater to individuals' religious and spiritual needs means that there is a large demand for their services from, for example, secular women's refuges, mental health services and schools (Ahmad and Sheriff, 2003).

Over the past four decades there has been much research exploring the process of victimisation, and of course it appears that victims of crime often experience substantial psychological, emotional, behavioural, financial and physical impacts (Spalek, 2006). A growing body of work increasingly acknowledges ethno-cultural variables when documenting victims' experiences and processes of recovery. For example, Neville et al (2004) refer to an earlier study comparing black and white women's experiences of sexual assault, and found that black women were generally less likely to disclose the incident. Furthermore, they were more likely to believe that black women are generally at higher risk of being sexually assaulted than white women. Commensurate with the discussion in Chapter Five, a study by Choudry (1996, p 1), exploring Pakistani women's experiences of domestic violence, revealed that the Pakistani women who took part in this project felt they faced dishonour and rejection within their own community if their marriages failed. In addition, they felt that language difficulties and restrictions of their personal freedom outside the family home made it very difficult for women to seek help from external agencies.

It is interesting to note that studies suggest that religion can be an important form of support for victims of crime. For example, a study by Shorter-Gooden (2004) reveals that some African American women may participate in a congregation or spiritual community as part of their coping strategies against the debilitating consequences of racism and sexism. Turning specifically to Muslim communities, Spalek (2002) suggests that some Muslim women who experience victimisation may turn to prayer, meditation and their local *imam* as a way of helping them cope in the aftermath of crime. According to a study of South Asians living in Karachi and Haslingden, Yorkshire, there was a commonly shared sense of victimisation among the South Asian Muslims. Such feelings were linked to the concept of the *ummah*, so that religious oppression and Islamophobia constitute important aspects to Muslims' perceptions as oppressed minorities (Quraishi, 2005).

It is important to highlight that mainstream victim services are secular in nature, which means that people's religious and spiritual needs are not addressed. For example, support services for the victims of domestic and sexual violence generally lack an appreciation of the centrality of faith in some women's lives. Once again, as indicated in Chapter Five, this means that women who hold religious beliefs may choose to stay in their abusive relationships rather than to go to seek help from an organisation which might ignore women's religious requirements, or, additionally, which may negatively judge them for conforming to what are prejudiced assumptions about the controlling and patriarchal nature of religion (Ahmad and Sheriff, 2003). These kinds of circumstances indicate that non-judgemental, culturally competent, outreach social work services, in conjunction with spiritual support, are needed to combat the sense of isolation, helplessness and probably misplaced loyalty that victims of domestic violence may experience.

It is also important to highlight that in the current climate, Muslim minorities are experiencing increased attention from the police and security forces. Community groups are consequently raising concerns that institutional racism, as highlighted by the Macpherson Report (1999), has developed into institutional prejudice against Muslims. In the UK, a series of anti-terror laws have been implemented, including the 2000 Terrorism Act, the 2001 Anti-Terrorism, Crime and Security Act, the 2005 Prevention of Terrorism Act, and the 2006 Terrorism Act. These new anti-terror laws have been criticised by civil liberties organisations as being draconian, and making little, if any, impact on national security. These laws have also provoked criticism from Muslim communities, who feel that they are being unfairly targeted. For instance, the Preventing Extremism Together Working Group on security/policing, set up in the aftermath of the 7 July 2005 London bombings and consisting of representatives of Muslim communities, has raised concerns about the possible breadth of new powers being introduced by the 2006 Terrorism Act, thus:

> Inciting, justifying or glorifying terrorism as currently
> formulated could lead to a significant chill factor in the
> Muslim community in expressing legitimate support for
> self-determination struggles around the world and in using
> legitimate concepts and terminology because of fear of
> being misunderstood and implicated for terrorism by the
> authorities. (Home Office, 2005, p 77)

Muslims are being asked by governments to help combat extremism
from within their own communities. However, the disproportionate
use of anti-terror laws against Muslims might serve to alienate those
communities that are needed to work in partnership with the police
for the purposes of counter-terrorism.

Similar strategies are taking place on the Continent. Soon after 9/11
a new set of emergency measures were passed in Germany. The new
laws created by these measures have lifted the privileges traditionally
afforded to religious organisations in Germany (which used to be
viewed as needing extra protection, permitting religious organisations
to form with relative ease) and have led to databases being created
holding the profiles of German Muslims as well as other members of
potentially extremist groups. Muslim organisations have been put under
surveillance and those accused of having associations with terrorism
or holding dangerous ideologies have been banned. The police have
carried out massive raids on mosques that have yet to yield results.
These policies have had a negative impact on community–state relations
between Muslim groups and the authorities, leading to the greater
isolation and segregation of Muslim communities from mainstream
society (Bakir and Harburg, 2007).

Furthermore, in Australia a raft of anti-terrorism legislation has
been passed at both state and federal level, which gives wide-ranging
powers to the Australian Federal Police and the Australian Security and
Intelligence Organisation. These include the power to detain suspects
for up to 28 days, during which time it is an offence (carrying the
maximum penalty of five years) for the detainee to notify anyone,
including a family member, that they were detained. There is also the
power to conduct strip searches on detainees of 16 and 17 years of age
(Spalek and Imtoual, 2007). Poynting and Mason (2006) argue that
the pursuit of the 'war on terror' since 9/11 in Australia has seen an
increasing intrusion of the state into cultural and religious matters for
minorities, particularly for Muslim communities. Political leaders are
found to be routinely commenting on religious matters: for example,
what is acceptable in a sermon and what is deemed as 'extreme'

or 'radical'. The Muslim Community Reference Group (MCRG) constitutes the major federal government initiative with regards to engagement with Muslim communities. The MCRG's Statement of Principles and its National Action Plan indicate that the main task of the MCRG lies in assisting the Commonwealth government to identify, isolate and detain Muslim community members who are seen as 'extremists' or 'potential terrorists'. The MCRG has been severely criticised for supporting a government agenda that has little to do with the lives of most Australian Muslims and for promoting an association between 'terrorist' and 'Muslim' (Spalek and Imtoual, 2007).

Muslim communities and crime

In the aftermath of a series of bombings and attempted bombings in the UK, as well as in other liberal democratic societies, there has been considerable discussion and concern within the media and political arenas about the possible pathways to radicalisation that young men in particular may take, and the sites at which radicalisation or extremist recruitment may occur. Within these discussions, populations deemed 'at risk' from radicalisation have been identified. These feature North African male immigrants, second- or third-generation Muslims, particularly Pakistani males, and those (predominantly black Caribbean and East African) males who have converted to Islam. Places recognised as 'at risk' include universities, mosques, Islamic book shops, youth centres and prisons. It is important to stress, however, that sustained and detailed research exploring potential pathways to 'radicalisation' is rare, as is public information about Islamist terrorists (Pargeter, 2006).

However, it should also be noted that in certain communities some Muslim men have policed women's behaviour and inflicted psychological and physical violence on women who transgress cultural norms and dress codes (Macey, 1999). As mentioned in Chapter One, it is also claimed that within some Muslim youth subcultures religion may be used to justify and/or absolve deviant or criminal acts. Justifications may include claims that the victims are not Muslim or that they belong to a different religious community. Moreover, perpetrators may resort to paying some of the proceeds from crime to Islamic causes or centres as a way of absolving themselves from guilt. The Muslim Boys Gang in London consists of Muslim converts who use their newly-created Muslim identities as a justification for committing crimes of violence (Spalek et al, 2008). Such gangs are coming to the attention of the media. Shiv Malik writing in *The Observer* (30 September 2007), notes in reference to the atrocious gang problem in Tower Hamlets that, of the 27 known gangs there, 26 are Bangladeshi, and comments that early racist oppression towards the Bangladeshi community appears to have bred a culture of brutalisation in turn.

These issues need to be placed within a broader context that takes into consideration not only religious factors but also other dimensions, such as culture, class, ethnicity and masculinity. This is because although religion may be used as an identity marker by individuals, and, indeed, may be used to justify crime and forms of anti-social behaviour, other factors are also at play. These suggest that Islam in relation to crime and violence should be approached from a multidimensional perspective, particularly when considering that in the present era Islam can be misrepresented and vilified as a result of geopolitical power plays that take place in the international arena.

The significant decline of the manufacturing sector in Britain over the past 30 years, alongside the reduction of secure long-term employment and the rise of short-term, unstable employment, has had a particularly severe impact on young men. This is especially the case for those who are unskilled and who live in areas where factories were once based, these having been closed down, reduced in size or replaced by supermarkets and other retail outlets. Young (1999) argues that some young men attempt to cope with the social and economic climate that surrounds them by creating subcultures based on the construction of strong or aggressive masculinities, where physical strength and other masculine powers are valued. Almost inevitably, without sufficiently influential moral guidance from leaders, mentors or similar beneficial outlets, this may lead to such outcomes as crime and harassment.

In Chapter One we referred to the underprivileged socioeconomic backgrounds experienced by many Muslim families, while in Chapter Two we discussed the low employment figures experienced by Muslims across Europe. To counteract this psychologically, the allegiance to a global community, as exemplified by the concept of *ummah*, may make oppressed groups feel less marginalised in society. This connection with a global Islamic identity, one which has a rich and powerful history, may serve to undo local stereotypes of Islam, which may be particularly negative. So it might be argued that young Muslim men who are experiencing social and economic deprivation are reacting to their social situations in ways that are very similar to other marginalised male youth. It is important, however, to stress that in working to place Muslim offenders' experiences within a broader social and economic context we do not bypass the issue of faith altogether. If religion is, at times, used by offenders as a cultural resource when attempting to legitimise criminal activities, it might be argued that agencies of the criminal justice system must engage with offenders' faith identities as well as other aspects of their identities, such as class, 'race'/ethnic identities and other relevant properties.

It is also important to stress that participation in religious activities, as well as having religious beliefs, may in certain contexts serve to reduce an individual's propensity to commit crime. According to a study of Pakistani Muslim communities in Edinburgh by Wardak (2000), for instance, the mosque is a site at which various educational, social, recreational as well as religious activities take place. Wardak (2000) argues that the greater the involvement of Muslim youths in their community's social and religious life, the less likely they are to engage in crime. Wardak (2000) maintains that Islam constitutes a framework around which order is maintained in this particular community in Edinburgh.

Muslim communities, prisons and rehabilitation

The over-representation of Muslims in jails in England and Wales, coupled with concerns about conversion to Islam in prisons and the issue of radicalisation, have meant that Muslims in prison are increasingly featuring in policy agendas. The social characteristics of the prison population suggest that religious conversion is going to be a feature of prison life. Studies on religious conversion suggest that personal problems that characterise life situations before religious conversion involve a number of factors. Kose (1996), in reference to Snow and Phillips (1980), refers to these as the *spiritual* (involving the meaninglessness of life, a lack of direction and poor self-image); the *interpersonal* (including marital problems and parental problems); the *material* (unemployment, school-related problems); and, finally, *character* (including drugs, alcohol and uncontrollable temper). The social characteristics of prisoners resemble these, thus, the prison population is socially and economically disadvantaged, with 43% of prisoners having no educational qualifications at all and 23% of prisoners having been in local authority care – this figure rises to 38% for prisoners aged under 21, compared with only 2% of people who have been in local authority care from among the general population. A large proportion of prisoners have also engaged in hazardous activities, such as drug taking, prior to their incarceration. Of sentenced males, 63% have engaged in heavy drinking and between a third and a half have used heroin. Of male prisoners, 10% have been mental health patients at some point prior to their incarceration and 64% of sentenced males have some form of personality disorder (Morgan, 2002, p 1139). It seems plausible to suggest therefore that many prisoners will have experienced situations conducive to religious conversion prior to their imprisonment.

Added to this, the prison context itself is favourable to conversion. Prisoner autobiographies reveal the brutalising aspects of everyday life in prison. The lack of control over one's daily routine, the regular exposure to verbal, physical or sexual abuse, directly and/or indirectly, or indeed the constant stress of the potential of being victimised, form the backdrop to prison life (see Carter, 1974; McVicar, 1982; Cook and Wilkinson, 1998). These conditions can profoundly affect prisoners and turning to a religion may be one way of coping with prison life.

A small-scale study of Muslim converts in jails in England reveals that converting to Islam in prison may serve to protect an inmate by providing them with a social network that may reduce their risk of being victimised. At the same time, Islam can help inmates to cope with imprisonment in other ways; for instance, by lowering their levels of aggression so that their interactions with other inmates are less stressed, and reducing their likelihood of committing crimes while incarcerated (Spalek and El-Hassan, 2007). Although, as Case study 10 indicates, the beneficial effects of conversion can be difficult to maintain beyond the prison walls.

Case study 10: Muslim converts in prison

Conversion to Islam appears to provide some prisoners with a sense of identity and belongingness that was largely missing in their lives prior to religious conversion. This is perhaps unsurprising, given that social theorists have argued that contemporary Western society is at a stage of late modernity, where traditional social affiliations, based on family or social class, have been eroded, as evidenced by, for example, the reduction in union and party political membership and the rise in the numbers of people living alone (Furedi, 1997; James, 1997; Bauman, 2004).

Prisoner A: I was out in the world, not knowing anything, who I was, yeah? And Islam sort of gives you the thing 'you are a slave of Allah'. And what you're here for on this Earth, partly why you are brotherhood, part of a believer, ummah is it?

Prisoner B: It's definitely a brotherhood in Islam…. I did have a sense of belonging before but to belong to people that have the exact same beliefs as me that's more important. Cos obviously I know where I'm from, I mean I know my people in terms of my country but they don't all believe in the same things as me and they don't even believe the same thing as each other. But as Muslims we have an identity and we all believe in Allah, Mohammed. (Spalek and El-Hassan, 2007, p 110)

Islam was seen by the participants as being inclusive of all, regardless of 'race', ethnicity or nationality:

Prisoner A: In the Qur'an that's what it says, it says brotherhood. It doesn't matter what nation, it's a religion for the world, innit? That's one of the things I love about it because you go to the mosque and you see white, brown, black, you just see all the colours, that unity init. (Spalek and El-Hassan, 2007, pp 110-11)

In relation to religious conversion, in some cases, converts may feel that they have little religious, spiritual and practical support upon leaving prison, and this may lead them back to their lives of crime:

Interviewer: Do you think that it will be more difficult to practise Islam on the outside of prison?

Prisoner B: Much more difficult. On the outside I have no foundation for Islam, I'm living in a non-Islamic household and my friends are non-Islamic. The ones that are, they're not practising Muslims, they don't go to the mosque every Friday, they talk about Islam but they don't practise the rules as such. (Spalek and El-Hassan, 2007, p 111)

Prison authorities would like to develop interventions with violent extremists who are incarcerated. Policy and research attention is being placed on examining: which regime characteristics are effective with violently extreme prisoners; what style of facilitation constitutes effective intervention; and the significance of a faith-based programme of intervention with this group of offenders. These developments are in their infancy and so currently little research exists addressing these concerns. It is important to stress that, currently, criminal justice practitioners rarely discuss religious or spiritual issues with their clients. In light of the importance of religion as a cultural resource for some offenders, it might be argued that a key policy development should be to train practitioners to open up space for considering religious and spiritual issues. Empirical research and exploration of this issue is needed, particularly in terms of how this should be done.

At the same time, offender resettlement programmes are increasingly involving Muslim community groups. In relation to offenders who convert to Islam while in prison, evidence suggests that there are specific resettlement issues to consider when these prisoners are released into their local communities (Spalek and El-Hassan, 2007). Therefore, the involvement of Muslim groups in planning releases is to be encouraged, as these may be able to address released prisoners' specific religious, spiritual, cultural and social needs. For example, resettlement programmes run by Muslim communities through the use of local mosques can help provide wide-ranging support to ex-offenders, such as practical help in finding accommodation and work. An additional source of assistance would be the provision of spiritual and religious assistance and guidance where this is requested. What is abundantly clear, however, is that in a post-9/11 context, religion as an identity marker can no longer be bypassed.

Probation work also needs to increasingly incorporate religious identities. For example, in Britain the probation service runs programmes for black and Asian offenders: separate provision and specialist provision. In separate provision, programmes are provided in groups exclusively for black and Asian offenders, and the work done is the same or similar to that done by white offenders. In specialist provision, black and Asian offenders are offered interventions that specifically address their perceived needs where they are different from those for white offenders. Specialist programmes are likely to focus on empowerment, and there is likely to be an acknowledgement that minority ethnic offenders have encountered both direct and institutional racism, and so specialist forms of rehabilitation are required. It may be the case that in those probation areas where there is a high proportion of minority ethnic offenders, discussion needs to be generated around whether there might be separate or specialist provision for Muslim offenders. The pervasiveness of Islamophobia in society means that Muslim offenders are likely to have experienced prejudice not only on the grounds of their 'race' but also due to their faith identity. The significance of this is likely to have increased in the aftermath of 9/11. Even when individuals are not particularly observant of their faith, religion might be strongly linked to culture and how individuals make sense of the world, so that the effectiveness of work with offenders could be enhanced by focusing on individuals' faith. Indeed, probation officers who have worked with young Muslim men have reported that these young men have to negotiate their way between two mutually exclusive worlds – the street, drugs and clubs versus the home, the mosque and work. When considering implementing programmes specifically catering to Muslim offenders, the possibility of using Muslim speakers and mentors should be explored (Spalek, 2005).

EIGHT

Concluding remarks

Reflecting on aims

This book is the culmination of an ambitious undertaking attempting to offer an introduction for social workers to Islamic philosophy and practice. Although the scope of the book is wide there is of course much more to be said on the subject, it being impossible to give it full justice within the confines of a single volume.

As proposed in Chapter One, our aim has been to create a dialogic and discursive space, in which to interweave our own individual experiences and perspectives of Islam with those of our reader. Coming from different but complementary disciplines we regard our work as a synergistic collaboration in the spirit of a multidisciplinary (and multi-faith) partnership. In this respect the notion of reflectivity is one that is highly congruent with Islamic thought, as Barise (2005) seeks to convey.

The central purpose of the book has been an attempt to expand on many of the assumptions and stereotypes that underpin the way Islam is perceived in a post-9/11 culture. A further aim has been to highlight both the conspicuous and, sometimes, less evident needs of Muslim individuals, families and communities. Finally, we have attempted to offer some useful guidelines for practitioners attempting to transform social work values into practical forms of anti-oppressive practice with Muslim clients.

Values revisited

Given this kind of approach, a risk is thereby run of stereotyping individuals into a set of crude properties that can be classified as typically 'Muslim'. This is clearly not our intention, given our emphasis on the diversity and heterogeneity of the Muslim *ummah* both nationally and globally. For this reason we have avoided a prescriptive approach to practice in favour of a person-centred focus. More to the point, to date there is no comprehensive evidence-based practice on 'how to' work with Muslim clients that can be offered; and given the issue of diversity this seems unlikely to be methodologically feasible.

Instead, we urge readers to return to basic social work principles which make up the foundations of good practice. In this regard the principle of *individualisation*, as defined by Biestek cited in Banks (2006), comes to the fore and refers to the recognition of the client's uniqueness (Banks, 2006). This is a highly pertinent principle in terms of considering diversity, and is congruent with another principle: *respect for persons*.

Furthermore the social work value of *service to humanity* is one that fits in well with the Islamic principle of *ashan*, which emphasises care and nurturance (Beckett and Maynard, 2005). Standing alongside the concern for social justice that is found in the concept of *zakat*, this principle may well have provided the ethical basis for the traditional Islamic emphasis on medical and social care. Both of these principles have in turn a close correspondence to the professional value base of social work. Consequently these could well provide inspiration for Muslim social work practitioners, in addition to their other personal values and codes of ethics.

Considering oppression

In considering oppression one needs look no further than the economic and social deprivation and disadvantages that many British Muslim families experience. This is the effect of, and is exacerbated by, multiple forms of discrimination at many levels, including employment, housing, health and education. Social work as a profession is dedicated to analysing, challenging and working with oppression at many levels, including that of 'race'/ethnicity as a significant issue. This has been justly viewed as a valuable form of emancipatory practice (Thompson, 2005). To this end, social work values, as described by the National Association of Social Workers (BASW's American counterpart), accommodate the view of many minority ethnic groups regarding the 'importance of human relationships' (Beckett and Maynard, 2005, p 77). This can include working across the family as well as a wider collective of similarly oppressed groups, such as Muslim minorities, which ties in once again with emancipatory and anti-oppressive practices.

Yet, discrimination against those of particular faith backgrounds is less notable in most recognised categories of oppression, despite the fact that white Muslims are likely to feel marginalised in common with black members of the *ummah*. Islamophobia, as a concept, overlaps racial discrimination but also stands distinct from it, and as such has yet to be fully understood and accommodated within social work. This is probably due to the predominantly secular focus of the profession in Britain, in addition to the prevailing use of ethnic-based classifications of clients.

Beckett and Maynard (2005) consider the issue of religion by locating it within the broad category of values. They further suggest that Neil Thompson's original PCS model (personal/psychological, cultural/commonalities and structural/social) (Thompson, 1993) remains a useful vehicle to explore more fully the role of faith in the lives of clients. Religion, however, is not viewed uncritically by Beckett and Maynard (2005) but is considered as a factor in tension: in that it may lead to resilience, as well as to inflexibility; to cohesion, as well as to exclusion and exclusiveness.

Taking due account of faith is becoming essential in social work intervention with clients, particularly in considering those religions that permeate all aspects of daily life, as is the case with Islam. Being knowledgeable of these ways of experiencing the world is a good example of anti-oppressive practice.

Equally, an awareness of the prevailing social and religious issues affecting the lives of Muslims is clearly important for social workers to be aware of in general. Yet, at the same time untested assumptions that certain social conditions are *necessarily* the ones affecting a particular Muslim client should be suspended until more evidence is gathered. Obviously such caveats apply to assumptions regarding religion in which it is believed that faith is of paramount consideration in the lives of all Muslims. To summarise therefore, the application of stereotypes to clients can be construed as essentially oppressive, despite any basic good intentions on the part of the practitioner (Thompson, 2005).

The resonances associated with the term 'Islam' are profound, where connotations of fanaticism and terrorism abound in the media, as well as in the minds of many members of the general public. This tends to completely obscure much that is excellent, such as the crucial contribution of Islamic scholarship to Western civilisation, as well as that Islam is essentially a religion that values conciliation (Irfan Coles, 2004). Negative associations of Islam and Muslims are continuously reinforced at various levels of society, leading to alarming rhetorical stances, such as the question of whether one can be both a Briton and a Muslim. Ironically this dangerous and deeply divisive point has been raised by both the proponents of extremist interpretations of Islam, as well as non-Muslim opponents. Such mutual antagonism tends to drown out the more subdued voices of moderate, law-abiding Muslim citizens. Their views by contrast should be viewed as of the greatest importance in the goal towards modifying extremist views and mediating across divisions to shape a better future for British Muslims. Where advocacy, partnership and negotiation is weak, the repercussions will be felt by vulnerable and impressionable members of society, as the following indicates:

> For some youths, the measure of their faith is proportionate to their rejection of the West, as if they defined Islam by what it is not, rather than what it is. (Irfan Cole, 2004, p 119)

Future directions for research

Many of the issues that we have raised require a much more rigorous investigation in order to facilitate a deeper understanding of the concerns and problems facing Muslim communities in Britain. There are urgent points to address regarding the underprivileged and oppressed status of many Muslims. A further concern lies in meeting the health needs of Muslim patients, particularly in the area of disability. Furthermore, research is needed to facilitate the prevention of the abuse of Muslim girls and women within their own families and communities. Finally, there is the issue of crime which dominates public thought in the way that Muslims are perceived to be involved. As we have shown, although they are largely the victims of crime, some are also implicated as perpetrators.

There are of course many other competing issues that deeply affect the lives of Muslims in Britain; many questions are duly raised but few answers are forthcoming. However, what has emerged strongly from our work is just how compatible social work as a profession is with traditional Islamic principles and evolving concepts. Thus the professional social work canon of knowledge can only be enriched by including Islamic perspectives. Furthermore it is hoped that in so doing the expertise of multicultural practitioners in Britain will be strengthened by a new and larger generation of Muslim social workers. It is in fact no exaggeration to say that their knowledge and professional collaboration have never before been so urgently needed.

References

0-19 Update (2003) *Children & Young People Now* (www.childrennow. co.uk/home/index.cfm).

Abdel Haleem, M.A.S. (2001) 'The blind and the Qur'an', *Journal of Qur'anic Studies/Majallat al-Dirasat al-Qur'anya*, vol 3, no 2, pp 123-5.

Algar, M. (2006) 'Ethical aspects and regulation of assisted reproduction in the Arabic-speaking world', *Ethics, Law and Moral Philosophy of Reproductive Biomedicine*, vol 2, no 1, pp 143-6.

About.com: Islam, 'Adopting a child in Islam' (http://islam.about. com/cs/parenting/a/adoption.htm).

Abu Baker, K. and Dwairy, M. (2003) 'Cultural norms versus state law in treating incest: a suggested model for Arab families', *Child Abuse & Neglect*, vol 27, no 1, pp 109-23.

Abu-Lughod, L. (1993) 'Islam and the gendered discourses of death', *International Journal of Middle East Studies*, vol 25, pp 187-205.

Abumalham, M. (1996) 'The Muslim presence in Spain: policy and society', in W.A.R. Shadid and P.S. van Koningsveld (eds) *Muslims in the Margin*, Kampen: Kok Pharos Publishing House, pp 80-92.

Acharyya, S. (1996) 'Practising cultural psychiatry: the doctor's dilemma', in T. Heller, J. Reynolds, R. Gomm, R. Muston and S. Pattison (eds) *Mental Health Matters*, London: The Open University/Macmillan Press, pp 339-45.

Afshar, H. (1996) 'Islam and feminism: an analysis of political strategies', in M. Yamani (ed) *Feminism and Islam*, New York: New York University Press.

Ahmad, B. (1990) *Black Perspectives in Social Work*, Birmingham: Ventura.

Ahmad, W.I.U. (1994) 'Reflections on the consanguinity and birth outcome debate', *Journal of Public Health Medicine*, vol 16, no 4, pp 423-28.

Ahmed, S. (1994) 'Anti-racist social work: a black perspective', in C. Hanvey and T. Philpot (eds) *Practising Social Work*, London: Routledge, pp 199-233.

Ahmad, F. and Sheriff, S. (2003) 'Muslim women of Europe: welfare needs and responses', *Social Work in Europe*, vol 8, no 1, pp 30-55.

Ahmed, T. (2005) 'Muslim "Marginal man"', *Policy*, vol 21, no 1, pp 35-41.

Ait Sabbah, F. (1986) *La Femme dans l'Inconscient Musulman*, Paris: Albin Michel.

Alcott, L. (1991) 'The problem of speaking for others', *Cultural Critique*, 1991-1992, Winter, pp 2-31.

Abu-Salieh, S.A.A. (1997) 'Jehovah, His cousins, Allah, and sexual mutilations', in G.C. Denniston and M. Fayre Milos (eds) *Sexual Mutilations: A Human Tragedy*, New York: Plenum Press, pp 41-62.

Alghazo, E.M., Dodeen, H. and Algaryouti, I. (2003) 'Attitudes of pre-service teachers towards persons with disabilities: predictions for the success of inclusion', *College Student Journal*, Dec 2003, vol 37, no 4, pp 515-22.

Al-Khateeb, S.A.H. (1998) 'Muslim women's perceptions of equality: case study of Saudi women', *Mediterranean Quarterly*, vol 9, no 2, pp 110-31.

Al-Krenawi, A. and Graham, J.R. (1999) 'Social work and Koranic mental health healers', *International Social Work*, vol 42, no 1, pp 53-65.

Al-Krenawi, A. and Graham, J.R. (2000) 'Islamic theology and prayer', *International Social Work*, vol 43, no 3, pp 289-304.

Al-Krenawi, A. and Graham, J.R. (2001) 'The cultural mediator: bridging the gap between a non-Western community and professional social work practice', *British Journal of Social Work*, vol 31, pp 665-85.

Al-Krenawi, A. and Graham, J.R. (2003) 'Principles of social work practice in the Muslim Arab world', *Arab Studies Quarterly*, vol 25, no 4, pp 75-92.

Al-Krenawi, A. and Graham, J.R. (2007) 'Social work intervention with Bedouin-Arab children in the context of blood vengeance', *Child Welfare*, vol LXXVIII, no 2, pp 283-96.

Al-Krenawi, A., Graham, J.R. and Slonim-Nevo, V. (2002) 'Mental health aspects of Arab-Israeli adolescents from polygamous versus monogamous families', *The Journal of Social Psychology*, vol 142, no 4, pp 446-60.

Al-Shamsi, M.S.A. and Fulcher, L.C. (2005) 'The impact of polygamy on United Arab Emirates' first wives and their children', *International Journal of Child & Family Welfare*, vol 8, no 1, pp 46-55.

Ammar, N.H. (2000) 'Simplistic stereotyping and complex reality of Arab-American immigrant identity: consequences and future strategies in policing wife battery', *Islam and Christian–Muslim Relations*, vol 11, no 1, pp 51-69.

Andrews, M. (2006) 'The globalization of transcultural nursing theory and research', in M.M. Leininger and M.R. McFarland (eds) *Culture, Care, Diversity and Universality: A Worldwide Nursing Theory*, Boston: Jones and Bartlett Publishers, pp 83-6.

Anwar, E. (2006) *Gender and Self in Islam*, London/New York: Routledge.

Archer, L. (2003) *Race, Masculinity and Schooling: Muslim Boys and Education*, Maidenhead: Open University Press.

Arkoun, M. (1994) *Rethinking Islam*, Oxford: Westview Press.

Ashencaen Crabtree, S. (1999) 'Teaching anti-discriminatory practice in Malaysia', *Social Work Education International Journal*, vol 18, no 3, pp 247-55.

Ashencaen Crabtree, S. (2007a) 'Maternal perceptions of care-giving of children with developmental disabilities in the United Arab Emirates', *Journal of Applied Research in Intellectual Disabilities*, vol 20, pp 247-55.

Ashencaen Crabtree, S. (2007b) 'Family responses to the social inclusion of children with developmental disabilities in the United Arab Emirates', *Disability & Society*, vol 22, no 1, pp 49-62.

Ashencaen Crabtree, S. (2007c) 'Culture, gender and the influence of social change amongst Emirati families in the United Arab Emirates', *Journal of Comparative Family Studies*, vol 38, no 4, pp 573-85.

Ashencaen Crabtree, S. (2008, forthcoming) 'Dilemmas in international social work education in the United Arab Emirates: Islam, localization and social need', *Social Work Education*.

Ashencaen Crabtree, S. and Baba, I. (2001) 'Islamic perspectives in social work education', *Social Work Education*, vol 20, no 4, pp 469-81.

Atshan, L. (1997) 'Disability and gender at a cross-roads: a Palestinian perspective', in L. Abu-Habib (ed) *Gender And Disability: Women's Experiences in the Middle East*, Oxford: Oxfam, pp 53-9.

Baer, Z. (1997) 'Are baby boys entitled to the same protection as baby girls regarding genital mutilation', in G.C. Denniston and M. Fayre Milos (eds) *Sexual Mutilations: A Human Tragedy*, New York: Plenum Press, pp 197-204.

Bahar, Z., Okçay, H., Özbiçakçi, Š., Bešer, A., Üstün, B. and Öztürk, M. (2005) 'The effects of Islam and traditional practices on women's health and reproduction', *Nursing Ethics*, vol 12, no 6, pp 557-70.

Bakir, S. and Harburg, B. (2007) '"Die Geister, die ich rief!" [The ghosts that I awoke]: German anti-terror law and religious extremism', preliminary report, Bochum, Germany: Ruhr University (www.humanityinaction.org/docs/Bakir_and_Harburg_Final%5B1%5D.doc).

Banks, S. (2006) *Ethics and Values in Social Work*, Basingstoke: BASW/Palgrave Macmillan.

Barise, A. (2003) 'Towards indigenization of social work in the United Arab Emirates', in *Advancing Indigenous Social Work*, conference proceedings, Kuching: Universiti Malaysia Sarawak, 20-21 October.

Barise, A. (2005) 'Social work with Muslims: insights from the teachings of Islam', *Critical Social Work*, vol 6, no 2 (www.uwindsor.ca/units/socialwork/critical.nsf/EditDoNotShowInTOC/554026006519AFC38525700F004B57B6).

Barn, R. and Sidhu, K. (2004) 'Understanding the interconnections between ethnicity, gender, social class and health: experiences of minority ethnic women in Britain', *Social Work in Health Care*, vol 39, no 1/2, pp 11-27.

Barnes, M. and Bowl, R. (2001) *Taking over the asylum*, Basingstoke: Palgrave.

Bauman, Z. (2004) *Identity: Conversations with Benedetto Vecchi*, Cambridge: Polity Press.

BBC News (2005) 'Bomber attacked UK Muslim leaders', 16 November (http://news.bbc.co.uk/1/hi/uk/4440772.stm).

BBC News (2006) 'One in 10 "backs honour killings"', 4 September (http://news.bbc.co.uk/2/hi/uk_news/5311244.stm).

BBC News (2008) 'Sharia law in the UK is "unavoidable"', 7 February (http://news.bbc.co.uk/1/hi/uk/7232661.stm).

Becher, H. and Husain, F. (2003) *South Asian Muslims and Hindus in Britain: Developments in Family Support*, London: NFPI.

Beckett, C. and Maynard, A. (2005) *Values and Ethics in Social Work*, London: Sage Publications.

Beckford, J., Joly, D. and Khosrokhavar, F. (2005) *Muslims in Prison: Challenge and Change in Britain and France*, Basingstoke: Palgrave.

Bedell, G. (2004) 'Death before dishonour', *The Observer*, 21 November.

Bell, D. (2007) 'In the name of the law', *The Guardian*, 14 June.

Bhatti-Sinclair, K. (1994) 'Asian women and violence from male partners', in C. Lupton and T. Gillespie (eds) *Working with Violence*, Basingstoke: Macmillan, pp 75-95.

Bhugra, D. (1997) 'Setting up psychiatric services: cross-cultural issues in planning and delivery', *International Journal of Social Psychiatry*, Spring, vol 43, no 1, pp 1-16.

Blackwood, E. (1995) 'Senior women, model mothers and dutiful wives: managing gender contradictions in a Minangkabau village', in A. Ong and M.G. Peletz (eds) *Bewitching Women, Pious Men: Gender and Body Politics in Southeast Asia*, Berkeley, CA: University of California, pp 124-58.

Blair, T. (2006) 'Our nation's future', speech delivered at 10 Downing Street, 3 December.

Bose, R. (1997) 'Psychiatry and the popular conception of possession among the Bangladeshis in London', *Journal of Social Psychiatry*, vol 43, no 1, Spring, pp 1-16.

Bouhdiba, A. (1997) 'The child and the mother in Arab-Muslim society', *Psychological Dimensions of Near Eastern Studies*, no 1997, pp 126-41.

Bowers, C.A. and Flinders, D.J. (1990) *Responsive Teaching*, New York: Teachers College Press, Columbia University.

Bowling, B. and Phillips, C. (2002) *Racism, Crime and Justice*, Harlow: Longman.

Bradby, H. (2007) 'Watch out for the aunties! Young British Asians' accounts of identity and substance use', *Sociology of Health & Illness*, vol 29, no 5, pp 656-72.

Brooks, G. (1995) *Nine Parts of Desire: The Hidden World of Islamic Women*, New York: Anchor Books/Doubleday.

Burr, E.G. (2005) 'Learning to teach Islam as a non-Muslim in the Twin Cities', *Teaching Theology and Religion*, vol 8, no 3, pp 155-63.

Burr, J. and Chapman, T. (2004) 'Contextualising experiences of depression in women from South Asian communities: a discursive approach', *Sociology of Health & Illness*, vol 26, no 4, pp 433-52.

Butalia, U. (2003) 'When culture kills', *New Internationalist*, December, p 5.

Bywaters, P., Ali, Z., Fazil, Q., Wallace, L.M. and Singh, G. (2003) 'Attitudes towards disability amongst Pakistani and Bangladeshi parents of disabled children in the UK: considerations for service providers and the disability movement', *Heath and Social Care in the Community*, vol 11, no 6, pp 502-9.

Carter, R. (1974) *'Hurricane': The 16th Round*, Ontario: Penguin.

Chakraborty, A. (1991) 'Culture, colonialism and psychiatry', *Lancet*, vol 337, no 8751, pp 1204-8.

Chand, A. (2000) 'The over-representation of Black children in the child protection system: possible causes, consequences and solutions', *Child & Family Social Work*, vol 5, no 1, pp 67-77.

Chand, A. and Thoburn, J. (2006) 'Research review: child protection referrals and minority ethnic children and families', *Child & Family Social Work*, vol 11, pp 368-77.

Chew-Graham, C., Bashir, C., Chantler, K. and Burman, E. (2002) 'South Asian women, psychological distress and self-harm: lessons for primary care trusts', *Health & Social Care in the Community*, vol 10, no 5, pp 339-47.

Choudhury, T. (2005) 'Overview' in, *Muslims in the UK: Policies for Engaged Citizens*, Budapest: Open Society Institute, pp 10-41.

Choudry, S. (1996) 'Pakistani women's experience of domestic violence in Great Britain', *Home Office Research Findings*, no 43, London: HMSO, pp 1-4.

Clancy, A., Hough, M., Aust, R. and Kershaw, C. (2001) *Crime, Policing and Justice: The Experiences of Ethnic Minorities*, London: Home Office.

Cohen, S. and Warren, R.D. (1990) 'The intersection of disability and child abuse in England and the United States', *Child Welfare*, vol 69, no 3, pp 253-63.

Cook, F. and Wilkinson, M. (1998) *Hard Cell*, Liverpool: Bluecoat Press.

Crabtree, S.A. (2006) 'A comparative analysis of social work responses to child abuse in the United Arab Emirates', *International Journal of Child & Family Welfare*, vol 9, no 4, pp 228-37.

Crampton, R. (2005) 'It's terrifying and shocking, said Ali, 19, then strode smartly away', *Times Online* (www.timesonline.co.uk/tol/news/uk/article541717.ece).

Croissant, J.L. (2005) 'Pain and culture', in S. Restivo (ed) *Science, Technology and Society: An Encyclopaedia*, Oxford: Oxford University Press, pp 363-7.

Crown Prosecution Service (2005) *Racist Incident Annual Monitoring Report 2004-2005*, London: CPS.

Da Costa, D.E., Ghazal, H. and Al Khusaiby, S. (2002) 'Do Not Resuscitate orders and ethical decisions in a neonatal intensive care unit in a Muslim community', *Archives Disease in Childhood: Fetal and Neonatal Edition*, vol 86, pp 115-19.

DCLG (Department for Communities and Local Government) (2006) *2005 Citizenship Survey Race and Faith Topic Report*, London: DCLG.

Dean, H. and Khan, Z. (1997) 'Muslim perspectives on welfare', *Journal of Social Policy*, vol 26, no 2, pp 193-209.

Derin, S. (2005-06) 'The tradition of *suhl* among the Sufis; with special reference to Ibn Arabi and Yunus Emre', *Journal of Academic Studies*, Nov 2005-Jan 2006, vol 27, issue 27, pp 1-12.

Dhami, S. and Sheikh, A. (2000) 'The family: predicament and promise', in A. Sheikh and A.R. Gatrad (eds) *Caring for Muslim Patients*, Oxon: Radcliffe Medical Press, pp 43-56.

Dienemann, J., Boyle, E., Baker, D., Resnick, W., Wiederhorn, N. and Campbell, J. (2000) 'Intimate partner abuse among women diagnosed with depression', *Issues in Mental Health Nursing*, vol 21, pp 499-513.

Doi, A.R.I. (1992) *Women in Shari'ah*, Kuala Lumpur: A.S. Noordeen.

Dominelli, L. (1988) *Anti-Racist Social Work*, Basingstoke: Macmillan Press/BASW.

Dominelli, L. (1996) 'Deprofessionalizing social work: anti-oppressive practice, competencies and postmodernism', *British Journal of Social Work*, vol 26, pp 153-75.

Dorfman, R.A. (1996) *Clinical Social Work*, New York: Brunner/Mazel.

Dorkenoo, E., Morison, L. and MacFarlane, A. (2007) *A Statistical Study To Estimate the Prevalence of Female Genital Mutilation in England and Wales: Summary Report*, London: FORWARD (Foundation for Women's Health, Research and Development).

Douki, S., Nacef, F., Belhadj, A., Bousaker, A. and Ghachem, R. (2003) 'Violence against women in Arab and Islamic countries', *Archives of Women's Mental Health*, vol 6, pp 165-71.

DuBois, B. and Miley, K.K. (2005) *Social Work: An Empowering Profession*, Boston: Pearson Education Ltd.

Dwairy, M. (2004) 'Culturally sensitive education: adapting self-orientated assertiveness training to collective minorities', *Journal of Social Issues*, vol 60, no 2, pp 423-36.

El Naggar Gaad, E. (2001) 'Educating children with Down's syndrome in the United Arab Emirates', *British Journal of Special Education*, vol 28, no 4, pp 195-203.

Ely, P. and Denney, D. (1987) *Social Work in a Multi-Racial Society*, Aldershot: Ashgate.

EOC (Equal Opportunities Commission) (2007) *Moving On Up: The Way Forward*, London: The Stationery Office.

Errington, S. (1990) 'Recasting sex, gender, and power: a theoretical and regional overview', in J. Monnig Atkinson and S. Errington (eds) *Power and Difference: Gender in Island Southeast Asia*, Stanford, CA: Stanford University Press, pp 1-58.

Esposito, J.L. (2002) *What Everyone Needs to Know About Islam*, New York: Oxford University Press.

EUMC (European Monitoring Centre on Racism and Xenophobia) (2005) *The Impact of 7 July 2005 London Bomb Attacks on Muslim Communities in the EU*, Vienna: EUMC.

EUMC (2006) *Muslims in the European Union: Discrimination and Islamophobia*, Vienna: EUMC.

Ewald, F. (1991) 'Insurance and risk', in G. Burchell, C. Gordon and P. Miller (eds) *The Foucault Effect: Studies in Governmentality*, London: Harvester Wheatsheaf, pp 197-210.

Faizi, N. (2001) 'Domestic violence in the Muslim community', *Journal of Women and the Law*, vol 10, no 2, pp 15-22.

Fazil, Q., Bywaters, P., Ali, Z., Wallace, L. and Singh, G. (2002) 'Disadvantage and discrimination compounded: the experience of Pakistani and Bangladeshi parents of disabled children in the UK', *Disability & Society*, vol 17, no 3, pp 237-53.

Fenton, S. and Sadiq, A. (1996) 'Asian women speak out', in T. Heller, J. Reynolds, R. Gomm, R. Muston and S. Pattison (eds) *Mental Health Matters*, Basingstoke: Macmillan/Open University Press, pp 252-9.

Fenton, S. and Sadiq-Sangster, A. (1996) 'Culture, relativism and the expression of mental distress: South Asian women in Britain', *Sociology of Health & Illness*, vol 18, no 1, pp 66-85.

Fernando, S., Ndegwa, D. and Wilson, M. (1998) *Forensic Psychiatry, Race and Culture*, London/New York: Routledge.

Fikree, F.F. and Bhatti, L.I. (1999) 'Domestic violence and health of Pakistani women', *International Journal of Gynaecological Obstetrics*, vol 62, no 2, pp 195-201.

Fikree, F.F. (2005) 'Attitudes of Pakistani men to domestic violence: a study from Karachi, Pakistan', *The Journal of Men's Health & Gender*, vol 2, no 1, pp 49-58.

Fook, J. (1996) 'The reflective researcher: Developing a reflective approach to practice', in J. Fook (ed) *The Reflective Researcher*, Australia: Allen & Unwin, pp 1-8.

Foreign and Commonwealth Office, 'Foreign Marriages. What we can do to help' (www.fco.gov.uk/).

Fowler, D. (1984) *The Evolution of the British Welfare State*, Basingstoke: Macmillan.

Fowler, H., Griffin, E. and Luesley, D. (1990) 'Antenatal attendance and fasting of pregnant Muslims during Ramadan', *British Journal of Obstetrics and Gynaecology*, vol 97, pp 861-2

Frazer, L. and Selwyn, J. (2005) 'Why are we waiting? The demography of adoption for children of black, Asian and black mixed parentage in England', *Child & Family Social Work*, vol 10, pp 135-47.

Fricker, M. (2000) 'Feminism in epistemology: pluralism without postmodernism', in M. Fricker and J. Hornsby (eds) *The Cambridge Companion to Feminism in Philosophy*, Cambridge: Cambridge University Press, pp 146-65.

Fuller, G.E. and Lesser, I.O. (1995) *A Sense of Siege*, Boulder, CO: Westview Press.

Furedi, F. (1997) *Culture of Fear: Risk-Taking and the Morality of Low Expectation*, London: Cassell.

Furman, L.D., Benson, P.W., Canda, E.R. and Grimwood, C. (2005) 'A comparative international analysis of religion and spirituality in social work: a survey of UK and US social workers', *Social Work Education*, vol 24, no 8, pp 813-39.

Garland, J., Spalek, B. and Chakraborti, N. (2006) 'Hearing lost voices: issues in researching hidden minority ethnic communities', *The British Journal of Criminology*, vol 46, pp 423-37.

Garr, M. and Marans, G. (2001) 'Ultra-orthodox women in Israel: a pilot project in social work education', *Social Work Education*, vol 20, no 4, pp 459-68.

Gatrad, A.R. and Sheikh, A. (2001) 'Medical ethics and Islam: principles and practice', *Archives of Disease in Childhood*, vol 84, pp 72-5.

Gatrad, A.R. and Sheikh, A. (2000) 'Birth customs: meanings and significance', in A. Sheikh and A.R. Gatrad (eds) *Caring for Muslim Patients*, Oxford: Radcliffe Medical Press, pp 57-72.

Gatrad, A.R. and Sheikh, A. (2002a) 'Palliative care for Muslims and issues before death', *International Journal of Palliative Nursing*, vol 8, no 11, pp 526-31.

Gatrad, A.R. and Sheikh, A. (2002b) 'Palliative care for Muslims and issues after death', *International Journal of Palliative Nursing*, vol 8, no 12, pp 594-7.

Gatrad, A.R. and Sheikh, A. (2001) 'Medical ethics and Islam: principles and practice', *Archives of Disease in Childhood*, vol 84, pp 72-5.

Goonesekere, S. (1994) 'The best interests of the child: a South Asian perspective', *International Journal of Law, Policy and the Family*, vol 8, no 1, pp 117-49.

Gough, D. and Lynch, M.A. (2002) 'Culture and child protection', *Child Abuse Review*, vol 11, pp 341-4.

Gowricharn, R. and Mungra, B. (1996) 'The politics of integration in the Netherlands', in W.A.R. Shadid and P.S. van Koningsveld (eds) *Muslims in the Margin*, Kampen: Kok Pharos Publishing House, pp 114-29.

Grassivaro Gallo, P., Viviani, F., Livio, M., Corsaro, R., De Cordova, F., Fortunato, G., Beccacini, S. and Salad Hassan, S. (1997) 'Epidemiological surveys on female genital mutilation in Italy', in G.C. Denniston and M. Fayre Milos (eds) *Sexual Mutilations: A Human Tragedy*, New York: Plenum Press, pp 153-7.

Haj-Yahia, M.M. (2003) 'Beliefs about wife beating among Arab men from Israel: the influence of their patriarchal ideology', *Journal of Family Violence*, vol 18, no 4, pp 193-206.

Halstead, M.J. and Lewicka, K. (1998) 'Should homosexuality be taught as an acceptable alternative lifestyle? A Muslim perspective', *Cambridge Journal of Education*, vol 28, no 1, pp 18-22.

Hamzah, M. (1996) 'In search of the female voice', *The Star* (Malaysia), 5 September.

Harron, E. (2002) 'Barriers to effective child protection in a multicultural society', *Child Abuse Review*, vol 11, pp 411-14.

Hartsock, N. (1990) 'Postmodernism and political change: issues for feminist theory', *Cultural Critique*, vol 14, pp 15-33.

Hassan, R. (1993) 'The interface between Islam and psychiatric practice in Malaysia: a personal viewpoint', *Malaysian Journal of Psychiatry*, vol 1, pp 93-101.

Hassouneh-Phillips, D. (2001) 'Polygamy and wife abuse: a qualitative study of Muslim women in America', *Health Care for Women International*, vol 22, no 8, pp 735-48.

Hastings, R.P. and Taunt, H.M. (2002) 'Positive perceptions of families of children with developmental disabilities', *American Journal on Mental Retardation*, vol 107, no 2, pp 116-27.

Hatta, S. (2001) 'Islamic issues in forensic psychiatry and the instinct theory: the Malaysian scenario', in A. Haque (ed) *Mental Health in Malaysia*, Kuala Lumpur: University of Malaya Press, pp 181-96.

Haw K.F. with Shah, S. and Hanifa, M. (1998) *Educating Muslim Girls: Shifting Discourses*, Buckingham: Open University Press.

Henkel, H. (2004) 'Rethinking the *dâr ak-harb*: social change and changing perceptions of the West in Turkish Islam', *Journal of Ethnic and Migration Studies*, vol 30, no 5, pp 961-77.

Hirsch, E. and Olson, G.A. (1995) 'Starting from marginalized lives: a conversation with Sandra Harding', in G.A. Olson and E. Hirsch (eds) *Women Writing Culture*, New York: State University of New York Press, pp 3-44.

Hodge, D.R. (2005) 'Social work and the house of Islam: orientating practitioners to the beliefs and values of Muslims in the United States', *Social Work*, vol 50, no 2, pp 162-73.

Hodge, D.R. (2006) 'A template for spiritual assessment: a review of the JCAHO requirements and guidelines for implementation', *Social Work*, vol 51, no 4, pp 317-26.

Home Office (2006) 'Offender Management Caseload Statistics', *Home Office Statistical Bulletin* (www.homeoffice.gov.uk/rds/pdfs06/hosb1806.pdfdate).

Home Office (2005) *Preventing Extremism Together Working Groups August-October*, London: The Stationery Office.

Hood, R. (1992) *Race and Sentencing*, Oxford: Clarendon Press.

Hopkins, S. (1999) 'A discussion of the legal aspects of female genital mutilation', *Journal of Advanced Nursing*, vol 30, no 4, pp 926–33.

Hourani, A. (1991) *A History of the Arab Peoples*, London: Faber & Faber.

Hugman, R. (2005) *New Approaches in Ethics for the Caring Professions*, Basingstoke: Palgrave Macmillan.

Humphries, B. (2003) 'What *else* counts as evidence in evidence-based social work?', *Social Work Education*, vol 22, no 1, pp 81–91.

Humphries, C., Sandeep, A. and Baldwin, N. (1999) 'Discrimination in child protection work: recurring themes in work with Asian families', *Child & Family Social Work*, vol 4, no 4, pp 283–91.

Huntingdon, S. (1997) *The Clash of Civilisation and the Remaking of World Order*, London: Simon & Schuster UK.

Husain, F. (2007) 'Educational underachievement and social disadvantage: a consultation with teachers', Unpublished, internal discussion paper, London: Save the Children.

Husain, N., Creed, F. and Tomenson, B. (1997) 'Adverse social circumstances and depression in people of Pakistani origin in the UK', *British Journal of Psychiatry*, vol 171, pp 434–8.

IHRC (Islamic Human Rights Commission) (2006) 'Islamophobia rampant in Ramadan in UK', press release (www.ihrc.org.uk/show.php?id=2147).

Irfan, S. and Cowburn, M. (2004) 'Disciplining, chastisement and physical child abuse: perceptions and attitudes of the British Pakistani community', *Journal of Muslim Affairs*, vol 24, no 1, pp 89-98.

Irfan Coles, M. (2004) 'Education and Islam: a new strategy', in B. van Driel (ed) *Confronting Islamophobia in Educational Practice*, Stoke-on-Trent: Trentham Books, pp 111-28.

Jack, C.M., Penny, L. and Nazar, W. (2001) 'Effective palliative care for minority ethnic groups: the role of a liaison worker', *International Journal of Palliative Nursing*, vol 7, no 8, pp 375-80.

James, O. (1997) *Britain on the Couch*, London: Century.

Jardine, L. (2007) 'Power of the headscarf', BBC News, 13 April, (http://news.bbc.co.uk/2/hi/uk_news/magazine/6553033.stm).

Jawad, H.A. (1998) *The Right of Women in Islam*, Basingstoke: Macmillan Press.

Jeffery, P. (1998) 'Agency, activism and agendas', in P. Jeffery and A. Basu (eds) *Appropriating Gender*, London: Routledge, pp 221-4.

Johnson, L.C. and Yanca, S.J. (2004) *Social Work Practice*, Boston: Pearson.

Johnston, P. (2006) 'Reid meets the furious face of Islam', *Telegraph. co.uk*, 21 September (www.telegraph.co.uk/news/main.jhtml?xml=/news/2006/09/21/nreid21.xml).

Kai, J. and Hedges, C. (1999) 'Minority ethnic community participation in needs assessment and service development in primary care: perceptions of Pakistani and Bangladeshi people about psychological distress', *Health Expectations*, vol 2, no 1, pp 7-20.

Kalunta-Crumpton, A. (1999) *Race and Drug Trials*, Aldershot: Avebury.

Karmi, G. (1996) 'Women, Islam and patriarchalism', in M. Yamani (ed) *Feminism and Islam*, New York: New York University Press, pp 69-86.

Katbamna, S., Waqar, A., Bhakta, P., Baker, R. and Parker, G. (2004) 'Do they look after their own? Informal support for South Asian carers', *Health & Social Care in the Community*, vol 12, no 5, pp 398-406.

Keating, F. (2000) 'Anti-racist perspectives: what are the gains for social work?' *Social Work Education*, vol 19, no 1, pp 77-87.

Khan, Z.H., Watson, P.J. and Habib, F. (2005) 'Muslim attitudes towards religion, religious orientation and empathy among Pakistanis', *Mental Health, Religion & Culture*, vol 8, no 1, pp 49-61.

Koenig, M.A., Ahmed, S., Hossein, M.B. and Mozumder, K.A. (2003) 'Women's status and domestic violence in rural Bangladesh', *Demography*, vol 40, no 2, pp 269-88.

Koramoa, J., Lynch, M.A. and Kinnair, D. (2002) 'A continuum of child-rearing: responding to traditional practices', *Child Abuse Review*, vol 11, pp 415-21.

Kort, A. (2005) 'Dar al-cyber Islam: women, domestic violence and the Islamic reformation on the world wide web', *Journal of Muslim Minority Affairs*, vol 25, no 3, pp 363-82.

Kose, A. (1996) *Conversion to Islam: A Study of Native British Converts*, London: Kegan Paul International.

Kübler-Ross, E. (1970) *On Death and Dying*, London/NY: Tavistock/Routledge.

Kuzu, M.A., Topçu, Ö., Keriman, U., Ulukent, S., Ekrem, Ü., Elhan, A. and Demirci, S. (2001) 'Effect of sphincter-sacrificing surgery for rectal carcinoma on quality of life in Muslim patients', conference proceedings, *The American Society of Colon and Rectal Surgeons*, 2-7 June, San Diego, CA: 1359-66.

Lea, V. (2004) 'The reflective cultural portfolio: identifying public cultural scripts in the private voices of White student teachers', *Journal of Teacher Education*, vol 55, no 2, pp 116-27.

Lerner, G. (1986) *The Creation of Patriarchy*, Oxford: Oxford University Press.

Levi-Strauss, C. (1967) *Les Structures Élementaires de la Parenté* [*The Elementary Structures of Kinship*], Paris: La Haye.

Lyon, W. (1995) 'Islam and Islamic women in Britain', *Women: A Cultural Review*, vol 6, no 2, pp 46-56.

Lyons, L. (1999) 'Re-telling "us": displacing the white feminist subject as knower', conference paper, 'Workshop on Southeast Asian women', Melbourne: Monash University.

Lyons, K., Manion, K. and Carlsen, M. (2006) *International Perspectives on Social Work*, Basingstoke: Palgrave Macmillan.

Macey, M. (1999) 'Class, gender and religious influences on changing patterns of Pakistani Muslim male violence in Bradford', *Ethnic and Racial Studies*, vol 22, no 5, pp 845-66.

Macpherson, W. (1999) *The Stephen Lawrence Inquiry*, Cm 4262-I, London: The Stationery Office.

Mahamud-Hassan, N. (2004) 'It doesn't happen in our society', *Index on Censorship*, vol 33, no 1, pp 38-41.

Malik, S. (2007) 'Support artistic truth, Prince Charles – go to see Brick Lane', *The Observer*, 30 September.

Malik, R., Shaikh, A. and Suleyman, M. (2007) *Providing Faith and Culturally Sensitive Support Services to Young British Muslims*, Leicester: National Youth Agency.

Mallon, G.P. (2005) 'Practice with families where sexual orientation is an issue: lesbian and gay individuals and their families', in E.P. Congress and M.J. González (eds) *Multicultural Perspectives in Working with Families, Second Edition*, New York: Springer Publishing Company Inc., pp 199-227.

Mama, A. (2000) 'Woman abuse in London's black communities', in K. Owusu (ed) *Black British Culture and Society*, London: Routledge, pp 89–110.

Mama, R.S. (2001) 'Preparing social work students to work in culturally diverse settings', *Social Work Education*, vol 20, no 3, pp 373-82.

Mansson McGinty, A. (2006) *Becoming Muslim*, New York: Palgrave Macmillan.

Marranci, G. (2004) 'Multiculturalism, Islam and the clash of civilizations theory: rethinking Islamophobia', *Culture and Religion*, vol 5, no 1, pp 105-17.

Maududi, S.A. (1986) *Purdah and the Status of Woman in Islam*, Lahore: Islamic Publications Ltd.

McAskill, E. (2007) 'US Muslims more assimilated than British', *The Guardian*, 23 May.

McCaffrey, M., Jankowska, A. and Gordon, H. (1995) 'Management of female genital mutilation: the Northwick Park Hospital experience', *British Journal of Obstetrics and Gynaecology*, vol 102, pp 787-90.

McClaurin, I. (2001) 'Theorizing a black feminist self in anthropology: toward an auto ethnographic approach', in I. McClaurin (ed) *Black Feminist Anthropology*, London: Rutgers University Press, pp 49-76.

McCloud, A.B. (1995) *African American Islam*, New York: Routledge.

McGrowther, C.W., Bhaumik, S., Thorp, C.F., Watson, J.M. and Taub, N.A. (2002) 'Prevalence, morbidity and service need among South Asian and white adults with intellectual disability in Leicestershire, UK', *Journal of Intellectual Disability Research*, vol 46, no 4, pp 299-309.

McNeill, T. (2006) 'Evidence-based practice in an age of relativism: toward a model for practice', *Social Work*, vol 52, no 2, pp 147-56.

McVeigh, K. (2007a) 'Special units to crack down on honour killing', *Guardian Unlimited*, 16 June (www.guardian.co.uk/crime/article/0,,2104428,00.html).

McVeigh, K. (2007b) 'Men who decided a daughter had to die – for the good of the family', *Guardian Unlimited*, 12 June (www.guardian.co.uk/crime/article/0,,2100831,00.html).

McVeigh, K. (2007) 'Murder victim told police four times she feared her family: each time in vain', *Guardian Unlimited*, 12 June (www.guardian.co.uk/crime/article/0,,2100800,00.html).

McVicar, J. (1982) 'Violence in prisons' in P. Marsh and A. Campbell (eds) *Aggression and Violence*, Oxford: Basil Blackwell, pp 200-14.

Mehdi, R. (1997) 'The Offence of Rape in the Islamic Law of Pakistan', *Women Living Under Muslim Laws*, Dossier 18, Grabels: WLUML Publications (www.wluml.org/english/pubsfulltxt.shtml?cmd%5B87%5D=i-87-2675).

Mernissi, F. (1975) *Beyond the Veil*, Cambridge, MA: Schenkman Publishing Company.

Mernissi, F. (1983) *Sexe, Ideologie, Islam*, Paris: Tierce.

Mernissi, F. (1991) *Women and Islam: An Historical and Theological Enquiry*, Oxford: Blackwell.

Mernissi, F. (2001) *Scheherezade Goes West*, New York: Washington Square Press.

Merry, M. (2005) 'Should educators accommodate intolerance? Mark Halstead, homosexuality and the Islamic case', *Journal of Moral Education*, vol 34, no 1, pp 19-36.

Middleton, L. (1997) *The Art of Assessment*, Birmingham: Venture Press.

Miles, M. (1996) 'Walking delicately around mental handicap, sex education and abuse in Pakistan', *Child Abuse Review*, vol 5, no 5, pp 263-74.

Millon Underwood, S., Shaikha, L. and Bakr, D. (1999) 'Veiled yet vulnerable', *Cancer Practice*, vol 7, no 6, pp 285-90.

Milne, S. (2007) 'This onslaught risks turning into a racist witch-hunt', *The Guardian*, 20 September.

Minces, J. (1992) *The House of Obedience*, London: Zed Press.

Minh-ha, Trinh T. (1989) *Woman, Native, Other*, Bloomington, IN: Indiana University Press.

Mir-Hosseini, Z. (1996) 'Stretching the limits: a feminist reading of the Shari'a in post-Khomeini Iran', in M. Yamani (ed) *Feminism and Islam*, New York: New York University Press, pp 285-319.

Modood, T., Berthoud, R., Lakey, J., Nazroo, J., Smith, P., Virdee, S. and Beishon, S. (1997) *Ethnic Minorities in Britain: Diversity and Disadvantage*, London: Policy Studies Institute.

Moffatt, P.G. and Thoburn, J. (2001) 'Outcomes of permanent family placement for children of minority ethnic origin', *Child & Family Social Work*, vol 6, pp 13-21.

Moghissi, H. (1999) *Feminism and Islamic Fundamentalism*, London: Zed Books.

Mohammad, R. (2005) 'Negotiating spaces of the home, the education system and the labor market', in G.W. Falah and C. Nagel (eds) *Geographies of Muslim Women*, New York/London: The Guilford Press, pp 178-202.

Mohan, B. (2002) 'The future of social work education: curriculum conundrums in an age of uncertainty', *Electronic Journal of Social Work*, vol 1, no 1, pp 1-10.

Monnig Atkinson, J. (1990) 'How gender makes a difference in Wana society', in J. Monnig Atkinson and S. Errington (eds) *Power and Difference: Gender in Island Southeast Asia*, Stanford, CA: Stanford University Press, pp 59-63.

Morgan, R. (2002) 'Imprisonment: a brief history, the contemporary scene and likely prospects', *The Oxford Handbook of Criminology, 3rd edition*, Oxford: Oxford University Press.

Morrison, W. (1995) *Theoretical Criminology: From Modernity to Post-modernism*, London: Cavendish Publishing Limited.

Moxley Rouse, C. (2004) *Engaged Surrender: African American Women and Islam*, Berkeley, CA: University of California Press.

Müller, C. (1997) 'Female genital mutilation in Germany, an update from (I)NTACT', in G.C. Denniston and M. Fayre Milos (eds) *Sexual Mutilations: A Human Tragedy*, New York: Plenum Press, pp 159-62.

Munir, A.B.B. (1993) 'Child protection: principles and applications', *Child Abuse Review*, vol 2, no 2, pp 119-26.

National Census (2001) *Religion in Britain*, London: Office for National Statistics (www.statistics.gov.uk/cci/nugget.asp?id=293).

Nazroo, J.Y. (1997) *Ethnicity and Mental Health*, London: Policy Studies Institute.

Neville, H., Oh, E., Spanierman, L., Heppner, M. and Clark, M. (2004) 'General and culturally specific factors influencing black and white rape survivors' self-esteem', *Psychology of Women Quarterly*, vol 28, pp 83-94.

Newland, L. (2006) 'Female circumcision: Muslim identities and zero tolerance policies in rural West Java', *Women's Studies International Forum*, vol 29, no 4, July–August, pp 394-404.

Nielsen, J.S. (1999) *Towards a European Islam*, Basingstoke: Macmillan Press.

Noh, S., Kaspar, V., Hou, F. and Rummens, J. (1999) 'Perceived racial discrimination, depression and coping: a study of Southeast Asian refugees in Canada', *Journal of Health and Social Behavior*, vol 40, pp 193-207.

NSPCC (National Society for the Prevention of Cruelty to Children) (2007) 'Family "honour" dilemma for British Asians reporting child abuse', press release (www.nspcc.org.uk/whatwedo/mediacentre/pressreleases/2007_19_march_family_honour_dilemma_for_british_asians_reporting_child_abuse_wdn43191.html).

Obermeyer, C.M. (1994) 'Religious doctrine, state ideology and reproductive options in Islam', in G. Sen and R.C. Snow (eds) *Power and Decision: The Social Control of Reproduction*, Boston, MA: Harvard University Press, pp 59-75.

O'Malley, P. (1992) 'Risk, power and crime prevention', *Economy and Society*, vol 21, no 3, pp 253–75.

Ong, A. (1995) 'State versus Islam: Malay families, women's bodies and the body politic in Malaysia', in A. Ong and M.G. Peletz (eds) *Bewitching Women, Pious Men: Gender and Body Politics in Southeast Asia*, Berkeley, CA: University of California, pp 159-94.

ONS (Office for National Statistics) (2002) *Social Focus in Brief: Ethnicity 2002*, London: ONS.

Pargeter, A. (2006) 'North African immigrants in Europe and political violence', *Studies in Conflict and Terrorism*, vol 29, no 8, pp 731-47.

Patai, D. (1991) 'US academics and third world women: is ethical research possible?' *Women's Words: The Feminist Practice of Oral History*, New York/London: Routledge, pp 137-54.

Patel, N., Humphries, B. and Naik, D. (1998) 'The 3 Rs in social work: religion, "race" and racism in Europe', in C. Williams, H. Soydan and M.R.D. Johnson (eds) *Social Work and Minorities*, London: Routledge, pp 182-208.

Payne, M. (2006) *The Origins of Social Work*, Basingstoke: Palgrave Macmillan.

Peach, C. (2006) 'Muslims in the 2001 Census of England and Wales: gender and economic disadvantage', *Ethnic and Racial Studies*, vol 29, no 4, pp 629-55.

Peletz, M.G. (1995) 'Neither reasonable nor responsible: contrasting representations of masculinity in a Malay society', in A. Ong and M.G. Peletz (eds) *Bewitching Women, Pious Men: Gender and Body Politics in Southeast Asia*, Berkeley, CA: University of California, pp 176-23.

Platt, L. (2002) *Parallel Lives? Poverty Among Ethnic Minority Groups in Britain*, London: Child Poverty Action Group.

Poynting, S. and Mason, V. (2006) '"Tolerance, freedom, justice and peace"? Britain, Australia and anti-Muslim racism since 11th September 2001', *Journal of Intercultural Studies*, vol 27, no 4, November, pp 365-91.

Press Association (2007) 'Veil should not be worn, says Muslim peer', *Guardian Unlimited*, 20 February (www.guardian.co.uk/religion/Story/0,,2017301,00.html).

Preston-Shoot, M. (2000) 'Stumbling towards oblivion or discovering new horizons? Observations on the relationship between social work education and practice', *Journal of Social Work Practice*, vol 14, no 2, pp 87-98.

Pritchard, C. and Amanullah, S. (2006) 'An analysis of suicide and undetermined deaths in 17 predominantly Islamic countries contrasted with the UK', *Psychological Medicine*, vol 37, pp 421-30.

Pryke, J. and Thomas, M. (1998) *Domestic Violence and Social Work*, Aldershot: Ashgate.

Quraishi, M. (2005) *Muslims and Crime: A Comparative Study*, Aldershot: Ashgate.

Raad, S.A. (1998) 'Grief: a Muslim perspective', in K.J. Doka and J.D. Davidson (eds) *Living with Grief: Who We Are, How We Grieve*, Philadelphia: Brunner/Mazel, pp 47-56.

Rack, P. (1982) *Race, Culture and Mental Disorder*, London/New York: Tavistock.

Rasanayagam, J. (2006) 'Healing with spirits and the formation of Muslim selfhood in post-Soviet Uzbekistan', *Journal of the Royal Anthropological Institute*, vol 12, no 2, pp 377-93.

Rassool, H. (2000) 'The crescent and Islam: healing, nursing and the spiritual dimension. Some considerations towards an understanding of the Islamic perspectives on caring', *Journal of Advanced Nursing*, vol 32, no 6, pp 1479–89.

Ras-Work, B. (1997) 'Female genital mutilation', in G.C. Denniston and M. Fayre Milos (eds) *Sexual Mutilations: A Human Tragedy*, New York: Plenum Press, pp 1137–52.

Razack, N. (2001) 'Diversity and difference in the field education encounter: racial minority students in the practicum', *Social Work Education*, vol 20, no 2, pp 219–32.

Read, J. (2003) *Disability, the Family and Society*, Maidenhead: Open University Press.

Reamer, F.G. (1995) *Social Work Values and Ethics*, New York: Columbia University Press.

Reavey, P., Ahmed, B. and Majumdar, A. (2006) '"How can we help when she won't tell us what's wrong?" Professionals working with South Asian women who have experienced sexual abuse', *Journal of Community & Applied Social Psychology*, vol 16, no 3, pp 171–88.

Rehman, T.F. and Dziegielewski, S.F. (2003) 'Women who choose Islam', *International Journal of Mental Health*, vol 32, no 3, pp 31–49.

Richardson, R. (2004) 'Curriculum, ethos and leadership: confronting Islamophobia in UK education', in B. van Driel (ed) *Confronting Islamophobia in Educational Practice*, Stoke-on-Trent: Trentham Books, pp 19–33.

Rousseau, J. (1991) 'Gender and class in Central Borneo', in V.H. Sutlive (ed) *Female and Male in Borneo: Contributions and Challenges to Gender Studies*, Borneo Research Council Monograph series, vol one, Williamsburg, VA: Borneo Research Council Inc., pp 403–14.

Saeed, A., Blain, N. and Forbes, D. (1999) 'New ethnic and national questions in Scotland: post-British identities among Glasgow Pakistani teenagers', *Ethnic and Racial Studies*, vol 22, no 5, pp 821–44.

Sarfraz, A. and Castle, D. (2002) 'A Muslim suicide', *Australasian Psychiatry*, vol 10, no 1, pp 48–50.

Sarhill, N., LeGrand, S., Islambouli, R., Davis, M.P. and Walsh, D. (2001) 'The terminally ill Muslim: death and dying from the Muslim perspective', *American Journal of Hospice and Palliative Medicine*, vol 18, no 4, pp 251–5.

Schott, J. and Henley, A. (1996) *Culture, Religion and Childbearing in a Multicultural Society*. Oxford: Butterworth Heinemann.

Sharifzadeh, V.-S. (1998) 'Families with Middle Eastern roots', in E.W. Lynch and M.J. Hanson (eds) *Developing Cross-Cultural Competence*, 2nd edition, Baltimore, MD: Paul H. Brookes Publishing Co., pp 441-78.

Sheikh, A. and Gatrad, A.R. (2000) 'Death and bereavement: an exploration and a meditation', in A. Sheikh and A.R. Gatrad (eds) *Caring for Muslim Patients*, Oxford: Radcliffe Medical Press Ltd, pp 97-110.

Shenk, G. (2006) 'What went right: two best cases of Islam in Europe – Cordoba, Spain and Sarajevo, Bosnia', *Religion in Eastern Europe*, vol XXVI, no 4, pp 1-14.

Sheridan, L., Gillett, R., Blaauw, E. and Winkel, F. (2003) *Effects of the Events of September 11th on Discrimination and Implicit Racism in Five Religious and Seven Ethnic Groups*, Leicester: University of Leicester School of Psychology.

Shimmel, A. (1992) *Islam: An Introduction*, New York: State University of New York.

Shorter-Gooden, K. (2004) 'Multiple resistance strategies: how African American women cope with racism and sexism', *Journal of Black Psychology*, vol 30, no 3, pp 406-25.

Shute, S., Hood, R. and Seemungal, F. (2005) *A Fair Hearing? Ethnic Minorities in the Criminal Courts*, Cullompton: Willan Publishing.

Simon, J. (1988) 'The ideological effects of actuarial practices', *Law & Society Review*, vol 22, no 4, pp 771-800.

Soliman, A.M. (1991) 'The role of counselling in developing countries', *International Journal for the Advancement of Counselling*, vol 14, no 1, pp 3-14.

Solomos, J. (2003) *Race and Racism in Britain*, Basingstoke: Palgrave Macmillan.

Sonuga-Barke, E.J.S. and Mistry, M. (2000) 'The effect of extended family living on the mental health of three generations within two Asian communities', *British Journal of Clinical Psychology*, vol 39, no 2, pp 129-41.

Spalek, B. (2002) 'Muslim women's safety talk and their experiences of victimisation', in B. Spalek (ed) *Islam, Crime and Criminal Justice*, Cullompton: Willan Publishing, pp 50-71.

Spalek, B. (2005) 'Muslims and the criminal justice system', in T. Choudhury (ed) *Muslims in the UK: Policies for Engaged Citizens*, Budapest: Open Society Institute, pp 253-340.

Spalek, B. (2006) *Crime Victims: Theory, Policy And Practice*, Basingstoke: Palgrave Macmillan.

Spalek, B. (2007) 'Disconnection and exclusion: pathways to radicalisation?', in T. Abbas (ed) *Islamic Political Radicalism: A European Perspective*, Edinburgh: Edinburgh University Press, pp 192-206.

Spalek, B. and El-Hassan, S. (2007) 'Muslim converts in prison', *Howard Journal of Criminal Justice*, vol 46, no 2, pp 99-114.

Spalek, B. and Imtoual, A. (2007) '"Hard" approaches to community engagement in the UK and Australia: Muslim communities and counter-terror responses', *Journal of Muslim Minority Affairs*, vol 27, no 2, pp 185-202.

Spalek, B., Lambert, B. and Haqq-Baker, A. (2008, in press) 'Muslims and crime', in H. Bui (ed) *Race and the Criminal Justice System*, London: Sage Publications.

Spruyt, B.J. (2007) '"Can't we discuss this?" Liberalism and the challenge of Islam in the Netherlands', *Orbis*, vol 51, no 2, pp 313-29.

Spruyt, O. (1999) 'Community-based palliative care for Bangladeshi patients in east London: accounts of bereaved carers', *Palliative Medicine*, vol 13, no 2, pp 119-29.

Stang Dahl, T. (1997) *The Muslim family: a study of women's rights in Islam*, Oxford/Oslo: Scandinavian University Press.

Stoesz, D. (2002) 'From social work to human services', *Journal of Sociology and Social Welfare*, December, vol XXIX, no 4, pp 19-37.

Suárez-Orozco, M.M. (2005) 'Rethinking education in the global era', *Phi Delta Kappan*, November, vol 85, no 3, pp 209-12.

Svoboda, S.J. (1997) 'Routine infant male circumcision: examining human rights and constitutional issues', in G.C. Denniston and M. Fayre Milos (eds) *Sexual Mutilations: A Human Tragedy*, New York: Plenum Press, pp 205-15.

Swerdlow, A.J., Laing, S.P., dos Santos Silva, I., Slater, S.D., Burden, A.C., Botha, J.L., Waugh, N.R., Morris, A.D., Gatling, W., Bingley, P.J., Patterson, C.C., Qaio, Z. and Keen, H. (2004) 'Mortality of South Asian patients with insulin-treated diabetes mellitus in the United Kingdom: a cohort study', *Diabetic Medicine*, vol 21, pp 845-51.

Taseer, A. (2005) 'Made in Britain', *The Sunday Times News Review*, 31 July, p 3.

Taylor, I. (1997) *Developing Learning in Professional Education*, Buckingham: Society for Research into Higher Education/Open University Press.

Taylor, V. (2003) 'Female genital mutilation: cultural practice or child abuse?', *Paediatric Nursing*, vol 15, no 1, pp 31-3.

Thompson, N. (1993) *Anti-Discriminatory Practice*, Basingstoke: Macmillan/BASW.

Thompson, N. (2005) *Understanding Social Work*, Basingstoke: Palgrave Macmillan.

Thornton, S. and Garrett, K.J. (1995) 'Ethnography as a bridge to multicultural practice', *Journal of Social Work Education*, vol 31, no 1, pp 67-74.

Tickle, L. (2006) 'Do not contact the parents', *The Guardian*, 10 October.

Tripathi, A. and Yadav, S. (2004) 'For the sake of honour: but whose honour? "Honour crimes" against women', *Asia-Pacific Journal on Human Rights and the Law*, vol 5, no 2, pp 63-78.

Tsang, A.K.T. (2001) 'Representation of ethnic identity in North American social work literature: a dossier of the Chinese people', *Social Work*, vol 46, number 3, pp 229-43.

TUC (Trades Union Congress) (2005) 'End UK Pakistani and Bangladeshi poverty and deprivation', press release (www.tuc.org.uk/equality/tuc-10401-f0.cfm).

Udwadia, F.E (2001) *Man and Medicine: A History*, New Delhi/Oxford: Oxford University Press.

Van Dam, J. and Anastasi, M.-C. (2000) *Male Circumcision and HIV Prevention: Directions For Future Research*, Washington, DC: Horizons at Population Council (www.popcouncil.org/pdfs/circumcision.pdf).

Waines, D. (2003) *An Introduction to Islam*, 2nd edition, Cambridge: Cambridge University Press.

Wardak, A. (2000) *Social Control and Deviance*, Aldershot: Ashgate.

Warnock Fernea, E. (1995) 'Childhood in the Muslim Middle East', in E. Warnock Fernea (ed) *Children in the Muslim Middle East*, Austin, TX: University of Texas Press, pp 3-16.

Webb, E., Maddocks, A. and Bongili, J. (2002) 'Effectively protecting black and minority ethnic children from harm: overcoming barriers to the child protection process', *Child Abuse Review*, vol 11, no 6, pp 394-410.

Weller, P., Feldman, A. and Purdam, K. (2001) *Religious Discrimination in England and Wales*, Home Office Research Study 220, London: The Stationery Office.

Werbner, P. (1994) 'Diaspora and millennium: British Pakistani global–local fabulations of the Gulf War', in A.S. Ahmed and H. Donnan (eds) *Islam, Globalization and Postmodernity*, London/New York: Routledge, pp 213-36.

Werth, J.L., Blevins, D., Toussaint, K.L. and Durham, M.K. (2002) 'The influence of cultural diversity on end-of-life care and decisions', *American Behavioral Scientist*, vol 46, no 2, pp 204-19.

Wihtol de Wenden, C. (1996) 'Muslims in France', in W.A.R. Shadid and P.S. van Koningsveld (eds) *Muslims in the Margin*, Kampen: Kok Pharos Publishing House, pp 52-65.

Wikan, U. (1991) *Behind the Veil in Arabia: Women in Oman*, Chicago IL/London: University of Chicago Press.

Williams, C. (1998) 'Towards an emancipatory pedagogy? Social work education for a multicultural, multi-ethnic Europe', in C. Williams, H. Soydan and M.R.D. Johnson (eds) *Social Work and Minorities*, London: Routledge, pp 211-30.

Williams, R. (2007) '21,000 girls at risk of genital mutilation, say campaigners', *The Guardian*, 10 October (www.guardian.co.uk/uk/2007/oct/10/gender.ukcrime).

Wintour, P. (2007) 'Minister gives schools right to ban Muslim veil', *Guardian Unlimited*, 20 March (http://education.guardian.co.uk/schools/story/0,,2038239,00.html).

Wood Wetzel, J. (2000) 'Women and mental health: a global perspective', *International Social Work*, vol 43, no 2, pp 205-16.

Yasien-Esmael, H. and Rubin, S.S. (2005) 'The meaning structures of Muslim bereavements in Israel: religious traditions, mourning practices and human experience', *Death Studies*, vol 29, no 2, pp 495-518.

Yeprem, S. (2007) 'Current assisted reproduction treatment practices from an Islamic perspective', *Reproductive BioMedicine Online*, vol 14, no 1, pp 44-7 (www.rbmonline.com/Article/2445).

Yoshioka, M.R., Gilbert, L., El-Bassel, N. and Baig-Amin, M. (2003) 'Social support and disclosure of abuse: comparing South Asian, African American and Hispanic battered women', *Journal of Family Violence*, vol 18, no 3, pp 171-9.

Young, J. (1999) *The Exclusive Society*, London: Sage Publications.

Websites

An-Nisa Society: www.an-nisa.org

Foundation for Women's Health, Research and Development (FORWARD): www.forwarduk.org.uk

Muslim Youth Helpline: www.myh.org.uk

NAZ Project London: www.naz.org.uk

The Safra Project: www.safraproject.org

Southall Black Sisters: www.southallblacksisters.org.uk

Index